FORGED
IN FIRE

Advance Praise for Forged in Fire

"The story of Blanche Barnes's life during World War II is heart-breaking and inspirational, a quintessential American war story that is somehow unique and universal at the same time ... Rich in historical detail yet deeply human, this book sheds new light on women's roles in the war effort and is a fitting tribute to their service and sacrifice. I loved it!"

—**Jane Healey, award-winning author of** *The Beantown Girls*

"Described by an Army Major as a 'cute little redhead,' Blanche Gregory Barnes was among the heroic women who worked in a Red Cross clubmobile during World War II. Robert Gangwere tells her story with compelling details and engaging perspectives to help us understand one among many heroes."

—**Professor James H. Madison, author of**
Slinging Doughnuts for the Boys

"Compelling, important, moving, and absolutely fascinating, Blanche Barnes's story adds significantly to our understanding of the extremely important role women played in World War II. Sustaining the morale of our soldiers and airmen was no easy matter, and the clubmobile program put American women on the front lines of that critical effort."

—**Professor Charles B. Dew, author of**
The Making of a Racist

"Robert Gangwere has crafted a wonderful, fact-based story about his mother's service in the clubmobile program, delivering donuts, coffee, and warm smiles to America's GIs across the entire European Theater of Operations. *Forged in Fire* is a fitting tribute to all the Red Cross clubmobile girls."

—**Historian Dennis G. Pregent, author of the**
Berkshire Heroes in World War II

"*Forged in Fire* is a carefully researched work that will enlighten readers to the accomplishments and sacrifices made by the Red Cross clubmobile girls during World War II. It is a fitting tribute to the female members of 'The Greatest Generation.'

—**Harold G. Speer Jr., editor of** *From Kingdom Come to the Fringes of Outer Space*

FORGED IN FIRE

Grief, Purpose, and Devotion of a Woman at War

ROBERT L. GANGWERE

M·P·P
www.MissionPointPress.com

Published by Mission Point Press

 Mission Point Press

2554 Chandler Rd.
Traverse City, MI 49696
(231) 421-9513
MissionPointPress.com

Hardcover ISBN: 978-1-965278-72-7
Paperback ISBN: 978-1-965278-42-0

Library of Congress Control Number: 2025900038

Printed in the United States of America

"The Greatest generation serving our country on the front lines in World War II was not limited to one gender ..."
U.S. Senator Barbara Mikulski, May 2012

"In my opinion the Clubmobile Girls of the American Red Cross have performed ... a very major work in maintaining the morale of the front-line troops and in keeping before the eyes of our soldiers the best traditions of American womanhood."
General George S. Patton Jr., November 1944

For Kay, Stephanie, and Rachel

===============================

This Book is dedicated to the women who served in the American
Red Cross's Clubmobile Department during World War II,
and especially those who died while serving in the
European Theater of Operations:

Marie Ann Basso, Yonkers, New York,
1913–1945

Dorothy Jane Canton Burdge, Canton, Ohio,
1915–1945

Anne Kathleen Cullen, Larchmont, New York,
1918–1944

Harriet Pinkston Englehardt, Montgomery, Alabama,
1919–1945

Leonora Ashton Lindsley, Boston, Massachusetts,
1917–1945

Jean Lundy Jackson McCormick, Williamsport, Pennsylvania,
1914–1945

Alice Rae Meacham, Washington, D.C.,
1923–1946

Portia Appleton Miller, Milton, Massachusetts,
1920–1945

Elizabeth Ann Richardson, Mishawaka, Indiana,
1919–1945

Dorothy Alison Stretch, Detroit, Michigan,
1908–1943

Helen R. Thompson, Yoakum, Texas,
1914–1945

This book is also dedicated to four members of the author's
immediate family who served their country during World War II:

2nd Lt. Leslie C. Barnes, U.S. Army Air Corps,
1914–1942

Capt. George H. Gangwere Jr., U.S. Army,
1917–2003

Machinist Mate, 2nd Class, Benjamin LeRoy Kain, U.S. Navy,
1926–2009

1st Sgt. Herbert A. Kramer, U.S. Army,
1922–2008

Contents

Chapter 5 – *"Girls, don't think you're Theda Bara ..."*

Chapter 6 – *"A darn shaking experience ..."*

Chapter 7 – *"The hardest part [was] watching [the] planes crash ..."*

Chapter 8 – *"Hey, small fry, did you get that load of gravel we sent?"*

Chapter 9 – *"We would not have traded our right to drive for anything."*

Chapter 10 – *"Hey, look, a real, live American girl!"*

Introduction

"It is not the strength of the body that counts, but the strength of the spirit."

—*Anonymous*

The Second World War (1939–1945) was a watershed event by any standards. The sheer scale of the conflict, the number of countries involved, and the millions of people killed, wounded, or left homeless ensures its status as one of the most momentous events in world history. It was also a watershed moment in American history on multiple levels. One direct result of the war was the unprecedented opportunities it provided American women to join the workforce and break out of their traditional roles as homemakers. Over 350,000 women served in the American armed forces during the war, and millions served in auxiliary organizations such as the American Red Cross (ARC) and the United Service Organization (USO). Three and a half million American women volunteered their services to the ARC alone.

A small portion of these women signed up to serve overseas with the ARC and ultimately serve near combat zones. In doing so, they had to overcome traditional cultural stereotypes, sometimes the disapproval of their families and friends, and the dangers inherent in operating in a war environment. Minority women, like their male counterparts, had the added burden of dealing with systemic discrimination that was pervasive in American culture and in the

American military in the 1940s. The study of these women's achievements helps honor the important part they played in the movement toward gender and racial equality.

During the war, the ARC established what turned out to be a unique and highly successful branch of its operations referred to as the clubmobile program (based on a fleet of mobile kitchens set up in the back of buses and trucks). It was unique in that there had never been anything quite like it, and it successfully supplemented the traditional stationary Red Cross clubs located in major cities. In Great Britain, the clubmobile program delivered Red Cross services directly to where American GIs lived and worked and, because of the concept's success in Great Britain, after the Normandy Invasion in June 1944 (D-Day), numerous clubmobiles and their crews followed American forces to the continent. The crews of these vehicles were made up almost entirely of women, often serving within only a few miles of the front lines. Previously, only military nurses had been that close to harm's way. Approximately 850 women participated in the clubmobile program in the European Theater of Operations (ETO) and at least 11 of them never returned. Many hundreds more served in the Mediterranean Theater of Operations and in the Pacific.

This book is about one Red Cross clubmobile girl, Blanche Gregory Barnes Gangwere (1918–2019), who, at the beginning of the war, simply wanted to marry the man she loved, settle down, raise a family, and live the traditional life of a midwestern homemaker, wife, and mother. But fate had other things in store for her. Blanche had been born during the last year of World War I and raised in the heart of the nation, instilled with traditional midwestern values and, especially for her time, was extremely well educated. Her service during World War II was prompted less by raw patriotism than by personal loss and a sincere desire to assist the war effort. She joined the Red Cross because it was the only vehicle available to her for directly helping care for the welfare and morale of America's fighting men. Her story is one of heartbreak, determination, and ultimate salvation, and although she was less healthy, less physically capable, and less worldly than most of her fellow clubmobilers, her determination and fortitude was no less impressive.

Although Blanche's personal story is not unique among World War II clubmobilers, the history of the clubmobile program is unique and deserves to be honored and remembered. It underscores the fact that the story of America's participation in World War II was not limited to a single sex or race. Although a few general histories of the ARC attempted to cover the history of the clubmobile program, and several chapters of the autobiography of Harvey D. Gibson, the creator of the program, discussed its creation and operation, the clubmobile program was otherwise ignored by historians.

Decades after the war, a former clubmobile girl named Marjorie Lee Morgan compiled and edited the diary entries of numerous clubmobilers to highlight their experiences during the war. Afterward, a handful of former clubmobilers (or their families) published their personal stories through collections of their letters, diaries, and journals, which in turn sparked a new interest in their contributions to the war effort. In the past few decades, a new generation of professional historians have shown an interest in the clubmobile program as part of the overall history of women's roles during World War II. A few novelists, such as author Jane Healey, have even used the clubmobile story as a historical backdrop for their popular fictional stories. Finally, educational institutions and museums throughout the country included the stories of former Red Cross girls as part of their oral history programs. For example, the National World War II Museum in New Orleans, Louisiana, began interviewing women who had served during the war in support functions, like the Red Cross, as part of their ongoing World War II oral history project. Blanche was interviewed by museum staff in October 2014, and her interview is now a part of the museum's permanent online Digital Collection. Hopefully, that interview and this book will help preserve Blanche's story, and in some measure add to the history of the clubmobile service during World War II.

It is worth noting that clubmobile is spelled as one word throughout this book because that is how its creator, and the Red Cross, spelled it. It is also important to note that the women of the clubmobile program were usually referred to by the Red Cross, GIs and the military brass, and the American press as "Red Cross girls," and I have retained that nomenclature for consistency with the original sources, but the clubmobilers were uniformly older, more mature, and better educated than the average GI. They were college-educated women in their late twenties or early thirties with working experience, whereas the GIs were often young men right out of high school. As noted by historian Julia A. Ramsey, clubmobile girls were "girls in name only," and they proved to be exceptionally strong, independent, and self-motivated women who participated in war to an extent that few American women had ever done before.

Robert L. Gangwere
July 2024

Prologue

Near Bad Neuenahr, Germany April 1945

The evening air was cool and crisp, and Blanche's breath bellowed forth from each exhale and formed into small gray clouds that slowly rose and dissipated into the night sky. As the darkness and cold enveloped her, she felt a chill that quickly spread down her spine. The moon offered little assistance in illuminating her way along the narrow path to the outer perimeter of the military camp since she was surrounded by trees and dense underbrush. Each step had to be taken slowly and deliberately to avoid tripping over some unforeseen obstacle and dropping her precious cargo. It was daunting and exhilarating at the same time, but she was determined to accomplish her mission.[1]

Blanche was fully aware that her task included an element of danger. She and her fellow American Red Cross volunteers had been stationed with different divisions of the Fifteenth U.S. Army since March, and during the past several weeks, the Army's sentries had been trading potshots with German snipers. There was also concern about German infiltrators. Consequently, everyone was nervous and on edge. Being so close to the front lines, Blanche and the other American Red Cross clubmobile girls were required to be back at their tents before blackout. In addition, they were forbidden to enter or leave their living quarters at night without informing the guard on duty and receiving a password—something that was changed every night. The women often "wondered who made up the ludicrous-sounding passwords that ranged from the simple 'black' and 'white' to 'applesauce' and 'dipsy doodle'."[2] But they knew that the passwords served a serious purpose. They were part of the precautions taken by the Army to avoid "friendly fire" casualties and to protect the Army from enemy surprise.

Due to the nature of their work, clubmobile girls necessarily had to operate near forward positions and therefore their security was of continuing concern to local commanders, especially as the Army advanced deeper into captured German territory.[3] If someone approached that could not be readily identified, Army sentries were trained to call out "Halt!" and demand the nightly password. Failure to provide it or to provide it incorrectly could prove fatal. The Battle of the Bulge, concluded just three months before, had driven home the importance of this procedure after scores of specially trained English-speaking German Waffen-SS commandos had infiltrated American lines and caused major problems with unit communication and transportation.[4]

This evening, Blanche had been given the required permission to deliver coffee and doughnuts to the forward sentries, and the sentries had been notified accordingly before going on duty, but that had been hours ago. Naturally, Blanche had been provided the nightly password and thus armed, carefully felt her way in the dark toward the forward areas. After only a short distance, however, she stopped to take in the full measure of her surroundings. Through a break in the trees, she could see billions of stars and the Milky Way stretching across the night sky, and she could hear a chorus of insects and small animals as they went about their secret nocturnal activities. It was a soul-cleansing experience that stood in sharp contrast to the death and destruction that she had witnessed during her nine months in Europe. In that single moment, somewhere in west central Germany, the war seemed oceans away and the world appeared at peace.

As Blanche continued her trek toward the camp's perimeter, her silent reverie was suddenly shattered. First, Blanche felt a rush of chilly air on her face, as if an insect had just flown by, and that was quickly followed by the sharp and distinctive report of an American Garand M1 rifle. She knew instantly what had just happened. A nervous sentry had shot at her without yelling "Halt!" or demanding the required password. Blanche's knees almost buckled, and she instinctively yelled out the required password, "horse feathers," and, as calmly as she could muster, begged the hidden sentry to "please don't shoot again!" Even after the embarrassed, trigger-happy soldier apologized for his failure to follow protocol and instructed Blanche to come forward without fear, Blanche found it difficult at first. A cold shiver ran down her body. It was a narrow escape, and although the bullet missed its mark, it was an extremely close call.

Later that evening, back in the safety of her tent, Blanche quietly pondered how a sheltered midwestern girl who, prior to joining the Red Cross, had never been east of Chicago, now found herself halfway around the world in the middle of a great world war, and how she had almost lost her life for a doughnut. Despite such metaphysical musings, she never seriously questioned the importance of what she and the other clubmobile girls were doing or her earnest desire to be a part of it. The war had stirred something deep inside of her—a strong unwavering desire to help America's fighting men and to be a part of something larger than herself. The American Red Cross had given her that opportunity and she never regretted volunteering for overseas service. However, just three short years before, she never would have dreamed of how much her life was going to be transformed by global war and by her love for one special man.

Chapter 1

"Blanche, whatever you're doing, stop it!"

Kansas City, Missouri, April 1942

Three years earlier, in the spring of 1942, Blanche Gregory was as far away from the forests of east central Germany as one could be, both physically and psychologically. She was halfway around the world and firmly established in her hometown of Kansas City, Missouri. Kansas City, known as the "City of Fountains," is located smack-dab in the middle of the country at the junction of the Kaw and Missouri Rivers. It is a beautiful city, especially its southern suburbs, which are interlaced with wide, rambling boulevards bordered by large trees and numerous public parks and adorned with hundreds of fountains and statuary. In springtime, when thousands of oaks, elms, and maple trees begin to turn green, and flowering bushes and trees such as magnolias and dogwoods flourish, all accentuated by spring flowers such as tulips, iris, wisteria, daffodils, peonies, hyacinths, and black-eyed Susans that burst forth in color and native splendor, Kansas City's residential neighborhoods are truly breathtaking. The spring of 1942 was no exception.

Blanche was teaching music at a junior high school and giving piano lessons to indifferent teenagers—just biding her time really. For her and her family the war was something abstract and oceans away; merely the stuff of newspaper and magazine articles and the occasional newsreel at the local movie theater, even though the signs of change were everywhere.[5] Since Japan's surprise attack on Pearl Harbor the December before, the Gregorys' hometown had been quickly developing a local war industry and an extensive civilian defense program. In other words, Kansas Citians, like Americans throughout the country, were "snapping out of their former smug complacency and were ready and eager for an 'all-out effort'" in support of the war.[6] Men in uniform were everywhere, especially in and around Kansas City's massive and beautiful Beaux-Arts train depot, Union Station, and men who were not already in uniform were wrapping up their personal affairs and preparing to join up.

Even with all this external activity, however, the war had not touched Blanche personally, nor had it touched anyone within her family or social circle (with perhaps the exception of the government's rationing of rubber, sugar, coffee, and metal), even though they all knew, almost instinctively, that the worst was yet to come. They knew that the war was not going to be won quickly or without tremendous human cost. It was as if she and everyone around her were trying to act normally while at the same time silently bracing themselves for what was coming. They knew that war on such a global scale was not going to be won by the United States and its allies without the personal sacrifice of millions of Americans.

This dichotomy was reflected in the local newspapers. During the first week of April, the papers mixed their coverage of local political news with advertisements for the most recent spring fashions, and they entertained their readers with syndicated cartoons such as *Blondie, Gasoline Alley, Little Orphan Annie, Dick Tracy, Li'l Abner*, and *Superman*. On the other hand, war-themed movies, such as *The Fleet's In*, starring Dorothy Lamour and William Holden; *They Died with Their Boots On*, featuring Olivia de Havilland; and *The Bugle Sounds*, starring Kansas City's own Wallace Beery, reminded Kansas Citians that they were at war. In addition, the front pages were dominated by reports of the Soviet Union's defense of Leningrad, renewed aerial attacks on Great Britain by the German Luftwaffe, and the deteriorating Allied situation on the Bataan peninsula in the Philippine Islands.[7]

Blanche's ultimate involvement in the American war effort was, at this point, the farthest thing from her mind. When she finally did get involved, it would not be predicated on an overriding patriotism. It was simply based on her love for a special man and a desire to, in some small way, help the boys fighting the war. In fact, in the spring of 1942, all Blanche could think about was her fiancé and the wonderful future she envisioned for the two of them. Just the thought of getting married and embarking on a new life together was exhilarating.

Little about the background of the bride-to-be indicated anything particularly unusual or out of the ordinary. She had been born and raised in Kansas City, the daughter of Charles H. "Harry" Gregory and Grace Baum Gregory and had grown up in the old Northeast area of town overlooking the Missouri River and situated amid the stately homes and well-manicured lawns of the city's upper crust. The Northeast area was also surrounded by beautiful sections of Kansas City's famous park and boulevard system. Her family, however, was respectably middle-class, even though her father was directly descended from a Mayflower passenger.[8] In her youth, Blanche had received a solid public-school education and a typical midwestern upbringing founded upon friendliness, informality, hard work, and a healthy dose of common sense. As a result, her worldview was limited and somewhat parochial. She had never been west of the Rocky Mountains, east of Chicago, or further south than the Ozarks.

Nevertheless, the one thing that did set her apart was her passion and raw natural talent for music. She was a gifted piano student from an early age, and in her teens, she learned how to play the pipe organ under the careful tutelage of Hans Christian Feil,[9] and she did so with amazing skill and dexterity for one so young.

"Pop Feil," as he was affectionately known to all, was rightly considered one of the best organists in the Midwest, and Blanche was one of his star pupils. Her love for music was a passion and a vocation that would remain with her and sustain her for the rest of her life.

Nothing about Blanche's physical appearance or personality would have suggested, to the casual observer, the life she was destined to live over the next three years. She was pretty and petite and, as a result, never failed to attract the attention of the opposite sex (which she clearly enjoyed). Her lovely oval face and alabaster skin was framed by dark auburn hair streaked with red highlights that sparkled in the sunlight and gave her a prolonged youthful appearance. Strangers often assumed that she was much younger than she really was; consequently, her overall appearance made it difficult for her to get people to take her seriously. Her manners and speech were quiet, reserved, unassuming, and midwestern polite; but below the façade was a determined and intelligent young woman. She knew her own mind and was often the quiet leader among her youthful peers, and she never hesitated to follow the dictates of her own heart.

These personality traits manifested themselves at an early age. When Blanche was young, she and her sister, Vera, who was a year and a half older, were constant companions, playmates, and best friends. When they were playing out of their mother's sight, if Grace could hear them in the other room or outside her kitchen window, she knew all was well. If all she heard was an eerie silence, however, she knew the girls were up to something. But instead of assuming that Vera, the eldest, was leading Blanche astray, Grace would call out, "Blanche, whatever you're doing, stop it!" In other words, her mother always assumed, and rightfully so, that it was Blanche who was leading her older sister in the wrong direction.

A perfect example of this unusual sibling dynamic was when Blanche was about six years old, and she and Vera were playing in their backyard. Blanche was trying to convince Vera that they should cross the street to visit some neighborhood children, even though their mother had specifically forbidden them from doing so. Vera, logically and maturely, pointed out that they were not supposed to cross the street by themselves, and if they got caught, they would be punished. After all other arguments had failed, and in frustration, Blanche loudly scolded Vera to quit worrying since Blanche was confident that they were not going to get caught; and even if they were, Blanche pointed out, "All mother will do is spank us and that doesn't hurt for long." With that bit of twisted logic, Vera capitulated, and the girls took off across the street. What the girls had not realized was that their next-door neighbor was in his backyard and had overheard their conversation. Naturally, he promptly informed Grace and soon the girls received the predicted spanking, and Blanche got an extra hard one!

As Blanche grew older, her rebellious streak slowly disappeared and her life became sedate, if not pleasingly comfortable. Perhaps the only thing she had done that most young adults of her generation didn't do was attend college. In 1942 most Americans only had an eighth-grade education or less, and few women attended college. However, obtaining the best education possible was something her father insisted on for all his children. So, she and Vera attended Northwestern University in Evanston, Illinois (Blanche for its music school and Vera for its drama department), and Blanche ultimately and simultaneously earned two bachelor's degrees in 1939, one in music and one in music education, thereby becoming the first student to earn double degrees from Northwestern's prestigious School of Music. Receiving such a rare and marvelous education certainly helped instill in Blanche a certain level of self-confidence and poise that she had previously lacked, and yet her goals for the future were fundamentally the same as most of her female contemporaries.

A Life-Affirming Decision

By April 1942, the only part of Blanche's life that had been directly impacted by the war was her wedding plans. She and her fiancé, Les, grew up in the same neighborhood, went to the same high school and church, and were even in the church choir together.

They became engaged just four weeks after Pearl Harbor. Since he was already in the military, they both understood that he was going to be "in for the duration," and that he could be shipped overseas within a matter of months. In this regard they were not alone. Throughout the country "… literally hundreds of soldiers, sailors, and their sweethearts [were] getting married every day …" The fact that the new brides might end up young widows "encouraged life-affirming" decisions. While some weddings were "impetuous, with partners who had only known each other a few days, it [was] also true that many had planned to marry anyway and simply moved up the date in response to war."[10] That was the case with Blanche and Les. They were determined to get married regardless of the war. The only nod to the realities of wartime was their decision to move up the date and tone down the festivities.[11]

Of course, Blanche understood that her life was about to change forever, but she could not wait to embark on the journey. In her mind she had her whole life laid out in front of her, and for one so young, she knew exactly what she wanted and how her life would turn out. She was going to get married, of course, have four children (two boys and two girls), live in the beautiful Country Club District of south Kansas City, take care of her family, and find ways to continue her love affair with music. She did not stop, not for a moment, wondering if she should go ahead and marry, even though her fiancé was only months away from being sent overseas. Blanche had given the question serious consideration. She had unequivocally decided that she was not going to marry anyone else, regardless of how long Les might be gone, so she figured that she might as well marry him now versus later. At least that way she would be considered by the military, by the U.S. government, and by society at-large as Les's "next of kin," thus entitling her to the right to know whatever the military routinely let soldiers' families know about their soldiers serving overseas. It would also let her fiancé know that she was fully committed to their relationship and that she would be waiting for him when he returned.

The would-be groom, Leslie C. "Les" Barnes, was a tall, thin, big-boned, good-looking young man with wavy light brown hair, a big smile, and an acute sense of humor. He was also an intelligent, fun-loving, good-natured 27-year-old who knew the meaning of hard work and responsibility. His father had left him and his mother when Les was just a boy, and Les had been the family's breadwinner ever since. That traumatic event, and the formidable responsibility that went with it for a boy so young, did not jade him, however. Instead, his struggle to survive and to support his mother amid one of America's worst depressions, even to the point of him going hungry at times, made him "serious," "grounded," and "worldly" compared to most young men his age. Plus, his strong unwavering faith in God helped keep him away from many of the vices that attracted other young men and helped keep Les on the "straight and narrow."[12]

More than anything else, however, Les was crazy about Blanche, a fact she readily admitted to anyone who bothered to ask. Les "spoiled her rotten," as she loved to say. Regardless of the subject, all she had to do was give him a mild look of approval or disapproval and he would strive to make her wish a reality. What Blanche wanted, Les was determined to provide, for they were young and very much in love.

Even with all the momentous changes occurring around her during the first six months of America's entry into World War II, Blanche's life was in a holding pattern. She was living with her parents and working part-time jobs while waiting for Les to complete his military training at the West Coast Air Corps Training Center in Albuquerque, New Mexico. Her wait and her pedestrian existence, however, ended abruptly on Wednesday, April 1, 1942, when her fiancé received his "wings" and was commissioned a second lieutenant in the U.S. Army Air Forces.[13] When his wings were pinned on his chest, he also received a precious three-day pass. Not wishing to waste such an excellent opportunity, Les quickly decided that the pass might be his last chance to "seal the deal" with Blanche before he was shipped overseas. So, he immediately sent her a short, cryptic telegram informing her that he would be in Kansas City on the

second and that they could be married on the third. The telegram
came as a complete surprise, so much so that Blanche briefly wondered if it was her fiancé's idea of an unbelievably bad April Fool's
Day joke.

Once Blanche decided that Les's telegram was in earnest, she
immediately responded with her unqualified assent. It is what she
wanted. Her hopes and dreams for the future were no more complicated than a desire to be married to the man she loved, create a
wonderful home together, and raise a family. Yes, the war was going
to temporarily suspend a part of that dream, but the first step was
marriage. She was delighted and extremely happy at the prospect.
What came later they would face together and that is all that
mattered.

Wedding Bells

With her telegram of acceptance winging its way back to Les in New
Mexico, Blanche and her mother frantically got down to the business of preparing for a wedding ceremony and reception that was to
take place in exactly two days. The first order of business was spending an entire day calling family and friends and asking them to
"spread the word." Oddly enough, procuring a venue for the wedding on such short notice proved to be the easy part. Blanche and
her family had been active members of Independence Boulevard
Christian Church for nearly 20 years.[14] The church was the epicen-
ter of her family's religious and social life. Her father, Harry, had
served as the church's treasurer and was a member of the church's
men's club; Grace was active in the women's club; and Blanche
assisted with the adult and girls' choirs.

During their high school years, Blanche and her sister, Vera, had
been in the girls' choir and active members of the local chapter of
Christian Endeavor (a cross-denominational organization that met
at the church on a weekly basis). The club sponsored a host of activities for teenagers, and it was the focal point of the Gregory girls'
social lives. Among the club's many activities, members would visit

homes for the elderly and entertain the residents with music and song; attend services at other churches (including African American congregations); organize dances; and arrange social functions at local parks. As an accomplished pianist, Blanche always enjoyed entertaining the elderly and she was fascinated with the music performed in the African American churches. She came to admire and respect their musical talent and traditions, as well as their religious fervor. It was that connection, and the example set by her father, which served as a foundation for her developing a progressive attitude regarding race relations.

So it was with relative ease that Blanche was able to reserve the church's main sanctuary and the services of their minister for the afternoon of Friday the third. Naturally, Pop Feil agreed to play the organ and his wife, "Mom Feil," who was a professionally trained and gifted singer, also agreed to perform. The news of the impending marriage quickly spread among church members, and given the closeness of the church community, many felt free to attend the ceremony without formal invitations. The wedding guests numbered over five hundred people. Even the children's choir volunteered to sing at the ceremony in appreciative recognition of the bride's services as their volunteer choir director.

The most challenging part of the wedding preparations was obtaining a wedding dress on such short notice. As noted, Blanche was petite—barely five feet tall and weighing no more than a hundred pounds. Dresses her size were not then nor now easy to come by, but fate was with her and within a day she found a beautiful white satin wedding dress that did not require a single alteration. She could not believe her luck. Everything was quickly coming together, and she and her mother had all the plans in place by the end of the next day.

Meanwhile, the prospective groom was making his way to Kansas City by train. He too was excited about the coming nuptials, but his excitement quickly turned to anger and frustration. Upon his arrival at Union Station in Kansas City, he received unexplained orders to immediately return to the Training Center in New

Mexico. Canceling the wedding one day before the ceremony, after he was the one who had set everything in motion, was a nightmare scenario that he was determined to avoid. But orders were orders. Not sure what to do, Les ultimately rationalized that since his commanding officer knew that he planned to return to New Mexico with his car (and driving back would take two full days, counting a stop for the night), if, after leaving Kansas City on the fourth, he drove through the night instead of stopping, he could return to his base on time and still get married on the third. It would be cutting it close, but Les was determined. Confident of his solution, but fearful that if he informed his commanding officer of his new plan, he might receive a new order to return a day early, Les did not reply. Absent confirmation of receipt, his commanding officer enlisted the help of the local office of the Federal Bureau of Investigation (FBI) to track Les down and find out what he was up to.

That level of official concern for a lowly lieutenant was out of the ordinary, even for wartime, but it was prompted by the type of training Les had received as an aerial bombardier. The U.S. government was concerned about anyone who worked with its new Norden bombsight. Prior to the formation of the Manhattan Project (which successfully developed the first atomic bomb), one of America's major military secrets during World War II was the development and refinement of the Norden bombsight. The 1942 version was a significant improvement over earlier ones, so much so that some argued that it played a major role in ensuring Allied victory in World War II.[15] Once the local FBI agent tracked Les down, interviewed him, and learned of Les's pending marriage, the agent was convinced that the new lieutenant was "on the up and up" and not a national security risk. However, just to be sure, the FBI agent decided to attend the wedding and stay with Les until he left town and headed back to base.

The next day, Good Friday, April 3, 1942, dawned cool and clear in Kansas City, and by afternoon it was a stunning spring day with temperatures in the low 70s, and Blanche and Les's wedding went off without a hitch. The groom proudly wore his Army Air Corps uniform, his chest adorned with his brand-new silver wings and his shoulders sporting his officer's gold bars, and the bride wore her new white satin wedding dress and carried a large bouquet of spring flowers. Given the times, she gladly gave up some wedding traditions and formalities that her mother's generation had felt were so essential. Plus, the couple wrote their own wedding vows. Predating modern practice by decades and shocking most of the older women in attendance, Blanche took the opportunity to purposely delete the bride's traditional promise to "honor and obey." In addition to such deviations from established tradition, at least one wedding guest had other reasons for not being altogether pleased.

Her father liked the groom and thought that he was a good man, but Harry was deeply concerned about the couple's future together. Blanche's father was convinced that, without a college degree, Les was going to struggle to properly provide for her. Harry knew that Blanche also had special health problems that would command constant attention and expense. She had a serious heart problem that sapped her strength, and she suffered from severe allergies and asthma that, at times, could be life-threatening. Harry's concerns were so overpowering that, to the bride's surprise and embarrassment and the groom's annoyance, Harry quietly wept during the wedding ceremony.

Of course, the bride did not share her father's concerns. She knew that Les had already completed two years of community college and that he had done so while working full-time to support his mother. She had absolute faith in Les's ambition, character, intelligence, raw abilities, and innate work ethic. She was confident that he would finish college after the conclusion of his military service and would prove to be "an excellent provider." Les wanted to be an engineer, and he hoped that his military service would serve as a springboard to his future education and profession. Given Blanche's age (she was 24), her father simply had to accept her decision and he did so.

Following the simple but beautiful ceremony, the wedding party walked down the block to Pop and Mom Feils' house so that the bride could change into street clothes before driving to the reception. While doing so, Pop informed the newlyweds that some of their male friends were planning to "kidnap" the groom prior to the reception (an obscure wedding tradition from the Far East that has thankfully lost favor in America). So, Pop recommended that the rest of the wedding party should leave by his front door and serve as a decoy, while the newlyweds should escape out his back door, climb over the back fence, and head for their car from the other side of the block—thus eluding the would-be kidnappers. Pop's plan worked like a charm. The newlyweds made their escape, with the diligent FBI agent struggling to keep up. The agent stuck with the couple every step of the way. In fact, he attended the wedding reception and, later that night, remained in the hall outside the couple's room at the Pickwick Hotel in downtown Kansas City. Now that's professional dedication!

The U.S. Army Air Corps and "Killer Kane"

Regrettably, the newlyweds only had one night together before Les had to drive back to Albuquerque (without stopping for the night, of course). Blanche reluctantly remained behind because of her job. She was under contract with the Kansas City Board of Education until the end of the semester. However, several weeks later, her boss became aware of Blanche's peculiar situation and released Blanche from her contract and encouraged her to join her new husband in New Mexico.

Informed of this wonderful development, Les implored Blanche to make haste. His pet name for her was "Sir" (a humorous but accurate acknowledgment of the superior position he believed she had in the hierarchy of their relationship), and in a letter to her dated several weeks after their wedding, Les admitted that he was so lonesome that he didn't know what to do. "Dear Sir, ... I have a date every night—with a dream—but that is not quite satisfactory. I want you!"[16] Within the week, Blanche joined Les in Albuquerque and was present when he graduated from the Advanced Bombardier

School on May 2. She could not have been prouder, but she had little time to acclimatize herself to the desert or her new surroundings before Les received orders to report to Tampa, Florida, for additional training.

The newlyweds drove to his new post, and with a slight detour north, they were able to briefly visit their families in Kansas City. The quickest way to drive from Albuquerque to Kansas City in 1942 was the old Route 66 (of song, movie, and television fame) and that is what they utilized. Their first stop was for dinner in Amarillo, Texas. Although Blanche never figured out why (it could have been food poisoning or a reaction triggered by one of her many food allergies), within an hour after their meal Blanche became horribly ill. At that moment they were in open country with no gas stations or restaurants within miles, so Les had to stop along the side of the road so Blanche could exit the car and "take care of business." Les was more than understanding, but Blanche was totally embarrassed and mortified. Her new husband had pledged to be with her for better or for worse, but he had not expected to see her at her worst so early in their marriage.

After a short visit with their families, the newlyweds drove to Tampa, Florida, and Les promptly reported to MacDill Army Airfield. In May 1942, MacDill was being used as a transitional training facility for heavy bombers. Its primary mission was the training of bombardment units under the III Bomber Command. It was also one of 40 Florida airfields that the American military had developed prior to World War II. The fields were designed for training, national defense, and deployment of U.S. air forces overseas. The climate, topography, strategic location, and sparse population all combined to make Florida an ideal location for aviation development. "The year-round blue skies were ideal for training. ... The peninsula was never more than 150 miles from the sea, allowing for unlimited gunnery practice. The large empty National Forests and State Forests were available for bombing ranges [and] the flatness of the terrain invited landing fields ..."[17]

The newlyweds did not see much of Tampa, however, as Les's

stay at MacDill was short-lived. In less than a week he was transferred again to complete his final per-combat training, this time to
the new Sarasota Army Air Base. It was probably at MacDill that he
was assigned to the bomber crew commanded by 1st Lt. Robert G.
McCormick, 344th Bomber Squadron, 98th Bombardment Group.
The 98th was activated in early February 1942 and assigned to the
U.S. Ninth Air Force later in the year. Lieutenant McCormick commanded a pink Consolidated B-24D Liberator, #41-11814, which was
a four-engine heavy bomber with a wingspan of 110 feet, an operational cruising speed of about 180 miles per hour, a maximum
speed more than 300 mph, a service ceiling of 32,000 feet, and a
maximum range of nearly 3,000 nautical miles. It carried 500- or
1,000-pound bombs and its maximum bomb load was 8,000 pounds.
For protection, the B-24D carried ten .50 caliber machine guns.[18] It
was an impressive fighting machine, but there was nothing refined
about it. Its slab-sided fuselage prompted American aviators to nickname it the "Flying Boxcar," or if they were in a more macabre
mood, the "Flying Coffin," since it only had one exit near the tail
which made it impossible for the crew to escape during an emergency. On the inside it had no pressurized cabin, no heat, no bathroom, nothing to warm up food or coffee, and no padded or
reclining seats; in fact, it had nothing that could be remotely
referred to as creature comforts. The bomber served one deadly
purpose and one purpose only—to carry a heavy load of bombs a
great distance and drop them on enemy targets.[19]

Lieutenant McCormick's B-24 was named *Rose Bud*, no doubt
inspired by the famous wooden snow sled featured in the classic
Orson Welles's movie *Citizen Kane*, which had been released the
year before. Perhaps the idea came to Lieutenant McCormick from
the fact that the crew's new squadron commander was none other
than Major John Riley Kane of Shreveport, Louisiana. Major Kane
was already well known in the 98th Bombardment Group, and he
later became the commander of all the Group's B-24 Liberators,
often referred to as "The Pyramiders." Before the war was over,
Major Kane had flown 43 combat missions over Europe, North

Africa, and the Middle East; his daring missions earned him the nickname "Killer Kane" in intelligence reports written by none other than the German Luftwaffe. He also won a Medal of Honor for leading his bombers on their famous raid on the Ploiesti (Romania) oil fields in 1943.[20]

Although Sarasota County at the beginning of the war was an ideal place for the U.S. Army to train its bomber crews, in May of 1942, construction of the base had not yet been completed and the accommodations were primitive at best. Nevertheless, for young soldiers and airmen unfamiliar with a tropical climate, Sarasota looked and felt like a tropical paradise—with beautiful white sandy beaches and friendly inhabitants anxious to welcome the military and its money. The training Les received at Sarasota included the use of nonexplosive bombs containing white and black powder which, upon impact, produced a huge cloud of smoke and debris. This allowed spotters to report on the accuracy of the bomb drops and to make necessary recommendations for improvement.[21]

The Little House by the Sea

Thankfully, as a married officer, Les was not required to live on base, so upon their arrival in Sarasota, the newlyweds spent a day trying to find a place to live. Each time Les thought he had found a good rental prospect within his price range, he would look over at Blanche and notice the expression on her face. Les could always tell when she was not impressed. So, without her having to say a word, he would insist on continuing the search. However, her face lit up when they checked out a pretty, little, ranch-style house on a secluded beach overlooking the gulf. It had a full kitchen, living room, and screened-in side porch. She absolutely loved it, so Les promptly rented it.

Once settled in, Blanche easily fell into a comfortable routine. She would get up early to make her new husband breakfast and drive him to the airfield, and then, upon her return, she would take a quiet morning walk on the beach. While doing so she would think about how lucky they were to have each other in such uncertain times, and she would daydream about their lives together after the war and what their future might bring. Decades later she still fondly remembered that little house by the gulf and the time that they had spent there together, the sound of the waves, the gentle sea breeze, and how happy they were in their first real home together.

It was in that little house by the shore that Blanche first tried to do her husband's laundry. While ironing and starching his dress uniform shirts, she accidentally used too much starch. The next morning, when Les tried to put one of them on, they both exploded with laughter. The shirt was so stiff that Les could stand it up on its own. Unfortunately, the newlyweds were not able to enjoy their home for long. Since "... the runways at Sarasota were not suitable to accommodate the heavy bombers ...",[22] in early June, Les and his squadron were transferred to the yet to be completed Lakeland Army Airfield (previously Drane Field) near Lakeland, Florida. Lakeland is halfway between Tampa and Orlando. In 1942 the airfield was being used as a simulated forward combat base and operational training facility for heavy bombers such as the B-17 and the B-24.[23] Five squadrons of the 98th Bombardment Group were housed and trained there, and they used various gunnery and bombing ranges in the Tampa area.[24]

The couple were at Lakeland throughout the month of June, and it was there that Les decided to surprise his bride with a honey-colored female Cocker Spaniel puppy. He figured that the puppy would help keep Blanche company while he was overseas. She loved the little dog and named it "Lady Paderewski" (after the wife of the famous pianist) or just "Paddy" for short.

In an era long before home air-conditioning, the summer heat and humidity at Lakeland was suffocating and debilitating for Blanche; and, because of her heart condition and asthma, by mid-afternoon she was often drained of energy and extremely weak. To combat those symptoms, she quickly got into the habit of lying down after lunch and taking a nap during the worst part of the afternoon heat. Normally those naps were restful reprieves, but one day, while napping, the temperature suddenly dropped and a violent rainstorm rolled through the Lakeland area, accompanied by booming thunder and periodic lightning strikes. Being a native Midwesterner and no stranger to thunderstorms, Blanche was more fascinated than frightened. Even though she understood the potential danger, she could not resist lying near a slightly open window to take in the full effect of the sounds and the ferocity of the summer storm. Suddenly, a lightning bolt came shooting down from a gigantic black cumulus cloud and struck the wrought iron railing on the porch just outside of her window. Blanche watched in awe and terror as the lightning danced along the railing, frantically seeking an outlet. Luckily, it was not her, and she remained unharmed; but it occurred to her that she had been extremely lucky, and the lesson was not lost on her. In an uncertain world there is a fine line between life and death, and the side you end up on is often determined by blind luck and what the ancients referred to as "the fates."

Chapter 2

"Pray for me as much as you can, for He is the one who can bring us together ..."

The Florida-Brazil Coastal Corridor

Several weeks after Blanche's brush with death at Lakeland, and shortly before the Fourth of July, Les and the entire 98th Bombardment Group were transferred to Morrison Army Airfield, about three and a half miles southwest of West Palm Beach. At the time, the West Palm Beach area only contained a civilian population of around 34,000 people.[25] Blanche really did not care where they were as long as they were together. With each successive move, however, she was painfully aware that Les's training was coming to an end and that they were inching closer and closer to the day that he would leave. She did her best to put such thoughts out of her mind and savor every moment that they still had together.

In 1942, Morrison Field was being used as the jumping-off point for American heavy bombers headed for the Mediterranean and Europe. The route being used had become known as the "Florida-Brazil coastal corridor." Although the shortest route to Europe was the North Atlantic route made famous by Charles Lindbergh in

1927, which took planes from the U.S. to the British Isles via refueling stops in Montreal and Newfoundland, it was also impractical.

> It was a relatively short 2,700 miles, and specially fitted four-engine planes [such as the B-24] could fly it non-stop. But weather conditions made the route dangerous half the year, and often impossible. ... [Thus,] military geography suggested a safer route to both Europe and Asia by flying south by southwest from Florida. Theoretically, Florida-based aircraft could fly safely all year long across the Caribbean to Brazil, then across the Atlantic Narrows to Africa. From Africa, airplanes could fly north to the Mediterranean and Europe, or fly easterly across Africa to the British base in Egypt.[26]

On the other hand, the African route was thousands of miles longer. To fly from West Palm Beach to Egypt safely, American aircraft had to fly in separate legs—generally refueling at each stop. The first leg was from West Palm Beach to the newly constructed Borinquen Army Airfield on the west coast of Puerto Rico. The second leg was from Puerto Rico to Waller Airfield on the island of Trinidad off the coast of Venezuela. The third leg was a short hop to Atkinson Airfield in British Guiana, or the heavy bombers could skip Atkinson and fly directly to Belém, Brazil. The fourth leg took the aircraft from Belém to Natal, Brazil, the easternmost tip of the South American continent, which was the last fueling stop and jumping off point across the narrows of the Atlantic to Africa.[27]

Beginning in July 1942, the month Les and his squadron left Florida, a brief stop on Ascension Island was added to the route. That British-held island in the south Atlantic is about 1,437 miles from the coast of Brazil. After refueling at the newly American-built airfield dubbed "Wide-Awake" (because of the constant danger of thousands of birds in flight near the airfield), American aircraft would fly the last leg of the trip to one of three different airfields in west Africa. The main one was at Accra on the Gold Coast. After refueling and a short rest for the crew, aircraft would begin their first land-based leg to Kano, Nigeria, located in north central Africa. From Kano the planes could either fly due north to Algeria or due east to Khartoum in the Egyptian-controlled Sudan, and from Khartoum on north to Cairo. The entire route from Florida to Egypt was a grueling and physically demanding flight of over 10,000 miles, but when all factors were considered, it was still the safest.[28]

The African route was the option Les and his squadron would be utilizing, and about two weeks after arriving in West Palm Beach, they received their orders. The day the squadron was to report to the airfield was set for July 17, 1942, and Blanche and Les spent their last night together discussing what she should do while he was overseas, including looking after Les's mother and managing their joint finances. Les did his best to calm Blanche's fears, and although he readily acknowledged that his squadron's training had been accelerated to meet the Army Air Forces' urgent need to get American planes and crews over to the Mediterranean as soon as possible, he assured her that he had been assigned to a good plane and pilot, and they had an outstanding squadron commander.

The next morning Les placed Blanche's luggage, Paddy, and the couple's meager belongings into their car in anticipation of Blanche's return to Kansas City. At the last minute Les's squadron commander, Major Kane, who was staying nearby, requested a ride to the base. Of course, Les was not about to say no to his commanding officer, so the three of them piled into the front seat and they took off for the airfield. What Blanche remembered about that short trip was that it was "a cozy ride," and that Major Kane was polite and appreciative. He even volunteered to hold the couple's puppy.

After their last embrace and a long kiss goodbye, Les left a teary-eyed Blanche behind at the airfield's main gate and he and Major Kane disappeared into a nearby building to begin their preflight preparations and briefings. When the squadron finally left West Palm Beach, they headed southeast toward their first stop in Puerto Rico. The squadron made it to Brazil a few days later and prepared for the trip across the south Atlantic narrows. On the 22nd, the night before the squadron was scheduled to leave Natal, Brazil, and head for Ascension Island, Les took a moment to write a quick letter to his new bride:

> Dear Sir, I don't know if you are home or not so here's hoping you made the trip all right. I made mine O.K. and am doing fine. This is the winter season here and right on the equator, so it is neither hot nor cold but just right. I love you very much and wish I had you with me. I dreamed last night that I was back there with you and we were trying to be married and we had an awful time catching up with the minister, and we never did make it. Please write soon and often because it would give me a new lease on life if I could hear from you. I miss you terribly even though we have only been apart a few days. I hope it is only a few more until we are together again. I love you very much. Tell all hello and pray for me as much as you can, for He is the one who can bring us together. ... Love and kisses from your husband, Leslie[29]

Shock and Disbelief

On June 23, Les's squadron flew across the Atlantic toward to Gold Coast and landed in Accra on schedule. The squadron took off again that evening, after refueling, for a night flight to Khartoum, Egyptian-Sudan. Meanwhile, Blanche and little Paddy drove back to Kansas City. Within days she rented an apartment, but barely had time to start unpacking before she received an unexpected telegram from Major General James Alexander Ulio, the Adjutant General of the U.S. Army. For a heart-stopping moment Blanche hesitated to open it. An uncontrolled feeling of dread washed over her. During the war everyone knew what it meant for a family member of a serviceman to receive a telegram from the War or Navy Departments, but it just could not be. Les had only been gone for a week. Surely the telegram would prove benign; how could it be otherwise?

After slowly opening the envelope, her hands began to shake as she stared at the paper in front of her. She could not believe what she was reading:

> Deeply regret to inform you information received. Your husband Second Lieutenant Leslie Craven Barnes, United States Army, believed to have perished July twenty-second [*sic*] in airplane accident in the African Middle Eastern Theater. Further details will follow as received.[30]

Blanche was stunned! She carefully read and reread the telegram but at first refused to believe it. It simply was not possible. It's not that she didn't understand that Les could be killed or injured over enemy skies, but she was wholly unprepared for him to be lost just days after his departure because of an "accident." What kind of accident? How could such a thing happen? She wanted answers and the telegram provided none. As she reread the telegram a second and third time, her attention was drawn to the sentence that stated that Les was "*believed to have perished.*" So, it was anything but certain. He could be missing; or there could be some kind of horrible mistake. Les could be perfectly safe somewhere in Africa and the Army could be operating on false information. Certainly, such things did happen. It was what the GIs referred to as a "snafu," or "situation normal, all fucked up!" Frustratingly, the telegram did not give her advice on how to obtain more information; all it said was, "*Further details will follow as received.*" But when? How long was that going to take? What was she supposed to do in the meantime? She had no idea what to do or who to turn to for help.

The rest of that horrible day was a blur; Blanche could barely function. Naturally, her parents insisted that she remain with them for the night and her father even called their family physician who made an immediate house call and prescribed sleeping pills. By far the hardest task came the next day when her father took Blanche to visit Les's mother, who had not yet heard the awful news.

For five long, terrible, mind-numbing days Blanche heard

nothing further from the Adjutant General's Office. Not being able to wait any longer, she sat down and wrote a letter to General Ulio, begging him for more details. Since the telegram had said that the Army "*believed*" that Les had been killed, she refused to believe that he was dead; and, as every day passed in silence, she became more convinced that he would ultimately be found alive and that the whole episode would prove to be some awful bureaucratic foul-up—a classic Army "snafu." That made the need for more information more compelling. So that same day she also wrote to Major Kane in North Africa; but, given the delays in correspondence with service members abroad, it took a month for her letter to reach Major Kane and for him to respond.

When General Ulio responded several agonizing weeks after his initial telegram, he provided her some additional information but, again, nothing concrete:

> Dear Mrs. Barnes: Receipt is acknowledged of your letter ...,
> concerning your husband, Second Lieutenant Leslie Craven
> Barnes, ... who is believed to have perished on July 22nd [*sic*]
> in an airplane accident in the African Middle Eastern The-
> ater. The report stated that the wreckage of a plane of which
> it is believed that your husband was an occupant, has been
> sighted; however, due to the location of the crash, it was nec-
> essary to proceed to the scene of the crash by horseback. A
> further report has not been received.

After providing Blanche basic information about Les's government benefits, the General closed with a stark acknowledgment that the lack of information was regrettable but beyond his power to correct:

> The anguish and mental strain that you are experiencing as
> a result of the uncertainty during the past weeks is very under-
> standable and it is regretted that a more favorable reply can-
> not be made at this time. You may be assured, however, that

upon the receipt of any additional information, you will be immediately notified.[31]

It was all too surreal. In the blink of an eye Blanche had gone from unbelievable happiness to complete confusion and despair, followed by weeks of uncertainty and doubt. Although holding on to a hope for Les's survival, she concluded that anything would be better than the agony of going day after day not knowing. Blanche's reaction was anything but atypical. As one Red Cross worker explained, when a loved one received such a telegram,

> ... the conflict between hope and fear produces an almost unendurable tension which frequently finds expression in ceaseless effort to secure more information about [the missing GI]. The shock from the news that he is considered dead at least brings a certain kind of relief from the uncertainty of not knowing.[32]

The uncertainty of the situation for Blanche was pure torture, and to make matters worse, everywhere she went in her hometown she ran into well-meaning people who would stop and ask her about Les, or try to comfort her with worn-out cliches, or even worse, premature condolences. It was more than she could bear.

An Agonizing Wait

Harry Gregory saw what was happening to his daughter and the pain she was going through, so he decided that she needed to temporarily remove herself from Kansas City and go someplace where no one knew her; at least until such time as the government finally determined Les's fate. Surprisingly, she didn't need convincing, and she readily accepted her father's advice. Through the assistance of the Assistant Dean of the Northwestern University School of Music, Blanche quickly procured a job teaching voice at a junior high school in Wauwatosa, Wisconsin, near Milwaukee. She began her new job after Labor Day. At the time, Wauwatosa was a town of about 27,000 people, and places to rent during wartime were at a premium.

Blanche finally found a place to live in Milwaukee which, coincidentally, was located near an airport. That turned out to be an unfortunate coincidence, for the constant sound of airplanes taking off and landing only depressed her further. The sounds coming from the airport made Blanche think of her time with Les in Florida. The only thing that alleviated her depression were weekend visits to her sister Vera's home in Evanston, Illinois. While growing up, Vera and Blanche had been inseparable and they had even shared the same room all the way through college, that is until Vera married in 1938. By 1942, Vera and her husband, Lorin, had a baby girl named Jo Anne. Spending quality time with her sister and her little niece was just the tonic Blanche needed. As Blanche explained it years later, "There is nothing like playing with a child to make one forget about one's problems and put things into proper perspective."

During the last few days of September, Blanche finally received a reply from Major Kane. He couldn't have been kinder or more consoling, while at the same time trying to explain to her, as diplomatically as possible, that there was little hope that Les and his crew survived:

My dear Mrs. Barnes: I received your letter last week and have delayed this long in answering hoping that I can send you better news. The last we saw of all Lt. McCormick's crew was at Accra, Gold Coast, British West Africa. We all took off late in the evening and flew all night to Khartoum, Egypt. Mac's plane came up missing. We spent two anxious days waiting for word by radio before we were forced to leave. About two weeks later Pan-African Airlines notified us they had seen a pink B-24 crashed near Lake Tchad, north of Ft. Lamy. The Arabs had made eleven graves and erected a fence around the place. A search party was sent out from Accra. ... I have been hoping for favorable news for the last two weeks.

Mrs. Barnes, we grieve with you in your loss. Never a day has gone by but the boys have said, "Wish the rest were here. Sure do miss them." We hope to see them someday, but we have become convinced that it will be in the other world. Please express our deepest sympathy to Lt. Barnes' mother. If we receive any information, I will let you know as soon as possible. Very truly yours, ...[33]

Nevertheless, against all logic, Blanche held firm to her belief that the B-24 sighted near Lake Chad was not Les's plane, and through some miraculous turn of events, he would still be found alive. After all, the military had not officially confirmed his death; but as the weeks wore on, each new piece of information received drew her closer and closer to the painful conclusion that she would never see Les again. It nearly crushed the life out of her. When Les's mother received a letter from 2nd Lt. John R. Burger, a buddy of Les's in the Air Corps, and forwarded it to Blanche in Wisconsin, all remaining hope evaporated.

Dear Mrs. Barnes: I am I think Leslie's best friend in the group as we went all through school together in the same squadron. ... Leslie's accident happened just before arriving at our last stop prior to our present destination [Cairo, Egypt]. From what I can gather the ship was caught in a thunderhead making navigation very difficult. There are some very high mountains close to the course followed and it seems they were a little off course and crashed into the mountain [sic]. It was just one of those things that do occasionally happen and [that] we all risk every time we fly. ... When the search party arrived ... [it] found that the natives in the vicinity had given the men a Christian burial. They were all buried and crude crosses were at the head of the graves to mark them. It was very unfortunate, but I believe Les realized the possibilities and chances. It happened fast and they no doubt never knew anything about it, which is a consolation. ... It was an awful blow I know, happening so soon, but Mrs. Barnes it all happened for a cause, a good cause. The good Lord will look after Leslie in Heaven, and he gave his life so that his country may live, as many more of us will do before it's over. I am hoping that this letter may help to alleviate the pain in the hearts of the two people closest to him, his mother and his wife. He would have done the same for me, I know that. Hoping and praying for a speedy end to this war, I remain, Sincerely yours, ...[34]

Now the waiting for official word from the government was almost akin to a death watch. Every day the nightmare continued. Finally, near the end of October, Blanche received a phone call from an employee in the Western Union office in Milwaukee. The employee informed her that they had a telegram for her from the War Department. She knew that it was the telegram she had been waiting for but, at the same time, what she had been absolutely dreading, and it could not have arrived at a worse moment. A snowstorm had hit the area, and the Western Union office had so many telegrams to deliver that the employee informed her that his office could not deliver her message until the next day. Considering the obvious import of the message, she requested that the employee read the telegram to her over the phone, but he refused. He told her that it was against company policy and no amount of pleading on Blanche's part would get him to relent.

Waiting an entire day to find out what the telegram contained was, of course, out of the question. So, angry, frustrated, and filled with dread, and despite the horrible weather, Blanche got in her car and drove the seven to eight miles to the Western Union office on icy and treacherous roads. She carefully navigated her way to the office and was finally able to obtain and read the War Department's telegram. It confirmed her worst fears. Les was dead. Two and a half months of not knowing had mercifully ended, but with the worst possible outcome. Les would not be coming home, and she knew that her life would never be the same. In her short 24 years of life, Blanche's only personal experience with death had been the death of her maternal grandfather in 1931, when she was still quite young, but that had been different. She hardly knew what to do with her grief. She tried to drive herself back home, but she was crying so hard, and she was so distracted that she nearly wandered off the road several times. Then, as she approached a car in front of her waiting for a red light, she reacted too slowly and slowly slid into it. There was some minor damage to the other car, but the other driver was so moved by Blanche's situation that he didn't ask for her name or phone number and simply sent her on her way with his sincere condolences.

Upon renewing her trek home, she became so overwhelmed that she pulled the car over, stopped, and completely broke down. She felt so terribly alone—hundreds of miles from Kansas City and her family and friends. At that moment life did not seem to matter anymore, as she couldn't conceive of living without Les. When her parents were informed of Les's death, her mother immediately took a train to Milwaukee and spent several weeks with her grief-stricken daughter. Although on the one hand Blanche wanted to grieve alone, on the other hand, she desperately needed the support. She had no idea what to do next. It was as if her purpose for living had suddenly evaporated somewhere in the skies over west central Africa along with a pink B-24 Liberator named *Rose Bud*.

Among the condolences received over the next few weeks, a particularly poignant one was from the Chief of Staff of the United States Armed Forces (and future U.S. Secretary of State), Lieutenant General George C. Marshall:

My dear Mrs. Barnes: My deepest personal sympathy goes to you in this time of sadness. ... There are few words which would be helpful in your sorrow, but I hope you may find consolation in the knowledge that your husband, Leslie

Barnes, has made the great sacrifice in order that Americans may continue to live as a free people under a government of their own choosing. He died while serving as a soldier of his country. More cannot be said in honor of his memory. Again, with deepest sympathy, Faithfully yours, G.C. Marshall[35]

Gen. Marshall's letter was immediately followed by a similar message from Lieutenant General Henry H. "Hap" Arnold, the Commanding General of the U.S. Army Air Forces:

My dear Mrs. Barnes: It is with the deepest regret that I have learned of the untimely death of your husband, Second Lieutenant Leslie Craven Barnes, July 24, 1942, in an airplane accident in the African Area. Lieutenant Barnes, I am informed, was an unusually determined officer whose initiative, self-reliance and devotion to the Service captured the respect of all who knew him. Prior military training in the Missouri National Guard was reflected in the precision and dispatch with which Lieutenant Barnes discharged his assignments as a bombardier. It is my hope that time will alleviate your grief and that you will find comfort in the knowledge that Lieutenant Barnes died in the service of his Country. My deepest sympathy to you and to other members of the family. Very sincerely, H.H. Arnold[36]

Dead Reckoning

Based on the official U.S. Army Air Corps accident report, completed months later, Les and the crew of the *Rose Bud* had left Accra with their squadron on the evening of July 23 and headed northeast to Kano, and from Kano they continued toward Khartoum. However, unexpectedly, the squadron ran into a massive storm front that included lightning, thunder, and high winds. Since the moon had just set, visual markers were nonexistent. Naturally the squadron had difficulty maintaining its formation. At that point all the B-24s had to fly by dead reckoning, "a method of navigation which involved charting a given course, noting the required directional bearings, and computing the airplane headings and air speeds necessary to fly the charted course"[37] and *Rose Bud* got separated from the rest of the squadron. In other words, the navigator miscalculated, and they got lost.

Soon thereafter, at around four o'clock in the morning on the 24th, *Rose Bud* crashed near the village of Fallah, to the north of N'Djamena (originally Ft. Lamy) and near the shore of Lake Chad (or "Lac Tshad" in French), in French Equatorial Africa (which is now the independent country of Chad).

The local natives were the only witnesses to the accident, and, from their individual accounts, it appears as if the plane was either struck by lightning or brought down by severe winds. It started to break up while still in the air, as the debris field extended over 2,000 meters and yet the plane neither skimmed the ground on impact nor broke or sheared off surrounding trees and underbrush.

After having heard several large explosions, the natives left their village and rushed through the darkness to the crash site. They found three bodies outside of the main fuselage as all three appeared to have fallen from the plane as it broke up in the air. Their injuries were consistent with falls from a great height. Another five crew members were still in the main fuselage of the plane, and because of the fire ignited from the aviation fuel, the natives were unable to pull them from the wreckage. The bodies were so severely burned that the U.S. military could only identify them from their dog tags, personal belongings, and dental records. The natives also found two aviators under the severed right wing of the plane. Les Barnes was one of them. The natives pulled his body out from under the burning wing and discovered that the lower half of his body was already "carbonized." None of the crew survived.[38]

Of course, Les and his crewmates had known, especially at that early and critical point in the war, that they and the other bomber crews were "expendable," and that risks existed that were out of their control.[39] They accepted that fact with equanimity and resignation. They all firmly believed in what they were doing. The only concern Les ever voiced to Blanche was his, and his crewmates', lack of faith in their new navigator. She remembered that after one particularly long and grueling day of training, Les had told Blanche that the *Rose Bud*'s navigator "did not seem to know what he was doing" and that he "was easily flustered." That is a dangerous combination for someone charged with performing such an important task.

There was an organizational reason for why such an inexperienced navigator was placed on an operational B-24 and sent on a flight covering thousands of miles that included flying over the Atlantic Ocean and flying at night. At the beginning of the war navigational training was suffering:

> Probably no other aircrew [training] program was started with so few qualified instructors, and the shortage lasted longer than in other programs. The demands of the operational air units for navigators far exceeded the supply of qualified specialists during the first year of war; as a result, practically no experienced personnel could be spared for teaching, and reliance had to be placed upon new graduates of the navigation schools.[40]

The lack of trained instructors was a problem that was solved in time, and bomber crews that went through the training process from early 1943 on were far more prepared for their important tasks. However, in early 1942, there simply was not enough time or trained personnel to do the job properly. A "compromise had to be made between the urgent need for the planes" and the relative unpreparedness of the crews. In the final analysis, the crash of *Rose Bud* and Les's death was just one of those tragic accidents that often happen during wartime. Les drew the short straw and Blanche was left behind to pick up the pieces.

Left Behind

After the initial shock, Blanche felt numb, brokenhearted, and lost. She even felt a little guilty. Les had given his life for his country, and she had done nothing; and, yet, she was alive, and he was gone. How fair was that? How did that make any sense? Of course, under any circumstances, losing a spouse is a life-changing experience and grief is a normal reaction. Sometimes, though, grief is so profound that it interferes with one's ability to move forward with life. That described Blanche to a T. She felt as if her life was effectively over and yet she was still breathing, still waking up every morning, and still going through the motions of everyday life. That netherworld between life and death was made worse by the fact that her husband's body was never returned home for burial. Blanche had reluctantly acquiesced to Les's mother's desire for his remains to be reinterred in a military cemetery in North Africa, instead of being brought back to Kansas City for burial. That lack of closure made Blanche's grief even worse as she was never able to say goodbye in any formal manner. Consequently, the next year and a half of her life was filled with loneliness, sadness, and regret as constant companions, supplemented with a quiet contemplation of what might have been.

The only relic Blanche kept from this period of her life was a small article pressed inside the scrapbook she had created to memorialize Les's life and military career. It is an article by an unknown author entitled "Because He Will Not Return."

You are sitting in the room he left. The open cupboard shows all his workaday and best clothes hanging cleaned and pressed against his return. ... And now the paper in your hand says he will not return. ... The paper says that he is dead, but that is not true. He went adventuring out ahead of us, following the call to give his life—no, not his real life but that part of it which he shared with us here. That part of life he gave wholly and freely, not careless of us but because he was so mindful of us all. So, he no longer needs the body we know. It is folded away in Mother Earth. ... His first taste of life, his apprentice work, is over.

   We had not thought it would be that way. We thought of him as following us in our long monotone of work and care, his vigor like ours slowing down at last to the anxious step of advancing age. ... But for him a trumpet sounded! We had thought the days of chivalry gone forever, and yet in an hour our plain man went away like a knight to rescue the innocent and the distressed. He has done his [duty] and now the trumpets are sounding for him on the other side. ... We taught him the faith of the Everlasting. ... In that faith he went out, ...

   Do you think that ... he would want us to sit and mourn with folded hands in his old empty room? To grieve and harden and grow bitter? To turn the room where once he was so gay into a museum and a morgue? No! He wants us to lift up our hearts and catch a glimpse of the vision [that was] so clear to him ...[41]

As implied by that anonymous author, Blanche ultimately did find a new meaning to her life and to Les's sacrifice. While Blanche quietly grieved, the American Red Cross was organizing its overseas operations in Great Britain and, in the process, came up with a unique idea that provided hundreds of mature, well-educated American women with a unique once-in-a-lifetime opportunity to serve their country and expand their horizons.

Chapter 3

"[The GIs] never seemed to get their fill of doughnuts ..."

The American Red Cross

While Blanche quietly grappled with her grief and the uncertainty of her immediate future, the United States government was focusing on creating an all-out war effort that, it was hoped, would lead the country and its allies to ultimate victory. Private and charitable organizations that had historically supported the military during wartime were focusing on doing the same thing. The American Red Cross (ARC), however, was unique in that it was the only organization authorized by the United States government to provide canteens on military posts, and that, along with its medical-related services, meant that the American people had a long tradition of giving the ARC its full support, especially during wartime.[42]

In fact, during World War II, the American people supported the ARC on an unprecedented scale by "donating their time, their money, and their energy" to its humanitarian mission. By the end of the war over seven and half million Americans, male and female, and from every walk of life, had volunteered their time to the ARC at some point during the war, and over 104,000 registered nurses served in military hospitals at home and abroad under the auspices of the Red Cross. In addition to its extensive operations within the continental United States, the ARC also had over 39,000 paid staff providing its services directly to American service members overseas.[43]

Under the terms of its charter, granted by the United States Congress in 1905, the ARC had the obligation, among other things, to act as the medium for communication between American military personnel and their families back at home. This was a responsibility that the ARC took seriously. It also took seriously its companion mission to provide recreational services to military personnel at home and abroad, thereby giving GIs "a taste of home while relieving boredom and homesickness."[44] By the end of 1942, the ARC was already doing so in England, Northern Ireland, Wales, and Scotland through its network of "clubs," through its smaller "aeroclubs" (ultimately established on practically every airfield operated by the Eighth, Ninth, and Fifteenth U.S. air forces), and through its rest homes for airmen.[45] Similar clubs were later established at most U.S. Naval bases throughout Great Britain and referred to as "fleet clubs." There were about 300 of them.

Therefore, at its peak, the Red Cross was operating approximately 700 clubs of one sort or another within Great Britain, and that number did not include the small "Donut Dugouts" that only served doughnuts, commonly referred to by the GIs as "sinkers," and coffee.[46] Originally, these different clubs were the only facilities the ARC planned to establish, in addition to its traditional hospital and field medical service operations. The mission of these clubs was to lift the morale and spirit of homesick American GIs. But in a move that had the opposite effect, because of the substantial difference in pay and buying power between American and non-American service members stationed in Great Britain, the U.S. Armed Services asked that the Red Cross charge a nominal fee for its food, drinks, and lodgings at all its installations. It was a request that the Red Cross reluctantly complied with and a move that engendered a lot of criticism from American GIs, airmen, and sailors.[47]

By the summer of 1942, the ARC's operations overseas were already so large and complex that the organization's leadership decided that it needed someone on-site in England with strong administrative, financial, and management capabilities to properly oversee those operations. Therefore, in August 1942, Norman H. Davis, the National Chairman of the American Red Cross, asked banker Harvey Dow Gibson to visit him at his office in Washington, D.C. Davis was aware of Gibson's experience and qualifications. During the First World War, Gibson had served as the ARC's Commissioner in France, plus he had a highly distinguished banking and business career since that time. Gibson had begun his career with the American Express Company and later became the president of the Manufacturers Trust Company in New York City. In addition, in 1939, he served as the Chief Operating Officer and Chairman of the Board of Directors of the successful New York World's Fair.[48] He seemed to be the perfect choice.

When Gibson met with Davis in his office in Washington, D.C., Davis asked Gibson to become the ARC's Commissioner to Great Britain and Western Europe. After what Gibson admitted later was some "insincere hesitancy" on his part, as he had hoped that he would be offered an overseas assignment, he agreed to the request on two conditions. First, that he would be allowed to take his wife with him as a volunteer staff member, and second, that the appointment would be for only six months. Davis accepted both of Gibson's conditions, and Gibson was at his new job in London within the month. The limitation on the term of service was soon forgotten by both men and Gibson ended up remaining in London until after V-E Day in May 1945.[49]

Organizing in Support of Victory

Importantly, Gibson received the full endorsement and support of the Allied Commander in Chief of the European Theater of Operations (ETO), General Dwight D. Eisenhower, and that support proved vital. During the entire time that the ARC was operating in

Great Britain, almost everything, including food, was strictly
rationed by the British government, and all U.S. armed forces stationed in Great Britain, when on leave or otherwise not in active
service, were required to observe those rationing rules.[50] However,
it was rather difficult to abide by British civilian food rationing
while at the same time trying to satisfy the appetite of young, healthy
American males.[51]

Luckily, Gibson required General Eisenhower's direct intervention only once. A supervisor in the British Ministry of Food refused
to sell the ARC the amount of flour the ARC needed to continue to
serve doughnuts through its numerous distribution points. When
raised with the supervisor's minister, the minister refused to inter-
vene. So, Gibson had to seek the assistance of General Eisenhower.
The general took the matter to the highest levels of the British government, and predictably, the ARC got its flour.[52]

After his arrival in London, Gibson got right down to work. He
began to carefully evaluate the ARC's organizational structure,
financing, staffing, services, and supply network. He was impressed
and awed by "the magnitude of the services to be rendered" if the
ARC was going to meet all the Army's and Navy's expectations. For
example, the military had requested that "the ARC establish recreational facilities for service men, with extensive quarters for sleeping and eating for those men on leave or stationed nearby, in every
sizable population center in Great Britain." The ARC had attempted
to do so, but when America's First Lady, Eleanor Roosevelt, visited
GIs stationed in Great Britain in the fall of 1942, she correctly
observed that "there were not enough [Red Cross] clubs for men
stationed some distance from towns and cities."[53] In response, the
ARC ultimately opened nearly 400 clubs in major cities throughout
Great Britain. This club system was "by far the largest chain hotel
operation in the world. In these clubs the ARC provided sleeping
accommodations for 200,000 to 250,000 men a week and served an
average of two million meals and snacks a week." Each club was run
by a small American staff, assisted by British employees and
volunteers.[54]

It was immediately evident to Gibson that the expense involved in providing all these services was going to exceed the ARC's pre-war resources. Therefore, with General Eisenhower's approval and assistance, Gibson met with W. Averell Harriman, an American politician and businessman (who later served as President Harry S. Truman's Secretary of Commerce, and as the Governor of New York). At the time, Harriman oversaw administering the American government's Lend-Lease Program with Great Britain, pursuant to which huge quantities of goods and military supplies were being shipped to Great Britain by the United States. What became known as "Reverse Lend-Lease" had just been implemented. It allowed Great Britain, in exchange for the goods and supplies it was receiving from the U.S., to directly assume certain specified expenses in direct support of the U.S. military.

Gibson suggested to Harriman that certain ARC expenditures, which were obviously in direct support of the U.S. armed forces, should be included in Reverse Lend-Lease, if approved, of course, in advance by the U.S. military. Specifically, Gibson pointed to the rental and administrative costs of the ARC's clubs in Great Britain, as well as certain types of motor vehicles and the garages and other facilities required to maintain them. He also suggested that the cost of railroad transportation within Great Britain for ARC members and staff should be included.[55]

To Gibson's delight, Harriman readily agreed and thereafter "fully cooperated in every way" in making it happen. By 1944, the ARC had over 1,000 pieces of motor equipment, most of which were of British manufacture. Since during the war motor vehicles and parts were scarce and new vehicles unobtainable, the receipt of these vehicles and the authority to use British maintenance depots to service them proved to be a tremendous boon to the ARC.[56]

Birth of the Clubmobile

Regarding the ARC's club system, Gibson also concluded that the First Lady had been correct; it was not going to meet the overall needs of American service members stationed in Great Britain, as the clubs were only available to men on leave visiting major cities and towns. So, he decided that the ARC had to find a way to bring its services directly to American service members, no matter where they were stationed and regardless of whether they were on duty or on leave. But finding a solution was no easy task. It was impractical and far too expensive to establish small brick and mortar clubs in hundreds of additional locations throughout Great Britain, so Gibson came upon an original and brilliant idea. Instead of expecting the American GI to come to the ARC, he would take the ARC to the GI, utilizing the motor vehicles that were now available through Reverse Lend-Lease. What Gibson envisioned was some kind of moving or mobile canteen service unit, a club literally on wheels. Drawing from his familiarity with skimobiles, he ultimately dubbed these new mobile units as "clubmobiles."[57]

Initially, the vehicles procured for the clubmobile service were primarily converted English-made half-ton Bedford trucks. Then, in early 1943, the ARC placed into service 40 single-decker passenger buses that were purchased from the British Ministry of Transportation from a former London bus company called "The Green Line."[58] The Green Liners, as they were called, were spacious enough for the field operations required, but overall performance was average at best and the buses were generally restricted to the flatter terrain in the English countryside. Refueling was required every 80 miles or so. Since each clubmobile had limited space, it was essential to select a food item for distribution that would be easy to make, required few ingredients, and could be served quickly. "Second only to hamburgers, doughnuts were a favorite food among American troops and were determined [by the ARC] to be the best option for mobile dispersal to troops. When served alongside coffee, doughnuts became a powerful tool in combating battle fatigue among enlisted men."

Willing to contribute to the war effort, the Doughnut Corporation of America loaned the Red Cross 468 electric-powered doughnut machines. Each one could turn out 48 dozen doughnuts each hour. Even so, as time went on, these proved inadequate in keeping up with demand. "[The GIs] never seemed to get their fill of doughnuts. They would take all of them they could get the first trip up the line and then frequently would go right back to the end of the line and come up again."[59] By December 1943, over 50 clubmobiles were in operation. By December 1944, their crews had already served an astonishing 4,659,728 doughnuts to American servicemen.[60]

Since the doughnut was what was going to be served, each "Green Liner," the largest of the clubmobiles used in England, was equipped with a built-in kitchen in the middle of the bus with a doughnut machine that would allow the crew to make fresh doughnuts several times a day, if necessary, as well as a primus stove for making coffee.[61] The obvious advantage of these converted buses was that they could be driven directly onto army camps, airfields, and naval bases and provide everything required to serve the servicemen right where they lived, worked, and relaxed. Later, building on the original concept, Gibson created what was referred to as "cinemobiles," which were trucks converted into mobile entertainment units with one side that dropped and made a mini stage. Each cinemobile had a miniature piano, a motion picture projector, generator, and an assortment of films.[62]

The "Donut Dolls"

Regardless of how well appointed, the heart and soul of these "clubs on wheels" were going to be the crews that ran them. Gibson instinctively understood that basic fact; he knew that the clubmobile crews would play a pivotal role in the overall success of the program. So, he quickly decided that the new clubmobiles should be staffed by two or three young American women, designated as "staff assistants," and recruited from all parts of the country. Each crew would also include a British civilian driver. In this way, Gibson avoided the problem of a lack of available manpower and offered American servicemen the opportunity to meet and converse with American women from their own state or region while serving overseas. It was an ingenious way to help remind the men just what they were fighting for and, more importantly, to help reassure them that the folks back home were remembering and appreciating their service. In addition, since the clubmobiles would be providing services away from established clubs and cities, and directly on American military bases, the ARC was able to avoid the requirement that they charge a nominal fee for the clubmobiles' services. Thus, everything the women distributed from a clubmobile was free of charge.[63] That too was a popular feature of Gibson's creation.

Obviously, the American women recruited for this important task had to be "the cream of the crop." To guarantee the American public's support for the program, it was vitally important that the ARC ensured that the use of a female crew overseas was acceptable and conformed to existing social norms regarding American womanhood, or the whole plan could backfire. Sending American women overseas to provide Red Cross services directly to American soldiers and sailors, apart and distinct from established clubs, was a gamble. The public might consider any plan that placed women too close to the action as unacceptable. It was one thing to have women serving as nurses in hospitals, or running recreational clubs in major cities, but having them work on military bases or, even worse, near the front lines was a different matter. Consequently, the women had to be of good character, well-educated, poised, dedicated, and semi-independent.

To attract the right kind of applicant, the ARC decided that the women had to be mature (between the ages of 25 and 35, although ultimately some were older and some were younger), have at least two years of college, and have practical work experience. Additionally, applicants had to be in good physical health, display an upbeat and positive attitude, be a good conversationalist, and possess poise and charm, as well as possess solid social and interpersonal skills. Talent for music, dance, or other forms of entertainment were desirable but not required.[64]

The ARC hoped that these requirements would ensure the selection of applicants who would prove to be strong, resourceful, brave, friendly, resilient, and most importantly would stay out of trouble. Attractiveness was also a plus, but not in the model or movie actress sense of the word. What the ARC was seeking was the "well-scrubbed, wholesome 'girl next door.'"[65] But the ARC also wanted a woman mature enough to be viewed by the servicemen as their older sister. In other words, a woman who could manage the type of situations that might arise when placed among thousands of young men far away from home. But to sell the program to the American public, the Red Cross insisted on referring to these mature, well-educated, confident women as "girls." As historian Julia Ramsey noted in her excellent thesis on the Red Cross's participation in World War II, "Referring to ARC volunteers as 'girls' helped maintain their non-threatening status and set them apart from the 'women' of the …" military's women's auxiliary services.[66]

Interestingly, the ARC did not require applicants to be unmarried, but nevertheless most of them were. This is because the ARC feared that the American public might oppose the idea of sending married women into harm's way. The few exceptions were women without children whose husbands were also serving overseas.[67] The ARC also hoped that selecting older, independent, well-educated, middle- to upper-class women would somehow create the impression in the public's mind that the clubmobile crews were more moral than the alternatives. This was also a key to selling the public on the idea of placing women in close contact with thousands of young, middle- to lower-class men. "That this would be acceptable [was] built on the presumption that these women, because of their class status, would be able to not only control themselves, but also [control] the lower-class men around them."[68]

The formal application process started with a written application and a physical examination; and, if the applicant got past these initial steps, a personal interview with a panel of ARC recruiters was arranged to assess the candidate's qualifications. This rigorous selection process resulted in only one in six applicants being selected for overseas duty. Requiring some college education, of course, effectively eliminated from consideration most working—and

lower-class women because higher education for women in the
1930s and early 1940s was largely reserved for the upper middle
class and above.[69] So it was hardly surprising that most clubmobile
crews had similar backgrounds and came from the same social
strata, since the recruitment criteria almost guaranteed it.

Once his clubmobile program was firmly established, Gibson
and his staff worked closely with the military to create scheduled
routes to locations where the need for the ARC's services was the
greatest.[70] Great Britain was divided into regional areas, "each one
with a base from which the service fanned out to remote locations.
At most bases, living accommodations and storage facilities were
provided."[71] The women selected for clubmobile service were then
assigned to an individual clubmobile and to a regional base. Next,
they were assigned specific Army bases or airfields to serve.

The sight of a Red Cross clubmobile driving up to their base or
airfield was both exciting and comforting to the men. It almost
immediately raised their spirits because that clubmobile contained
American women who had come a long way just to see them. The
clubmobilers were female, young, attractive, and all American! And,
because they had been carefully screened and selected, they knew
how to talk to the GIs. They knew their slang, their music, their
dances, and their culture. The "clubmobile girls" knew how to tell a
joke or return a wisecrack. They knew baseball, Bob Hope, Clark
Gable, and the latest American movie, record, or dance. Plus, the
men knew that they could walk right up to a Red Cross Girl and
strike up a conversation without worrying about being rebuffed or
belittled. The men were crazy about them.[72]

Thus, Harvey Gibson's clubmobile program proved to be a brilliant and popular innovation for the ARC and for the American
military, and American servicemen loved it. It was the first time in
American history that American women were officially made a part
of the military apparatus, and the women quickly became the stars
of the program. The clubmobile program was ultimately utilized in
all the main theaters of the war, including Great Britain, the Middle
East, North Africa, Australia, New Guinea, and India.[73] It provided

the American GIs the morale boost they needed, and the women a unique opportunity to directly assist the war effort overseas while at the same time broadening their own horizons. It was a perfect fit for Blanche too, although in 1943 and in early 1944 she did not know it yet.

Chapter 4

"Adventure is a state of mind ... and spirit."

Back to Northwestern

Far from the European Theater of Operations and from the policy and administrative challenges confronting Harvey Gibson and his staff in spring 1943, Blanche was still living in Wisconsin and teaching voice and music at a local junior high school. As fall turned into winter, and winter into spring, she had gone through the motions of trying to make sense of her dislocated and broken world. She had had eight months to try to decide, in relative privacy, what she wanted to do with the rest of her life. Although by the end of the school year she did not have a definitive answer, she knew what she *did not* want to do. Blanche never wanted to teach in a classroom again.

Not possessing the physical presence or the dominating personality required to properly control rowdy teenagers, she felt as if she had accomplished nothing as a teacher. The two highlights (or lowlights if you will) of her year teaching were when one of her teenaged students asked her out on a date, and when another teacher told her to leave the teachers' lounge since it was reserved for teachers and not students. No one took her seriously. In addition, she was physically and mentally exhausted, but permanently returning to Kansas City was not an attractive option. There were just too many memories there, too many familiar places that reminded her of Les. Ultimately, she turned to the one thing in her life that had always provided her comfort, enjoyment, and a feeling of self-worth—her music.[74]

Therefore, when the school year ended and her contract obligations with the Wauwatosa School District had been faithfully fulfilled, Blanche left Wisconsin and drove to Evanston, Illinois, to enroll in summer school at Northwestern University. She had decided to continue her education and earn a master's degree in music, with an emphasis on concert piano. Unfortunately, little Paddy could not accompany her. Her landlord in Milwaukee had refused to allow dogs, so Blanche had reluctantly asked Les's mother to take Paddy for the school year. Later, when Les's mother could no longer manage the little dog, Blanche's brother, Lloyd, offered to take Paddy. Lloyd and his wife became so attached to the little cocker spaniel that, although Blanche had a special attachment to Paddy (she had been a gift from Les), she never had the heart to ask for her back.

For her accommodations at Evanston, Blanche found a quaint little one-bedroom apartment over a grocery store near campus and for the next nine months she immersed herself in her studies. Besides her regular course work, she also practiced the piano four to six hours every day. Keeping that busy during the daylight hours certainly helped keep her mind off her grief and her intense loneliness, but at night the ghosts of times past would return with a vengeance and her dreams were often filled with memories of Les and their time together in Florida. She also suffered from nightmares, usually of planes that were carrying Les crashing and burning. As if that was not enough, every time she heard a plane overhead the magnitude of her loss was instantly revisited. She came to hate the sound of them. It was a psychological reaction that left a horrible taste in her mouth. She had always prided herself on her ability to manage whatever life threw at her; and, unlike her mother, who had an overpowering fear of water and had never learned to swim or drive, Blanche believed in facing her fears head on.

As winter faded and Blanche got closer to finishing her master's degree, she decided that enough was enough and that she needed to "take the bull by the horns" and do something about her aversion to planes and airports. She had already decided that once her graduate studies were concluded she would, in honor of her husband's supreme sacrifice, find some way to help the war effort, and preferably by doing something that directly assisted America's fighting men overseas.

Reaching for the Sky

Despite her newly acquired aversion, Blanche had always admired the women who blazed new trails in aviation. During the 1930s, women pilots such as Louise Thaden (who set airborne and altitude records, as well as winning the Women's Air Derby in 1929), Amelia Earhart (the first woman to fly solo from the United States to Europe in 1932), and Jacqueline "Jackie" Cochran, had caught Blanche's attention and fascination. She read all she could about Jackie Cochran, who was quickly becoming an authentic American hero. "She was a test pilot who constantly pushed the edge of the envelope, and routinely risked her life in unproven aircraft."[75] In 1937 Cochran was the only woman to compete in the Bendix Transcontinental Trophy Race (a point-to-point air race sponsored by industrialist Vincent Bendix, the founder of Bendix Corporation) and she won the race in 1938.

By 1944 Jackie Cochran was rightfully considered the best female pilot in the United States. Besides winning the Bendix Race, she had set new transcontinental speed and altitude records as well. She also was the first woman to fly a bomber across the Atlantic Ocean and win five Harmon Trophies (awarded annually to the world's outstanding aviator). Quite simply, she was one of the most gifted racing pilots of her generation—male or female. No other pilot held more speed, distance, or altitude records in aviation history than Jackie Cochran.[76] It was Jackie Cochran who famously said that "adventure is a state of mind ... and spirit," and Blanche was confident that she possessed the right spirit and the right sense of adventure to do more than sit idly by and watch the world move on without her.

Thus, the answer slowly became clear to Blanche; she needed to learn how to fly both figuratively and literally. Perhaps it would kill her, or perhaps it would kill two birds with one stone. It could end what she considered a silly fear, and it could make her eligible for the newly created Women Airforce Service Pilots (WASP) organization, headed by none other than her hero Jackie Cochran. The WASPs were not a part of the U.S. military or military reserves in 1944 like the Women's Army Corps (WACs) and the Women Accepted for Volunteer Emergency Service (WAVES) were. Instead, the WASPs were Federal civil service employees attached to the U.S. Army Air Corps and authorized to fly military aircraft. During its brief history, 1,074 female WASPs earned their wings and helped free up male pilots for military combat and other duties. They did so by transporting every major type of military aircraft from base to base as needed, transporting personnel and military cargo, towing targets for live anti-aircraft gunnery practice, and even testing new aircraft. As a result of these activities, some of which were highly dangerous, 38 WASPs died in the service of their country.[77]

Blanche knew that to be a WASP she needed a pilot's license, but what she did not know was that more than 25,000 women had already applied for the new organization and that only 1,830 would be accepted. To qualify, applicants had to be at least five feet four inches tall (and Blanche was barely five feet) and pass an Army physical (which she was unlikely to be able to do because of her heart condition).[78] Furthermore, her accumulated hours of flying would have been unimpressive. Of course, she did not know any of those things at the time. All she knew was that she was not interested in the WACs or WAVES because they were a part of the military and seemed "too military-like" and too masculine and regimented for her taste. Plus, they were generally assigned stateside duties, and that wasn't for her. Finally, the idea of being referred to as a "soldier" or a "sailor," with all the negative connotations those terms implied for females in the early 1940s, turned Blanche off.

So, with her decision made, Blanche identified the nearest airfield that offered flying lessons, which turned out to be the Palwaukee Municipal Airport (now part of the Chicago Executive Airport). It was located eighteen miles northwest of Chicago in the town of Wheeling. With her decision made, one beautiful spring morning Blanche drove to the Palwaukee airport and signed up for lessons. It was a gutsy move, and one she did not mention to her family. Obtaining a pilot's license in 1944 was an expensive proposition, costing around $750 at a time when the average teacher's salary was somewhere under $1,000 a year.[79] Since careers in commercial aviation were generally closed to women, it is no wonder that few women sought or obtained a pilot's license.[80]

In 1944 the conditions at the Palwaukee Airport were primitive at best. There was no control tower, and the runway was a cleared but unpaved field. The airport had first opened in 1925 and was named Palwaukee because of its location near the intersection of *Pal*atine Road and Mil*waukee* Avenue.[81] Blanche's instructor turned out to be a World War I fighter pilot, and the plane she was to train in was a 1930s version of the Piper Cub Army trainer (probably a model L-4 "Grasshopper") built by the Piper Aircraft Company. It was a lightweight, high-wing, strut-braced monoplane with a large rectangular wing powered by an air-cooled piston engine. Its fuselage was made of welded steel and covered in fabric. It had fixed landing gear and it seated two people in tandem in a cockpit open on either side under the wing. The aircraft had a maximum range of around 200 miles, and a cruising speed of around 70 miles per hour. It was perfect for training purposes as it had good low-speed handling properties and could easily take off and land on short airfields.[82] Most American pilots during World War II had learned to fly in a Piper Cub because it was so easy to fly. However, the Piper did not have a radio and the prop had to be hand-rotated to start its engine.

As part of Blanche's initial training, she had to learn how to operate the plane within normal flying conditions and manage typical emergency situations. Like today's basic flight training, the instructor focused on the importance of obtaining proficiency in slow flight, upset prevention and recovery, ways to avoid stalling and, if you did, how to recover from it without power and without killing yourself. To teach that last skill the instructor had Blanche turn the plane into a spin with the nose straight down, better known as a "spiral dive." After eight rotations she had to pull the plane out of its dive or else! The key to the maneuver was remembering which direction the plane had begun its roll, because to get out of the dive, she had to push the stick hard in the opposite direction.

Going Solo

Surprisingly, Blanche took to flying almost immediately and soon her fears were a thing of the past. Her plan had worked, at least in part. When the time came for her to "solo flight," her instructor walked her through the process and at the end added a stern warning. He informed her that Army planes from a nearby airfield were flying over the airport that day, but at a higher altitude; therefore, he instructed her to follow the set flight plan he had constructed for her without deviations. She was to take off with the wind in her face, go up to a predetermined altitude (and no higher), perform a 180-degree turn around the field, and come back down (with the wind in her face again).

Of course, as all pilots know, taking off into the wind (or with a "headwind") slows the plane down during its acceleration with respect to the ground, but it increases the flow of air over the wings, thus generating lift and allowing the pilot to achieve a higher altitude in less time and with less speed. "In essence, this reduces the amount of speed and distance needed to achieve 'wheels up'" and assists the pilot in clearing any obstacles at the end of the runway.[83]

Landing into the wind is even more important because it helps to decrease speed and bring the plane to a controlled stop. This was particularly important for Blanche's solo flight because the plane she was flying in did not have brakes and the field was relatively short. The wind in her face and a skid underneath the plane were the only things that were going to slow the plane down after landing. If a pilot is coming in too fast, another option is to land the plane with its nose slightly tilted upward to effect rapid deceleration. However, with the Piper Cub, as with most single prop planes of the time, this method would also result in the pilot temporarily losing sight of the runway—which is not advisable for a novice pilot. Although she was familiar with the nose up method, it had not been a part of her training.

After Blanche took off, with the wind in her face of course, she successfully reached her assigned maximum altitude, completed a half circle around the field, and proceeded to align the aircraft with the field for a landing. The feeling of flying on her own in an open cockpit, and being in total control, was exhilarating. Although the sound of the engine and of the wind was deafening, the view was breathtaking. But Blanche kept reminding herself that she was not up there to sightsee; she was on her first solo flight, and she needed to concentrate on what she was doing.

Everything was going well until she prepared to land. Since she had completed a 180-degree turn around the field, she was expecting that the wind would be in her face again when she landed. However, in the brief time she had been in the air, the wind had completely switched directions. Thus, if she landed as planned, she was going to have the wind at her back. Therefore, she had a serious decision to make, and she had to make it quickly. She could either abort her approach, regain altitude, and attempt another 180-degree turn around the field to land from the other direction, or keep going, land with the wind at her back in the nose up position, and hope that she could stop the plane before she ran out of runway.

Of course, Blanche also remembered her instructor's admonition before she took off; that under no circumstances was she to "deviate from her flight plan." Keeping that in mind, and since she felt confident that she could land the plane successfully with the wind behind her, she decided to keep going. It was a gutsy call as well as a potentially dangerous one. To come in at the correct angle of descent and have any hope of stopping on time, Blanche had to clear a row of trees and several power lines at low altitude and bring the plane down onto the runway as quickly as possible. She successfully cleared the obstacles, but to ensure that the plane slowed sufficiently she had to tilt the nose of the plane slightly upward just before the rear landing gear encountered the ground. That forced the front of the plane to come down with a thump—it nearly jarred Blanche out of her seat. It was just the reduction in speed she needed, however, since, once on the ground, she struggled to bring the plane to a stop before reaching the end of the runway.

Her instructor, watching from the ground, was duly impressed. He too had noticed the shift in wind and Blanche had reacted to it exactly the way he would have in the same situation. So, he rewarded her with a pilot's license from the new U.S. Civil Aeronautics Administration (CAA). It was an accomplishment most women in the United States had not attained. In 1935 only about 700 to 800 women were licensed pilots, and although World War II created new opportunities for women in aviation, by 1944 only 4,829 pilot licenses were issued to women—whereas over 127,000 had gone to men.[84]

The next logical step in Blanche's grand plan was adding time in the air and learning to parachute, but before doing so she made a thoroughly disheartening discovery. She learned of the WASP's requirement that its pilots be at least five feet four inches tall, and that eliminated her from consideration. So, for a while, she reluctantly gave up on the idea of getting into the war. She had more immediate concerns anyway. For her master's degree program, she was required to perform a public piano recital as part of the School of Music's Student Recital Series (its 53rd season) at the recently completed Lutkin Hall. On the day of her recital, May 9, 1944, she shared the stage with a clarinetist and a string quartet. Among the pieces she performed were "Papillons" by Schumann, "Andaluza" by de Falla, and the "Sonata No. 5, Opus 53" by Scriabin. Her training, practice, and preparation paid off and her recital was a resounding success. A month later she received her master's degree at the University's annual convocation, but she was not present to receive it. Shortly after her classes concluded, she returned to Kansas City, intent on trying to determine what she was going to do next.

At His Side

Blanche was, in fact, at a temporary loss. Now that her formal education was complete, she desperately wanted to get in the war and, thereby, gain a new purpose and mission for her life. If she got involved, however, she wanted to directly help American fighting men overseas and not be relegated to the home front. As explained by another young woman in the same position,

> I wanted to be in the thick of things, near where the fighting was. ... Being a girl made this difficult. True, one could enlist in the [military's women's auxiliary services], but when I looked into these different services, I discovered they could give no guarantee, in fact little possibility, of getting overseas. Further, if one did get sent overseas, it would no doubt be to a desk job behind a typewriter—way behind the lines. That was not my idea of being in the thick of things.[85]

Blanche also knew that working overseas would be the experience of a lifetime and might also allow her to see some of the oldest and grandest cities of Europe where many of the greatest composers in history had lived and worked. She had been well prepared for such an experience. As a young girl, she loved reading about the travels and adventures of American Richard Halliburton, as told through his letters home. Halliburton was a confirmed bachelor who lived for the moment and had a thirst for unmasking the unusual and the unknown. Tragically, he was lost at sea in March 1939 while attempting to sail across the Pacific Ocean on a Chinese junk. Nevertheless, Blanche found his descriptions and experiences in Europe, Russia, the Middle East, Africa, India, Southeast Asia, China, and Japan spellbinding. It had sparked a touch of wanderlust in her that she never thought she would be able to satisfy.[86]

As if an answer to a prayer, soon after arriving back in Kansas City, Blanche accepted an invitation to see a movie at a local theater with a high school friend. Truth be known, she did not have any interest in the movie and little interest in socializing, but she went anyway. As fate would have it, prior to the beginning of an otherwise nondescript movie, a newsreel flashed across the screen. At that moment, there in the darkened theater, the answer to Blanche's dilemma suddenly presented itself. It was a newsreel, probably "At His Side," which was about the American Red Cross and the significant role it was playing overseas, and even though the newsreel did not exactly glamorize what a handful of American women were doing for American fighting men, Blanche was inspired.

By 1944 American women, in unprecedented numbers and to do their part in the war effort, had accepted jobs formerly occupied by men, but the concept of service overseas with the Red Cross was new to Blanche. She always thought that female Red Cross personnel were limited to activities on the home front, unless you were a nurse and working in a Red Cross hospital overseas. She did not realize that thousands of women, without nursing credentials, were joining the Red Cross's foreign service and being sent to airfields, clubs, dockyards, and military posts all over Great Britain, North Africa, Italy, and the Pacific. It was a revelation!

Within days of seeing that short newsreel, Blanche had researched the requirements for joining the Red Cross's foreign service and discovered that applicants had to have at least two years of college, have work experience, and be over 25 years of age. She had three degrees, had work experience, and she was 26—even more thrilling was the fact that the ARC did not have a height requirement! So, she immediately obtained, completed, and submitted the formal application, including the necessary references, to the ARC office in St. Louis, Missouri.

For Blanche, her desire to join the Red Cross was not about having fun, nor was it about finding a husband. Even two years after Les's death she was still grieving, and his wedding ring was still on her finger. It was a visible sign for all who came near her that she still considered herself "taken." Her decision to join the Red Cross, however, was an attempt to forget her grief, become a part of something larger than herself, and re-enter the world of the living. And what better way to do it than by helping the war effort and by serving American GIs where they were serving. It was going to be her way of contributing to the war effort and honoring Les's memory. She also innately understood that it might prove to be the adventure of a lifetime, and she needed a little of that. She needed something that would help pull her out of the rut she had been in for the previous two years.

After receiving a favorable response to her written application, she was asked to travel to St. Louis to submit to a formal interview with Red Cross recruiters. So, within the week, she took a train across the state and appeared at the Red Cross office in St. Louis. Blanche knew that being asked for an interview did not mean acceptance. The Red Cross was known for having exacting standards. Women applying for work in the Red Cross's foreign service were required to have work experience, preferably in the recreational field. Plus, they had to be healthy, sociable, and attractive.[87]

Given how selective the Red Cross was, Blanche was understandably nervous about the interview. She was hoping that the interview would be short and rather perfunctory, but that did not prove to be the case. The recruiters (there were more than one) asked her questions about her education, her family, her health, her social life, her marriage, and her musical background. Having two bachelor's degrees, as well as a graduate degree, which was highly unusual in 1944 (especially for a woman), gave Blanche a decided advantage over other applicants. The interviewers were also impressed that she had a pilot's license, had taught school, and was a trained concert pianist.

So overall the interview went extremely well, and the last question posed was an obvious one. The recruiters wanted to know why Blanche wanted to join the Red Cross and serve overseas, considering that the work required was going to be demanding and dangerous. In response, Blanche admitted that she wanted to serve overseas because her husband had died in the war, and she had an ardent desire to do her part to ensure America's ultimate victory. She felt that the best way to do so, as a woman, was to directly help support the morale of America's fighting men. Naturally, that led to a follow-up question about how she was managing her husband's death, and she admitted that it had been difficult but that her faith in God had helped her get through it. That response worried one of the interviewers, perhaps thinking that Blanche would want to go overseas to spread "The Good Word" instead of doing her job, but Blanche quickly assured the interviewer that in her opinion one's religion is a private matter that should stay that way. That satisfied the panel, because after her interview she was directed to a heart specialist in St. Louis for a thorough physical exam. Although interested in hiring Blanche, the ARC was legitimately concerned about her health and her ability to withstand the rigors of overseas service.

After a thorough physical examination, the heart specialist approved Blanche for overseas service, but only for what he referred to as "light duty." Based on the specialist's recommendation, Blanche was hired as "a Staff Assistant for an overseas assignment." However, the "light duty" recommendation was never clearly defined, and once Blanche was overseas, the suggested limited nature of her service was completely forgotten. Perks of the new job were a monthly salary of $150, maintenance benefits, and free life insurance in case of death while overseas. Blanche was going to get her chance to serve! Surprisingly, when informed of her plans, Blanche's parents never voiced an objection, but they were, quite naturally, worried about her health and her safety throughout her overseas tour of duty. Consequently, her letters home constantly attempted to assure them that she was safe and healthy, even when that was not always the case.

Washington, D.C.

When Operation Overlord, the code name for the invasion of France, occurred on June 6, 1944, "D-Day," Blanche was still in Kansas City living with her parents. With the success of the invasion, the Allies were finally taking the war to Hitler's backyard, and the liberation of France was in sight.

Once Blanche was hired by the Red Cross, things moved quickly as the organization was anxious to get her and other new recruits trained and overseas as soon as possible. On Friday, June 9, 1944, just three days after D-Day and less than a week after being hired, Blanche's parents drove her to Kansas City's beautiful and stately Union Station. She hugged and kissed them goodbye and did her best to assure them that she would be fine, then climbed aboard a train headed east for Washington, D.C. The train was packed with hundreds of soldiers and sailors, as well as civilians like herself. "World War II would prove to be the zenith of public rail transportation. … In 1944, the peak war year, more than 75 percent of all commercial passengers traveled by rail, as did an astonishing 97 percent of military passengers."[88] Since she was traveling alone, she found it extremely difficult to avoid the constant attention of the soldiers and sailors all around her. The wedding ring on her finger helped, but still some were undeterred. However, Blanche "took it all in stride," and realized that it was good practice for what she was going to experience daily once she got overseas.

Upon Blanche's arrival at Washington D.C.'s historic Union Station, it was the first time she had been in the nation's capital and the first time she had been east of Chicago. Just as she had not known a single person on the train, she did not know a soul in Washington, D.C. either; but if the previous two years had taught her anything, it was how to manage isolation and be on her own.

Having received orders to immediately "report in" upon arriving in the city, Blanche found the main entrance to the station and hailed a taxi. She was simultaneously shocked that the nation's capital was even hotter and more humid than Kansas City and taken aback by the breathtaking view of the majestic dome of the U.S. Capitol off in the distance. But she had her orders. So, the only nod to the natural impulse to sightsee was a request that the driver get as close as possible to the White House as they headed to the northwest. Blanche was duly impressed by all the magnificent public buildings, the beautiful architecture, the wide lengthy and busy boulevards, and the air of power and importance that it all exuded. But there was also the unmistakable evidence of a city at war. The city's population had nearly doubled in size since 1941 as a mostly female workforce had moved to the city seeking government jobs. So temporary office buildings had been built along the mall, around the Washington Monument, and on three sides of the reflecting pool in front of the Lincoln Memorial just to house tens of thousands of clerical personnel, mostly women. The women were referred to by many as the "government girls."[89] In addition, and out of an abundance of caution, anti-aircraft guns were visible on the roofs of many of the public buildings and in front of the Smithsonian Arts and Industries Building.[90]

From the area around the White House, the taxi driver took Blanche up Massachusetts Avenue, around DuPont Circle, past Embassy Row, and the beautiful and impressive National Cathedral to the campus of American University and the Red Cross headquarters at Hurst Hall. The Hall was a two-story, neoclassical, white limestone building with two massive Ionic columns framing the front doors. It was part of a private, Methodist-affiliated, liberal arts and research institution located at the intersection of Nebraska and Massachusetts Avenues, N.W., at Ward Circle. Built in 1896, Hurst Hall was the university's first building, and it originally housed the College of History. The Red Cross was one of the many organizations that were using American University's campus and buildings during war.

As Blanche slowly walked up the front steps of Hurst Hall, the reality of her surroundings finally began to sink in. She was in her nation's capital, seeing up close the massive public buildings she had only seen before in picture books. It was all suddenly real, and she was there and in the middle of it. However, seeing those buildings armed to the teeth against possible enemy attack hammered home to her that she was on her way to playing a personal role, however small, in the great worldwide conflict that had taken her husband from her two years before. She was officially entering the war effort and she was going to get her opportunity to help the men fighting it. One historian has noted that, given the time and place, "[i]t took a certain uncommon independent streak [for Blanche and the other women joining her at Hurst Hall that hot, muggy July day] ... to leave home and family to serve overseas." It also exhibited a good measure of "tenacity, strength of will, and a keen sense of adventure," attributes Jackie Cochran and Richard Halliburton would have recognized and applauded.[91]

Plates I

Blanche Gregory and 2nd Lt. Leslie C. Barnes on their wedding day, April 3, 1942, Kansas City, Missouri. She's wearing the wedding dress she found the day before and he's wearing his newly awarded wings.

Harvey Dow Gibson (1882–1950), the American Red Cross's Commissioner to Great Britain and Western Europe, and the "father of the clubmobile." *(Courtesy of the American Red Cross.)*

"Volunteer for Victory." A typical World War II Red Cross recruitment poster. Such posters, as well as movie newsreels, promoting the Red Cross's mission helped encourage Blanche and millions of other Americans to volunteer for the war effort. *(Courtesy of the American Red Cross.)*

Resplendent in her new uniform, Blanche poses for her official Red Cross portrait, taken in Washington, D.C., June 1944. It was the beginning of a 15-month overseas tour of duty.

Red Cross girls during a break in front of Hurst Hall, American University, Washington, D.C. It is where Blanche received her initial Red Cross training in June 1944. *(Courtesy of American University and the American Red Cross.)*

The RMS *Queen Elizabeth* in New York Harbor, loaded down with thousands of American servicemen returning from the war, 1945. The ship was painted battleship gray, however, when Blanche sailed from New York City to Scotland in July 1944. *(Imperial War Museum, #NYP 74029.)*

The control tower at RAF Molesworth, September 28, 1944. Notice the loudspeaker system on top of the tower, which is what Blanche used to make routine field announcements. The men on base got a real kick out of her occasionally stumbling over technical words or when she went off script. *(Courtesy of 303rd Bomb Group Association.)*

B-17s of the 359th Bomb Squadron, 303rd Bombardment Group, prepared for takeoff, ca. 1944. When the planes took off and joined other groups to create their formations, the planes would darken the skies. *(Courtesy of 303rd Bomb Group Association.)*

Maj. Melvin L. "Mel" Schulstad Jr. of the 303rd Bombardment Group, Eighth Air Force, ca. 1944. He was handsome, charming, brave, and shouldered enormous responsibilities for one so young, and Blanche nearly fell for him. *(Courtesy of 303rd Bomb Group Association.)*

A Red Cross postcard showing combat troops taking a break around a Green Liner clubmobile at Molesworth Airfield outside Kettering, England, 1944—probably before the D-Day invasion. *(Courtesy of the American Red Cross.)*

A Red Cross postcard showing combat troops taking a break around a Green Liner clubmobile, somewhere in England, 1944—probably before the D-Day invasion. *(Courtesy of the American Red Cross.)*

"Greetings from the Donut Wagon." A humorous cartoon drawn in honor of the Clubmobile Department's second anniversary, October 1944. Note the clubmobile girl depicted as an angel and a GI depicted as a wolf chasing after her. *(Artist unknown.)*

Blanche in the nose of the B-17G "Sack Time," #42-102544, 360th Bomb Squadron, 303rd Bombardment Group, at Molesworth Airfield outside Kettering, England, December 1944. Naturally, she had no trouble fitting completely inside it.

The crew of *The Maine* serving GIs from the side panels at an airfield near Kettering, England, September 1944.

(L to R) Clubmobile driver Ted Scott, Blanche, Dottie Barrett, and Captain Lois Stone with journalist Ernie Pyle's short snorter at an airfield, near Kettering, England, fall 1944. Pyle's short snorter was reputed to be one of the longest in the Army because of the numerous places he had visited during the war.

Blanche at an airfield near Kettering, England, with journalist Ernie Pyle's short snorter around her shoulders, fall 1944.

Chapter 5

"Girls, don't think you're Theda Bara ..."

American University

The first bit of business Blanche faced after reporting to Hurst Hall was the assignment of temporary quarters selected and paid for by the Red Cross. Blanche and the other women freshly arrived were assigned to private homes and boarding houses on K Street and throughout the city. Of course, accommodations in wartime Washington were at a premium, so limited availability dictated that the women had to triple and quadruple up in a single room.[92]

Come Monday morning, June 12, 1944, and for each day thereafter during their training, Blanche and the other new recruits took buses to Hurst Hall to participate in a general, condensed, and highly accelerated two-week training course. It had to be general as the training was basically the same regardless of which theater of war or what department of the ARC the women were ultimately assigned to; it was condensed and accelerated because the time allotted for the training had been drastically cut. When the training for the Red Cross's overseas staff began in late 1942 it lasted six weeks, followed by two weeks of practical experience at nearby clubs

and military bases. But by the summer of 1944, the pressing demand
for more trained overseas staff required the ARC to speed up the
classroom training, reducing it to only two weeks by the time
Blanche arrived. The training had always been inadequate but cutting it by two-thirds almost ensured that the new recruits were
heading overseas without the practical knowledge they needed to
hit the ground running.

Blanche spent that first Monday morning in a large classroom
with scores of other women, all of them filling out paperwork and
listening to introductory lectures on the Red Cross, its programs,
and its history. The paperwork included a release in favor of the
ARC and a promise not to sue in case of injury or death while serving overseas, and a life insurance policy worth $2,000.[93] The paper-
work also included forms for health and accident insurance.

The new recruits also received practical information about their
schedule for the next two weeks, the required uniform, and their
financial responsibilities—which came as a surprise to Blanche.
They were told that at the end of the week they would be given, at
Red Cross expense, summer and winter uniforms, shoes, a cap with
a Red Cross pin on the front of it, a trench-style raincoat, and a
heavy-duty topcoat with red lining; the women would be responsible for shopping and buying all other clothing items and equipment
required for their overseas service. This included a specific number
of white blouses and handkerchiefs, slip and underwear, socks,
white cotton gloves, a robe, a towel and washcloth, plus a belt, boots,
musette bag (a large tote bag), a duffle bag, and a footlocker. It was
also recommended that the women consider purchasing additional
items such as stockings; socks; pajamas; underpants; sanitary nap-
kins; sanitary belt with safety pins; indelible ink for marking clothes;
a suitcase (not to exceed seven pounds empty or 40 pounds when
packed); a bathing suit; safety pins, bobby pins, hairnets, hairpins,
and hair curlers; and last but not least, a dress outfit for semi-formal
occasions.[94]

Blanche really liked the look, style, and the material of the Red
Cross summer uniform—so much so that when she first tried hers

on, with all the accessories, she had her roommate capture the moment with Blanche's movie camera.[95] But she was decidedly less enthused about the winter uniform, which was made of dark gray wool. Later, however, when she was working in England in the dead of winter, she was thankful for having it. During the one weekend sandwiched between the two weeks of classroom training, the women were free from Saturday noon to Monday morning, but Saturday afternoon was used for shopping at Abercrombie & Fitch or other department stores of their choosing. They were also told that under no circumstances were they to travel more than four hours away from Washington, D.C. There was little time for sightseeing, anyway, and Blanche did little of it while there.

Blanche was impressed with the quality, education, and experience of most of the other women who were in training with her, and through their regional accents, she realized that they had come from all over the country. As noted by another earlier trainee, "[t]he radio had to some extent homogenized the country ...: the [radio] announcers all talked with the same accent, and we all had the same magazines sitting on [our] coffee tables ... [However,] the sameness wasn't nearly as great as it might seem. There were girls from all parts of the country ... and each one brought ..." their own makeup, accents, colloquialism, slang, and regional biases.[96]

Blanche found the lectures and training interesting and informative, but she had no idea where she was going to be sent or exactly what she would be doing during her Red Cross tenure, and she was not able to judge. Topics of the lectures included military procedures and security rules, the recognition of military rank and insignia, the various types of work they might be required to perform in the different theaters of operation, a recreation course that covered the types of entertainment they could appropriately offer the GIs (music, cards, dancing, etc.), possible problems they might have to face as women in a war zone, and the importance of maintaining a good relationship with the military brass. The one topic that was excluded by the summer of 1944 was training in first aid, which Blanche thought odd. They were, however, carefully instructed on what the Red Cross expected of them regarding their attitude, deportment, manners, and appearance—basically rules that they all had to live by while serving in the Red Cross. They were reminded that when they were wearing their uniforms, they were ambassadors for the ARC, and if they created bad impressions, that could have a negative impact on the public's financial support for the organization.

One particular female instructor, who had served with the Red Cross during World War I, was dubbed "Theda Bara" (an American actress of the silent film era) by some of the trainees, because after a long lecture warning the women against "the pitfalls and perils women face in situations where they are sometimes outnumbered hundreds to one by men in uniform," she told them, "Girls, don't think you're Theda Bara just because of all the attention you get!"[97] It turned out to be wise advice that some of the trainees unfortunately forgot. The instructor knew what the trainees did not. Even by the summer of 1944, well under one percent of all American military personnel in Great Britain was female.[98]

The instructor also stressed that, if captured, the women would have the equivalent rank of a captain, and, thus, would have to be treated as such under the international rules of war—assuming the Germans, Italians, or Japanese chose to follow them. Consequently, Red Cross policy forbade them from dating enlisted men, which left a sour taste in the mouths of many of the women. If they were being sent overseas to provide services to, and help lift the morale of, the average GI, how could they do so effectively if they refused to socialize with them while off duty? It was one of the many contradictions between Red Cross rules and its mission that the women would face while overseas.

During the training in Washington, D.C., Blanche and the other women had their official individual Red Cross photographs taken, and they were given a series of shots (which included vaccines for smallpox, typhoid-paratyphoid, tetanus, yellow fever, typhus, and cholera) at the general dispensary at the new Pentagon Building across the Potomac River. When an inexperienced male Army nurse tried to give Blanche one of the required shots, he could not find her vein (her veins were notoriously loose and nimble), and after numerous unsuccessful attempts, *he* grew faint. Another senior nurse had to step in and take over. Blanche was not fazed in the least. With her medical history, she could have given herself the shot without blinking an eye.

New York City and the St. George

Blanche graduated from the Red Cross's initial two-week orientation on Saturday, June 24. She was now officially a "Red Cross Recreation Staff Assistant." Naturally, she was anxious to find out where she would go next for her field experience. By the following Monday morning, she was on her way to a Red Cross club in Richmond, Virginia, staying in a private residence at Red Cross expense, and receiving practical experience serving coffee and doughnuts to GIs. The training was designed to teach the new staff assistants how to interact with and relate to GIs in a war zone. Although Blanche made quite a few acquaintances during her stay in Washington, D.C. and in Richmond, she did not make any lasting friendships, primarily because most of the women were sent off in different directions and ultimately lost contact with each other.

Blanche's final orders came after the Fourth of July holiday. She and 21 other women, including Elizabeth "Liz" Richardson, Caroline Drane, Isabel "Ski" Seaton, Rosemary Langheldt, Eloise Reilly, Virginia May Allison, Mary Ruth Read, Margaret "Bettie" Gearhart, Lindsay Rand, Portia Miller, Josephine "Jo" Banichar, Dorothy "Dottie" Barrett, Margaret "Peggy" Evans, Lois Stone, Jean Hogg Rayl, and Mary Alice Grant, were ordered to New York City for eventual embarkation.[99] They all knew what being sent to New York City meant. They were headed for the ETO, and that was exactly where Blanche wanted to go, so she was delighted.

The next day the women grabbed their musette bags and footlockers and headed for the great concourse of Washington's Union Station, where they were divided into six groups, each with a section leader, and boarded a train for New York City. Inexplicably, the new Red Cross "Recreation Staff Assistants" were ordered to wear their winter wool uniforms even though it was July and extremely hot and humid! Plus, each woman had to carry her own musette bag and raincoat. The women were incredibly uncomfortable during the entire trip, as this was a time long before air-conditioning or under-arm antiperspirant were in common use. When one sweats, especially while wearing wool, the result can be uncomfortable and highly unappealing. Blanche remembered that when she and the other women sat down on the train wearing their heavy wool skirts, then remained sitting for several hours, they ended up being what she referred to as "butt sprung!" In other words, the wool fabric had been stretched and soaked in sweat, and when the women rose to detrain, their skirts refused to return to their original positions. In good humor the women all thought it was funny, but they were also a bit embarrassed as they walked through Pennsylvania Station with their skirts visibly deformed.

Upon the women's arrival at Pennsylvania Station in the heart of "The Big Apple," they were greeted by a motor corps unit with police escort and taken by truck directly to the old but still prestigious St. George Hotel, where around 80 other Red Cross girls were already staying. The St. George is in the heart of old Brooklyn Heights, and just a subway station away from the center of Manhattan. At that time, it was one of the largest hotels in the United States. It was a massive complex of buildings situated in a mostly residential area surrounded by beautiful shade trees. The hotel was known for hosting numerous celebrities during the 1920s and 1930s, but its biggest attraction was its indoor saltwater swimming pool with a gigantic, mirrored ceiling.[100]

The women were billeted on one of the upper floors with numerous interconnecting rooms that allowed them to socialize with a reasonable degree of privacy. Because of the extreme heat and humidity, they all immediately changed out of their wool uniforms, showered, and then wandered around the floor in their slips, played cards, borrowed magazines and hair curlers, and sat around and talked. Security was tight—so much so that they could not call home. However, while housed at the St. George, there was time for a brief subway ride into Manhattan to take in the sights, or to see a play, or go to a movie. It was Blanche's first visit to Manhattan, and she was awed by its sheer size, the thousands of people, the huge buildings, and, of course, the stores and all the wonderful items inside them.

While staying at the St. George, Blanche and the other women were bused over to the Brooklyn Navy Yard for what was referred to as "Army processing." They were given steel Army helmets and liners which they were to wear while boarding ship, during drills on shipboard, and, once in the ETO, while serving in combat areas. That last bit of news struck home just how serious Blanche's newly chosen endeavor would be. "Combat areas!" Nevertheless, it did not deter any of them in the least. The women were also issued their other Army equipment and dutifully signed for them. This additional equipment included a canteen, mess kit, first aid packet, and Army-like dog tags.[101] The dog tags were to be placed around their necks and not to be removed for any reason—until their tour of duty ended.

In addition, they were each given a gas mask and carefully drilled on pulling the masks out of their cases and properly placing them on their face quickly and securely. All the women paid close attention as this was serious business indeed. After the oral instructions were completed, the women were allowed a little time to practice using their masks. Then they were directed to a Quonset hut that was being used as a makeshift gas chamber, and they were hurdled into the chamber. Once the doors were shut, their Army instructor ordered them to immediately put on their masks as he was ready to release live gas.[102] Blanche's gas mask was a bit too big, of course, and she had to press it hard against her face to make sure it retained a tight seal against the incoming gas. Thankfully, there were no casualties, just some irritated skin and watery eyes and a new appreciation for such safety procedures and equipment.

After the Army processing and a brief physical were complete, the women were taken back to the St. George and confined to a couple of blocks around the hotel for the next several days. One of the women remembered that it was like "being locked into a sorority chapter house." But most of the women were having fun; it was "almost like a paid vacation ..." Many of them, based on their letters home and their after-war memoirs, felt that the women they were locked in with at the St. George were "a cut above ..."; "not a dull one in the bunch ..."[103] Blanche, on the other hand, didn't feel as if she fit in. Although all the women were well-educated, outgoing, and motivated to assist in the war effort, she also noted a cliquishness among many and a typical, 20-something fascination with all things male. Perhaps because she was a widow and more straitlaced and introverted than most of them, Blanche had a tough time feeling comfortable around her colleagues. It was to prove to be a continuing pattern for the rest of her Red Cross career, and she struggled to try to fit in without losing track of her own moral compass.

Embarkation

Several days before departing, Blanche and the other Red Cross girls were allowed to write letters home to inform their loved ones that they were getting ready to start "a new assignment." However, military censorship was in full play, and they were strictly forbidden to mention where they currently were, where they were going, or how they were going to get there. Then the letters were collected by the ARC and were not mailed until the women had arrived in Great Britain. On Thursday, July 13, the women were informed that they were to set sail that night and that they should be ready to leave the hotel by evening. The women were also told to be dressed in their winter uniforms (again) with all their equipment and bags packed and ready to go.

After hours of waiting, and shortly after midnight, Blanche and the rest of the women finally received orders to move. Since the departure was supposed to be top secret, everyone was ordered to maintain absolute silence, and instead of departing from the front lobby, they were herded through a dark hotel corridor out on to an old fire escape. According to another Red Cross girl "[a]t least three times we broke silence with colorful expressions as the person behind lost control and half fell into the person ahead. At first muf-fled chortles filled the air; the third time someone lost balance, a loud 'Oh, Shit!' filled the night and we didn't bother to stifle our giggles."[104]

As it turned out, the order for silence really was superfluous. Once successfully down the fire escape and out into the back alley of the hotel, the women climbed into waiting buses. But "[a]s the buses pulled out of the alley and turned into the street in front of the hotel, it was a real surprise to see a crowd of people gathered to watch. They were waving and one man called out, 'God bless you girls!'"[105] So much for secrecy!

The RMS Queen Elizabeth

In the morning darkness, the buses took the women across the Brooklyn Bridge to the main docks of the Port of New York. Quickly coming into view was the huge and impressive RMS *Queen Elizabeth*, towering over everything around it. *"The Queen,"* as the ship was reverently referred to, was, at the time, the largest passenger liner in the world and the pride of the Cunard-White Star Line. It was launched just before the war and was originally designed to carry paying passengers across the Atlantic in luxury, but in 1940, it was converted into a troop transport ship for the war. It was 1,031 feet long, 118.5 feet wide, and a draft of 38 feet. Its original gross ton-nage was 83,673. By war's end in 1945, almost a quarter of all U.S. troops and support staff had been shipped to Europe by either the *Queen Elizabeth* or by her older sister ship the *Queen Mary*.[106]

Unlike her pre-war colors of white, red, and black, *The Queen* had been repainted a boring pewter or battleship gray to make it more difficult for German U-boats to identify her and get a fix on her speed and bearing. All the ship's pre-war finery had been care-fully removed, packed, and stored away in a warehouse, and any hint of the ship's pre-war luxuries had been eliminated. Although *The Queen* was originally designed to carry 2,283 passengers and more than 1,000 crew members, nearly 5,000 enlisted men and a bevy of WACs were in line waiting to board *The Queen* when Blanche and the other Red Cross girls arrived.[107]

It was a sweltering summer night, and the air was filled with the aroma of sweat, cigarettes, diesel fuel, fish, and saltwater. Of course, each woman had to carry her own gear, and this is how one Red Cross girl described the scene:

> I've never seen such a top-heavy bunch in my life—full winter uniform, musette bag ... hanging over one shoulder, gas mask over the other, our heavy black leather Red Cross shoulder purse jockeying for position between the two ..., a pistol belt around our waists to which is attached first aid kit and canteen. We carried one suitcase and our official raincoat, a Humphrey Bogart–type trench coat we all agree [was] real classy. We had to wear our helmets, so [we] stuffed our ARC caps in our purses. ... The tiny girls, especially, looked like overloaded toadstools. It was hilarious.[108]

Blanche, of course, was one of those "tiny girls," and to make matters worse, her helmet was too big for her and was constantly falling forward and hitting the bridge of her nose. Her musette bag was so full and tall that as she tried to move forward in line, she had trouble reaching over it to pick up her suitcase. Her suitcase was so long that after she managed to pick it up, and she then straightened up to her full five feet in height, the suitcase was still touching the ground! During the nearly mile-long hike from the dock entrance to the gangplank, Blanche occasionally had to step over a curb. When she managed to get up on the sidewalk, her suitcase would not make it and would almost knock her over. Many of the GIs around her thought that it was great sport to constantly ask Blanche's musette bag what was carrying it or hollering for "shorty" to get off her knees! Since everyone had their own luggage, bags, and equipment, and no one was allowed to get out of line, Blanche was totally on her own and just had to do the best she could under the circumstances. But it provided some much-needed comic relief for everyone involved. Plus, she and the other Red Cross girls could tell that the GIs sincerely loved the fact that they were there. "They like to know that we eat the same K-rations that they do and that we [wear] a steel helmet, gas mask, musette bag, pistol belt, canteen, first aid pack and heavy luggage ..., just like they [do]."[109]

The Red Cross girls, based on their sex and unofficial status as officers, were given first class cabins below deck that were originally designed for between two and six people. With space at a premium, up to 12 women were assigned to the first-class staterooms, whereas six were assigned to the smaller first-class cabins. Blanche was assigned to one of the smaller cabins, which had three bunk beds to accommodate her and five other women. Since Blanche was short, the girls always insisted that she sleep on the lower bunk, and she quickly became tired of always bumping her head on the upper. If the women were lucky, they got a porthole to help alleviate the claustrophobic feeling of their cramped quarters. Blanche was not that lucky. Her cabin was located on the inside with no porthole and no natural light. The women also had to share a bathroom down the hall with dozens of other women. Trying to sleep in a small cabin with five other women was, of course, challenging, and every morning Blanche awakened stiff and tired from a restless night. To undress at night or to get dressed in the morning, each woman had to take their turn because of the cramped conditions, and they constantly struggled to avoid getting their clothes mixed up.[110]

The Trip Across

As *The Queen* prepared to depart on Saturday morning, July 15, 1944, the women were confined to their quarters. So, none of the women without portholes got to see the huge ship, with the help of harbor tugs and still in the blackness of night, slowly move away from its slip and head out into the harbor and the open sea.

Nevertheless, for Blanche it was an exhilarating feeling to finally be on her way. Unlike the officers and Red Cross personnel, the thousands of enlisted men and a handful of WACs were billeted somewhere down in the lower decks. Some of the GIs even had to sleep in the swimming pool. That's where the Army brass stuck the African American singing group, The Ink Spots, who were on their way overseas to entertain the troops. In fact, there were so many GIs on board that they had to sleep in shifts (because there weren't enough bunks for everyone to lie down and sleep at the same time). For meals, everyone ate in shifts in one of the ship's numerous dining rooms. The officers and Red Cross girls ate in the smaller tourist class dining room. Since *The Queen* was an English ship with an English crew, the fare was decidedly English, such as corned beef cakes and kippered herrings for breakfast. It was a new experience for Blanche and for almost all the other Americans.

One of the women Blanche was traveling with was Lois Stone of Dalton, Pennsylvania, whom Blanche later served with in England. As Blanche got to know Lois better, she decided that they had little in common. Lois was looking for romance. While on *The Queen*, Lois fell for an officer and immediately got engaged, only to find out later that he was already married. Lois repeated the same mistake later in the year while serving in England. Apparently, Lois didn't listen to the instructors at American University. Blanche did not want to draw that kind of attention to herself, and she had no interest in romance. She just wanted to do her job and be left alone; she even continued to wear her wedding ring overseas. Unlike Lois, Blanche assumed that every man she met was already married until she had proof to the contrary.

While en route, the Red Cross girls did not have any assigned work to perform. So, besides the daily lifeboat drills, they spent their time talking among themselves, playing cards, or socializing with the GIs (within Army restrictions) and entertaining them with music. Blanche had brought with her a little paperback booklet given to her by the Red Cross entitled, *Army Song Book*,[111] and she used it to provide piano accompaniment to the Red Cross girls who could sing. As Blanche described it to her parents in her first letter home, "[I] spent several hours each day entertaining the fellows, but I should say they entertained us instead."[112] Of course, the women had prepared themselves to be constantly surrounded by GIs, but the attention they received on board *The Queen* was so intense that it was a bit shocking. The men were everywhere, and each one of them wanted to talk with a real live "Red Cross girl," even though the women were uniformly older. Many of the women found the constant attention exhilarating and thrived on it, but Blanche found it daunting and a bit overwhelming at times.

During the day, the women also "spent much of their time on one of the sundecks, known to all as the 'Bird Cage' (Sports Deck) which they shared with officers over the rank of captain." Come evening they hung out in the Officers' Lounge (the ship's grand salon) and talked, played cards, and sang songs "ranging from 'God Bless America' to increasingly bawdy versions of 'Roll Me Over in the Clover.'"[113]

The highlight of the voyage for Blanche was being able to occasionally go "topside" with her life jacket on and walk around the upper decks to breathe in the salt air, watch flying fish leap above the waves, and take in the incredible view. The water was a lovely dark blue and the ocean breeze was invigorating. However, one of the lowlights was the bathing facilities. To clean, the women had to use a saltwater shower, and Blanche remembered it as a "not-very-pleasant experience." No matter how hard she rubbed and dried her skin, she always felt like she had a sticky film all over her body. Naturally, many on board were on their first ocean voyage and suffered from seasickness. Blanche did not, even though the ocean was often very rough. She was blessed with a well-balanced inner ear.

On several occasions during the voyage, the Red Cross girls were allowed to go down to the lower decks and meet with the GIs, which drew the men's positive and appreciative response. Or as another Red Cross girl described it, "After an hour of close contact with the troops, talking and singing with them and having an occasional few minutes with a shy guy who proudly shows you pictures of his family,

we were ordered back to our deck."[114] To Blanche, and no doubt to
the other women as well, when she was interacting with the enlisted
men she felt as if she was finally doing what she had signed up to do.
Therefore, it was a rewarding experience for both sexes, and that
meaningful interaction would repeat itself on a thousand little
occasions over the next year and a half.

The Queen made its crossing of the northern Atlantic in five days,
and because it was so fast, it did so without an escort or being a part
of a convoy. Speed was its main defense. Nevertheless, for safety, it
also took a more northerly route and adhered to a constant zig-zag
course, thereby hoping to avoid German U-boats being able to get a
bead on her. Every time the huge ship zigged or zagged "going full
throttle and heeling over just when [the passengers] least expect[ed]
it," the result was "card games, meals, and quite a few stomachs"
being interrupted.[115] The captain also ordered regular battle station drills, and at night blackouts were ordered to avoid detection
by German submarines.

One night The Queen's captain learned that a German subma-
rine had been spotted in the area. He immediately called for "general quarters," had the passengers brought up to the upper decks
with life preservers on and ready, and had the crew secure all
hatches. Everyone was told to be quiet—not even sneezing was
allowed. It was a "scary" ordeal for the thousands of passengers, and
Blanche silently wondered whether her new adventure was also
going to be her last. If the ship had been torpedoed, many of the
passengers and crew would have been lost since the ship didn't have
enough lifeboats for everyone and the water in the north Atlantic
was frigid and deadly.

Thankfully, The Queen completed its trip unmolested, and once
on Scottish soil, Blanche officially entered the ETO and the war
that would define her life over the next 15 months. It was exciting
and a bit overwhelming, but she felt that she was ready for whatever
came her way. It was what she wanted to do, and she believed in the
Red Cross's mission. Most importantly, she was confident that she
could make a positive contribution to the war effort.

Chapter 6

"A darn shaking experience ..."

Arriving in the ETO

While Blanche and the other Red Cross girls were crossing the Atlantic on the *Queen Elizabeth*, the Battle for Normandy continued. On the 18th of July, British and Canadian forces implemented Operation Goodwood. It was part of the Allies' continuing attempts to end the stalemate in Normandy. The immediate goal was the French city of Caen, which was taken. However, when the British and Canadians pushed toward Falaise, they were stopped in their tracks by firmly entrenched German forces. The resulting battle became what many claimed to be the greatest tank battle ever fought by the British Army. The British and Canadians lost more than 4,000 men and 500 tanks, more than one-third of the tanks they had deployed in Normandy. Nevertheless, Allied forces finally broke through and moved inland less than two weeks later. Then the battle for the rest of France began in earnest.[116]

Meanwhile, *The Queen* arrived at the Firth of Clyde on July 19, 1944. The Firth is located at the mouth of the River Clyde on the west coast of Scotland and lies only 20 miles west of Glasgow. It is the deepest coastal port in Great Britain and is sheltered from the North Atlantic by the Kintyre Peninsula. It provides a large anchorage near the little twin towns of Greenock and Gourock. The towns' major claim to fame was that both the *Queen Elizabeth* and her massive sister ship, the *Queen Mary*, had been built there during the 1930s.[117] During the war, the Firth of Clyde had become the main entry point to Great Britain for Allied merchant shipping and personnel, as well as the center for the "assembly, dispatch, and control" of the Allies' ocean convoys. Which is why three years earlier, in 1941, Greenock had been targeted by the German Luftwaffe for two relentless nights of bombing. The bombing killed 271 people, more than 10,200 were injured, and 5,000 homes were damaged or destroyed.[118] When Blanche and the other passengers of *The Queen* arrived, evidence of that attack was still visible.

Upon its arrival, the sheer size of *The Queen* forced it to anchor out in the harbor off the Isle of Arran. Blanche thought that the panoramic view from the edge of the Firth was "simply beautiful." As far as the eye could see there were small farms bound by hedges in a nearly treeless landscape. It was her first impression of Great Britain, and it was a scene she long remembered. Over the next few days, *The Queen*'s thousands of passengers took turns disembarking and boarding tenders (which Blanche naively referred to in her diary as "funny barges") for transportation to Greenock. When it was the Red Cross's personnel's turn, Blanche and the other women assembled in one of the ship's lounges and received a gracious welcome from a Royal Air Force officer who provided the women basic instructions on leaving the ship and boarding the tenders. He also mentioned, almost in passing, that when they arrived in London (their ultimate destination), they would likely be introduced to Adolf Hitler's new vengeance weapon, the "buzz bomb."[119] Blanche had no idea what he was talking about, nor did any of her colleagues, and he didn't bother to explain or entertain questions. Within only a few days, however, they were all duly enlightened.

Although the officer was welcoming and polite, his habit of referring to the war as "The Big Show" rubbed Blanche the wrong way. Having lost a husband in the war, she cringed whenever she heard someone refer to it like some giant sporting event. To her it was a deadly serious matter and was not to be made light of or joked about. As time went on, however, her attitude about the English and their habits went through a marked transformation. That evolution in thought was assisted by a pamphlet that was published by the U.S. War and Navy Departments entitled *A Short Guide to Great Britain for Military Personnel Only.* Anticipating the cultural differences that were bound to create misunderstandings between American military personnel and the British, the guide was handed out to all American military personnel headed for Great Britain. It was also shared with Red Cross personnel. It began by informing the reader that they were "… going to Great Britain as part of an Allied offensive to meet Hitler and beat him on his own ground. For the time being you will be Britain's guest. The purpose of this guide is to start getting you acquainted with the British, their country, and their ways."[120]

After briefly describing Britain's form of government, and some of the customs and manners of the British people (like driving on the left side of the road and drinking warm beer), the guide warned the reader not to rub "a Britisher the wrong way by telling him 'We came over and won the last one.' … Britain remembers that nearly a million of her best manhood died in the last war [World War I]. America lost 60,000 in action." Then the Guide went on to explain that "The Briton is just as outspoken and independent as we are, but … he is also the most law-abiding citizen in the world. … When you find differences between British and American ways of doing things, there's usually a good reason for them." The guide also reminded the American GI that "At home you were in a country at war. Since your ship left port, however, you have been in a war zone. Britain has been a war zone since September 1939, which has brought great changes in their way of life. …"[121]

When Blanche and the other Red Cross girls disembarked at Greenock, they were surprised by the sincere enthusiasm with which they were received by the locals. Later that evening they were all taken to the local train station where they boarded a compartment troop train for London. It was about a 15-hour ride with a brief station stop in Glasgow, followed by a scenic ride through the Scottish countryside which one Red Cross girl described as "green fields dotted with white-washed or stone houses, flaming red poppies, and black cows."[122] Blanche thought the countryside was beautiful, but she noted that the people looked poor and destitute.

At Edinburgh, the women had several hours to walk around the station and get at least a glimpse of the Royal Mile, as well as a totally forgettable bite to eat in the station's dining room. The train also made brief stops at several major cities as it worked its way south into the heart of England.[123] Blanche spent almost the entire trip, except during a few stops, in a "chair car," as there was little room to stand or move about. Naturally, the train was packed with military personnel, and during the night hours, it was "blacked out" with every opening to the outside world closed tight so as not to give off light and attract enemy aircraft. Few passengers were able to sleep in such cramped and uncomfortable conditions, and Blanche was no exception. She arrived in London stiff, sore, and dead tired.

Buzz Bombs and the Blitz

Then, as if on cue, just as the train was approaching the outskirts of London and the sun was beginning to rise in the east, a German buzz bomb attack commenced. One of the conductors came hurrying down the aisle instructing everyone to put their helmets on, turn out all the lights, and make sure that all window blinds were down.[124] The attack forced the train to suddenly come to a complete halt. So, there they were sitting motionless in the early morning darkness and at the complete mercy of blind fate. The passengers could hear the distant air raid sirens, the distinctive sound of the motors of the buzz bombs as they passed nearby or overhead, and the horrendous impacts in nearby neighborhoods—some of which hit close enough to rock the train where it stood—"a darn shaking experience" as Blanche remembered it. In fact, she experienced her first flicker of fear while serving in the ETO. She learned from other better-informed passengers, however, that if you hear the buzz bomb's motor running overhead, or what Blanche referred to as "a loud mechanical humming noise," you were safe—at least for the moment. It was when the motor suddenly stopped that the bomb began its plunge to earth, and that was the time to seek cover and pray. Another Red Cross girl on the same train described the experience this way:

> We sat waiting, listening hard in the darkness and silence …
> [Then we] heard the unmistakable sound of a single motor,
> like a little airplane, and abruptly stopped talking. The motor
> sound grew louder. We were all staring out the window [which
> they had been told not to do] when the steady putt-putt mate-
> rialized into the dark form of a little plane in the sky, headed
> right over the train, trailing a smoky, fiery tail. The sound
> seemed directly overhead when the motor abruptly cut off.
> Waiting for the explosion was the longest few seconds of my
> life.[125]

What made the buzz bombs, or "doodlebugs" as some people called them, so unnerving was the distinctive sound they made, their unpredictability, the absence of a pilot, and, of course, their destructive capabilities. The Germans launched the first V-1 against London in June 1944 within a week after the D-Day landings. During the first phase of Hitler's V-1 bombing campaign, hundreds of buzz bombs hit London every day and night, and in all types of weather. In fact, less than three weeks before Blanche's arrival in London a buzz bomb exploded at Sloane Court East, a residential road in Chelsea, London, where a company of U.S. Army soldiers were stationed, and at least 66 American servicemen and 9 civilians lost their lives.[126]

The train's passengers responded to the attack in a myriad of ways: some silently praying, some vainly searching for cover, and others making inappropriate comments or remarks to try to ease the tension. Hearing one of the V-1s overhead and then suddenly hearing its engine cut out and knowing what came next was a terrifying experience for everyone, but Blanche simply remained quiet, and silently prayed and waited. Then as quickly as it started it was all over. As far as she knew, no one on the train was injured during the attack, and after the raid ended, the train safely arrived at Charing Cross Station. She had made it! She was in historic London and now definitely "in the war," and the excitement of the attack and her surroundings temporarily offset her physical exhaustion.

After disembarking from the train, the Red Cross girls were herded through the station and reassembled at a designated area with all their gear. Once so assembled, they climbed into waiting British Army trucks with the help of British soldiers assigned to the task. Then the soldiers (nicknamed "Tommies"), the Red Cross girls, and the trucks were off toward Kensington, located in London's stylish West End. The drive through London to their new temporary billets was quick but extremely bouncy. The women were naturally thrilled each time they passed another historic building or landmark that they were familiar with through books and films back home. However, evidence of the war and of the horrendous damage caused by it was abundant. London had taken on the look of a worn and tattered metropolis. It was essentially an armed camp with whole sections of the city containing damaged or obliterated buildings, some completely leveled; large gaping holes caused by exploded bombs; broken glass, bricks, and rubble pushed to one side; and sandbags protecting key buildings and locations. Even Buckingham Palace had sustained considerable damage to one of its wings.

The evident destruction to an otherwise beautiful city saddened the women, but the spirit of its people gave everyone a renewed sense of purpose and hope. Even though the city was a gray, dim, broken version of its previous self, the British people were undaunted. Although visibly tired and worn by years of stress, rationing, and personal loss, and often wearing worn out or mismatched clothing, their inner spirit and determination did not appear diminished. They retained the famous British "stiff upper lip" and soldiered on as they went about their daily routines. Slowly Blanche developed a real admiration for the British people and realized that they had earned the right to refer to the war any way they wished.

Regardless of how London looked upon first inspection, portions of its economy were clearly booming, fueled by over a half-million American, French, Dutch, Polish, Czech, and other European soldiers, along with the British military and the sailors and airmen in from its far-flung empire such as Canada, Australia, and New Zealand. Thus, stores, restaurants, theaters, bars, and nightclubs were packed and doing a bang-up business, and the local police officers, or "Bobbies," were hard-pressed to control the traffic at key intersections as cars, trucks, bicycles, and red double-decker buses packed with people competed for dominance and the right-of-way.

Princes Gate and Grosvenor Square

The trucks finally deposited Blanche and the other Red Cross girls at Princes Gate, a stately row of white stone Georgian town houses that had, thus far, avoided major damage. Each town house entrance was adorned with a two Doric-columned portico, topped with a stone balcony, and each town house was about five stories tall. Princes Gate was located directly across the street from Hyde Park, near the Royal Albert Hall, and within walking distance of both Kensington Palace and Buckingham Palace. The Red Cross had been given one of the town houses, a former hotel called the Hans Crescent Club, for its use and that is where the women were to be temporarily housed.

Upon their arrival at Princes Gate, the women stood in line for what seemed like hours waiting for the club personnel to sign them in and assign them a floor, a room, a bed, and bedding. Although the Red Cross's town house and the neighborhood around it were impressive enough, because of a shortage of dormitory space many of the women had to sleep on cots. After being assigned a room and stowing their gear, the women showered, changed their clothes, and freshened up. Few of them slept that day. Instead, Blanche and a handful of other women left the club and took a walk through Hyde Park and Kensington Gardens, then they paid for a bus tour of the typical tourist sights of London, including the Houses of Parliament and Big Ben, Westminster Abbey, Buckingham Palace (and witnessed the changing of the guard), No. 10 Downing Street, Piccadilly Circus, and the famous River Thames.[127] The next day Blanche visited St. Paul's Cathedral, which stood majestically and untouched among ruined buildings on all sides.

During their first evening in London, the air raid sirens went off, and before Blanche and her roommates could seek shelter, a buzz bomb exploded several blocks away—close enough that they felt the concussion and later saw the smoke rising from the impact. The women had all fallen to the floor so as "to avoid [any] shattering glass." After picking herself up and dusting herself off, Blanche instinctively left the building and walked toward the impact zone to see if anyone had been injured or killed. But it was impossible to determine without interfering with the police and firefighters who soon appeared on the scene. However, she found a small piece of twisted metal lying on the sidewalk and using her handkerchief (just in case it was still hot), picked it up and kept it as a souvenir of yet another close call.[128]

Predictably, Blanche spent the rest of that first night under her bed. As exhausted as she was, she found it impossible to sleep soundly as one buzz bomb exploded so close to their building that some of the glass panes in the conservatory roof on the top floor were shattered. The West End was located right in the middle of what the locals referred to as "Buzz Bomb Alley," as it was where Buckingham Palace and many other government buildings were located.[129] Afterward, Blanche attempted to describe the V-1s to her parents:

They look just like an airplane shooting across the sky and at night you can see a flame shooting out behind it making it look like an airplane on fire. They also sound like an airplane which is flying very low. … The theme song around here is "Praise the Lord and keep the motor running."[130]

The next morning, Monday, July 24, was the second anniversary of Les's death, and Blanche could not help but dwell on that fact and feel a little depressed. Any time she thought of Les she would think about what might have been and, of course, what she had lost. But she also gained renewed strength from the thought that she was not sitting at home silently grieving, feeling sorry for herself, and letting the world and the war pass her by. She was doing her part, no matter how small, and ensuring that her life would continue to have meaning. It was what Les would have wanted. She was also a little surprised to realize that she had not once been homesick since leaving Kansas City. She was where she wanted to be and there was simply too much that was new, exciting, and challenging to be homesick.

After breakfast and the obligatory cup of hot tea, all the new arrivals were transported to the American Red Cross's headquarters at 12 Grosvenor Square for final clearance and processing. The Square is located on the east side of Hyde Park and consists of rows of connecting brick and stone buildings encompassing a beautiful green park. Although five stories tall, Number 12 was one of the smaller and narrower town houses. It had been converted into offices and was located near the American Embassy, which had been Supreme Allied Commander General Dwight D. Eisenhower's headquarters prior to the D-Day landings. The Square was also where the official residence of the American Ambassador to the Court of St. James had been located since John Adams first held the post and established the first American mission there in 1785.[131]

The group of new arrivals were so numerous, 133 of them in all, and the front door and entryway to the town house so narrow, that everyone had to wait their turn to enter the building. Instead, they all congregated outside on the sidewalk and around the front door, gazing at their surroundings, talking, and waiting for their turn to

be summoned (in alphabetical order of course) to enter the building. While doing so, Kathleen "Kick" Kennedy Cavendish, the
daughter of former American Ambassador Joseph P. Kennedy Sr.,
and the sister of future President John F. Kennedy, looking resplendent in her Red Cross uniform, exited the building. Blanche had no
idea who she was but many of the Red Cross girls, especially the
ones from New England, knew, and they did their best not to stare
while they whispered among themselves that she was reportedly
married to a British nobleman.[132]

Once all the women had made their way inside and reported in,
they assembled in a large ballroom, filled out more paperwork, and
had a group picture taken with Harvey Gibson, the ARC's Commissioner to Great Britain and Western Europe, and his senior staff.
Then Gibson and a host of other Red Cross officials took turns
briefing the women on their mission in the ETO, military censorship rules, and other administrative matters. Red Cross girl Rosemary Langheldt described the presentation made by one female
speaker and the humorous response she received from her
audience:

A lovely British lady, looking positively smashing in her uniform, welcomed us in a teddy top-drawer British accent. ...
She talked of the V bombs and assured us that many are shot
down by ack-ack fire long before they reach London. The
ones that make it through come at all hours, but she reas-
sured us, most buildings have a spotter on the roof during
alerts ready to sound a bell if a bomb heads directly for the
building. That is the only time it's necessary to take cover ...

[Then] she paused to consult her notes ... and a loud bell
sounded. For the briefest instant we all froze in horror, then
tried to get down to put our heads under our chairs—the
only halfway solid objects around—and in the process upset
most of the folding chairs. The bell rang loudly again. I've
never seen a roomful of girls turn red quicker when we realized it was the phone on the official's desk ringing. ... The

room rocked with embarrassed laughter as we turned our chairs back up and scrambled around to gather up our instruction papers …[133]

The Clubmobile Department

The last administrative matter was the assignment of each new arrival to one of three different Red Cross departments, all under the auspices of the division of the Red Cross in Great Britain that was tasked with providing direct "services" to U.S. armed forces. The three departments were the Club Department (which included the established clubs located in major cities and the rest and convalescent homes), the Field Service Department (which included temporary field clubs and Red Cross personnel stationed in military hospitals), and the Clubmobile Department.[134]

Initially, Blanche was assigned to clubmobiles, but after talking to one of the ARC's administrative staff, she switched to field services. The staff person convinced Blanche that being assigned to a major Red Cross club would be the best use of her musical talents, as the clubs had pianos and provided music to their customers on a regular basis. But by the next day, Blanche had changed her mind and successfully switched back to the clubmobiles because she had decided that she did not want to be tied down to just one location. She wanted to move around and see the country, and most importantly, she wanted the opportunity to ultimately serve on the continent.[135]

As part of the new group of clubmobilers, around 50 in all, Blanche and her compatriots were given written instructions on how to go about obtaining a British driver's license; what additional items of clothing they would receive, including fleece-lined boots; how to obtain their clubmobile insignia for their uniforms; and details about rail travel, cash advances, vouchers for laundry and lodging, and ration books. All these items were to be vouchered for reimbursement by the Red Cross.[136] The Red Cross also issued a new, bright blue topcoat and visor hat, and a new bright blue uniform that was referred to as the clubmobile girls' "battle dress." These articles were issued to the clubmobilers and not to the regular club staff because of the more strenuous field service they were expected to perform. "These uniforms were so named because they were fashioned after the English soldiers' battle uniform. Naturally, the name always brought a hoot from any GI who heard us use it."[137] Predictably, Blanche had difficulty finding anything in her size when she attempted to buy her additional clothing and equipment.

The Red Cross did not have official clubmobile boots in Blanche's petite size, so they had to have them specially ordered back in the states. In the interim, Blanche bought some WAC field shoes to help her get through the oceans of mud that she later encountered everywhere she went. In the meantime, some talented GIs made Blanche a pair of custom-made Army boots. As winter approached, Blanche also purchased "the warmest wool scarf [she] could find, a red one, which was considered [an] acceptable" accessory to her uniform. She also wrote to her mother and asked her to send red wool mittens. "The English winters were notoriously damp and cold" and she wanted to be as prepared as she could be.[138]

Later that same day, the clubmobilers were taken to an old garage where they were taught how to operate the big, bulky, dangerous doughnut machine that would soon become their constant companion and nemesis. Clubmobiler B.J. Olewiler described the process in detail:

First we learned how to mix the prepared flour with the right amount of water. Then when we got it to the right consistency [and put it] in a pressurized can, which could blow up if not secured correctly. ... The dough then was spewed automatically into the heated grease in the shape of a donut with its all-important hole in the middle. Around they went in a circle and at the right moment when they became just the right tinge of brown, we fetched them out with skewers and arranged them in rows in the serving tray. Learning to operate the donut machine was not difficult: the hard part was getting inured to the overwhelming odor. ... [B]ut it wasn't long before we were more or less immune to the assault on our olfactory sense.[139]

Blanche felt that getting the dough into the pressurized can was the hard part. She had to wrap it around her arms with a spinning motion and then, at just the right moment, throw it into the can. Once she got the knack of it, however, she succeeded in turning out approximately seven and a half doughnuts per minute.[140]

The next morning, Blanche and some of the other women were moved to a five-story brick town house located at 103 Park Street, only a few blocks from Grosvenor Square, which was being used as a Red Cross dormitory and where the women would remain until they left London for their initial assignments. The accommodations were Spartan at best, and like everywhere else they had been billeted, there were always at least nine women to every room which was originally designed for two. But she and her compatriots "... learned to stand in line for a bathtub, and other facilities. There is usually one of each for 38 girls." Nevertheless, Blanche was amazed at how fast she and the other women adjusted to such inconveniences. For example, she reported to her parents that she "hadn't seen an iron since [leaving] Washington, and for over a week [she] couldn't wash any clothes." But she was "learning to eat anything and to go without many things." Despite all of that, she had "... never felt better... and [was] having a perfectly marvelous time."[141]

Ranger Duty in Scotland

As directed, on July 28, Blanche reported to Miss Virginia Cook, the Assistant Director of Clubmobile Personnel in Great Britain, and was ordered back up to Scotland on temporary "Ranger" duty. The Ranger service in the Clubmobile Department was a grueling, exhausting, but highly rewarding job. It entailed providing services to thousands of GIs as they congregated and passed through a particular entry or departure point. *At His Side,* the history of the American Red Cross during World War II, provided a succinct description of how it worked.

> The Rangers served coffee and doughnuts in the compara-
> tively few minutes between the soldiers' arrival at the railroad
> station and their departure through the drizzle of a fogbound
> dawn to some undisclosed destination. The boys responded
> to this unexpected service with surprised delight and
> gratitude.
>   The Rangers, handpicked for this special branch of the ser-
> vice, ... worked on twelve-hour shifts, skipping breakfast,
> lunch and even dinner until a particular operation was over.
> ... Up and down the [train] platform the Rangers moved trol-
> ley push-mobiles weighing anywhere from 300 to 400 pounds
> when loaded. Each held 750 doughnuts and urns containing
> 400 cups of coffee. Grease-spotted, rain-soaked, hair plas-
> tered to their cheeks, dragging their feet, they were all but
> exhausted when they stumbled into bed at the end of an
> operation.[142]

On the 29th, just a few days before 100 V-1 bombs hit London (the most to hit the city in a single day), Blanche and three other Red Cross girls, Virginia Allison of Wauwatosa, Wisconsin, Jo Banichar of Leechburg, Pennsylvania, and Dottie Barrett of Garden City, New York (all "swell kids" according to Blanche), boarded a north-bound train and took a third-class sleeper to Glasgow. The diversity of their places of origin was an indication of the Clubmobile Depart-ment's commitment to not group women together based on their regional backgrounds; and, given the women's age, education, and maturity, the Red Cross brass obviously assumed that they would follow orders, handle working on their own, and cope with whatever situation might arise. That was a confidence-building realization for the women as they headed north. Of the hundreds of women Rosemary Langheldt came across during her Red Cross training and journey to Great Britain, "only a few seem to have slipped through the cracks of the qualifications" in her opinion.[143] For the next week, Blanche and the other women

> … worked tirelessly at the docks at Greenock and Gourock. The docks and railroad stations were constantly busy. As the men filed off the ships with their packs on their backs, rifles slung over their shoulders, their steel helmets tilted at every angle, they seemed to be in high spirits. It was easy to share their pride in being overseas. Our job was to grab a tray of doughnuts, a pitcher of coffee, or a tray of cigarettes, Life Savers, and chewing gum, and follow them to the railroad cars which were to take them inland. We never had much time for conversation other than "Hi! Where are you from?" before the whistle blew and we'd have to hop off and get ready for the next train. For hours on end the soldiers came in droves …[144]

Blanche noted in her diary that on their first full day at the docks they worked until midnight, but she absolutely loved it![145] She knew that she was already doing a lot of good. When the GIs first landed, she was struck by how young, tired, and homesick they appeared to be; but after the women talked and laughed with them for a little while, they perked up and seemed ready to fight the world if necessary. Her heart ached for them, and yet, when she went to bed after a long day's work, she thanked God that she was where she was and that she had witnessed how the GIs' faces lit up at the very sight of an American girl. She could tell that they could not get over the fact that American girls would give up all the comforts of home and voluntarily share their hardships just to help brighten their day and make them smile.[146] She was finally doing what she had signed up to do—providing direct morale-boosting support to American GIs.

After a week of Ranger work in Scotland, staying in a private home while there and taking a two-day vacation to Loch Lomond and Edinburgh, Blanche, Dottie Barrett, and a few other women were ordered back to London for reassignment. Taking a train back to London, they arrived at Red Cross headquarters on August 7.[147] Blanche was anxious to know where she was going to be assigned and who she would be working with for the foreseeable future, but wherever they decided to send her, she felt confident that she was physically and mentally ready. However, her confidence in her ability to physically do the job was severely tested over the next six months, and her faith in the wisdom and integrity of her clubmobile supervisors was deeply shaken on at least one occasion. However, her belief in the Red Cross's mission and her admiration and respect for most of the American military personnel she worked with was not diminished.

Chapter 7

"The hardest part [was] watching [the] planes crash ..."

The Maine and Kettering, England

As directed, Blanche and Dottie Barrett reported to Miss Virginia Cook at Red Cross headquarters on the morning of August 8, 1944. Miss Cook informed the women that they were to be stationed in Kettering, England, and would be part of the crew of the clubmobile *Maine*. Their clubmobile captain was to be Lois Stone, whom Blanche had roomed with on *The Queen*. Later that same day Blanche, Dottie, and Lois took a train to Kettering.[148] Blanche was delighted that she and Dottie were assigned to the same clubmobile, as they had become good friends during their brief Ranger duty in Scotland. Dottie was from Garden City, New York, and like Blanche, she had signed up because she wanted to help the war effort, and she was determined to do her part, whatever it took. It was one of the things that Blanche admired about her.

The town the women were to be stationed at, Kettering, Northamptonshire, was a midsized market and industrial town located 83 miles northwest of London and in what the English refer to as the "East Midlands." It is surrounded by beautiful undulating countryside and is known for its limestone and ironstone roads and villages. The town was built on high ground overlooking the Rivers Slade and Ise; the locals referred to their area as "Queen Eleanor Country," named for Eleanor of Castile, the wife of King Edward I of England.[149] Eleanor had had extensive properties throughout the region, and the royal couple had a summer home in the middle of Rockingham Forest near Geddington, a sleepy little village located between Kettering and Corby to the north. After Queen Eleanor's death in 1290, her body was transported in a slow and solemn procession, from Lincoln to Westminster Abbey in London. To mark the occasion, King Edward ordered that elaborate memorial crosses be erected at each stop in the royal procession. Only three of these memorials remain and the best preserved is at Geddington.[150]

The Maine was but one of 40 Green Liners operating throughout Great Britain by the summer of 1944. The Red Cross had divided Great Britain into regional areas, "each one with a base from which the service fanned out to remote locations." Living accommodations and storage facilities were also provided by the ARC.[151] The women selected for clubmobile service were then assigned to individual clubmobiles and to a regional base. Since the Red Cross had sent over 400 clubmobilers across the channel in the months immediately following the D-Day invasion, the Green Liners (which were too big to operate effectively on the narrow and often unpaved roads of France) were left behind. Thus, they had to be restaffed with the new arrivals who had come over with Blanche on *The Queen*.

Each clubmobile had been christened with an All-American name. The clubmobiles in England were all given the name of an American city or state such as *The Kansas City* and *The New York*. The clubmobiles on the continent were given the name of an American hero, regional name, or sobriquet such as *The General Grant, The Golden State,* and *The Pathfinder.*

Upon their arrival at Kettering, Blanche, Dottie, and Lois reported to their field supervisor, Lewis "Lew" Hauck, of St. Louis, Missouri, and, with his assistance, spent the next day cleaning and becoming familiar with the mechanical workings of their clubmobile. *The Maine* was a single-decker bus and was the largest model of the clubmobiles used in England. Even so, the back of the bus was a tight fit when all three women were working there at the same time; as one wag put it, the women "didn't have enough room to change [their] minds."[152] It was equipped with a doughnut machine that would allow the crew to make fresh doughnuts several times a day, and a primus stove used for heating water for coffee made fresh in large 50-cup urns. On the other side of the work area was a counter-top with a large flap that opened outward so the crew could serve the coffee and doughnuts to waiting servicemen directly from the vehicle. Everything in the clubmobile could be fastened down when not in use and when the clubmobile was on the move. Before leaving, the crew had to be careful to make sure everything was battened down for security. Failing to do so could have "unfortunate" results and create quite a mess.[153]

In the back of the clubmobile was a lounge with a built-in bench on either side (which could be converted to sleeping bunks, if necessary); a Victrola with loudspeakers (so the music could be heard outside of the vehicle); a large selection of 78 records of the vocal stars and big bands of the day; magazines and paperback books that could be loaned out; writing paper and envelopes for writing home; some of the latest American newspapers from different parts of the United States; and other small items such as cigarettes, Life Savers, and chewing gum.[154] Among the records available on *The Maine* were songs such as "Paper Doll" by the Mills Brothers, "I'll Walk Alone" by Dinah Shore, "G.I. Jive" by Louis Jordan, "Comin' In on a Wing and a Prayer" by the Song Spinners, "Mairzy Doats" by the Merry Macs, "Rum and Coca-Cola" by the Andrews Sisters, and "I'll Be Seeing You" by Bing Crosby. Bing was one of Blanche's favorite singers.

On their first day, just to make sure they were ready, the women produced 62 pounds of doughnuts in preparation for their first visit to a nearby Eighth Air Force airfield. A local lad from Kettering, Ted Scott, was hired by the Red Cross and assigned to the crew as their driver. He was responsible for keeping the clubmobile at his residence overnight, fueling and maintaining it, cleaning the equipment in the back of the clubmobile each night, and driving the women to the different air bases during the day.

The Eighth Air Force

Of course, the Red Cross had arranged for a place for the women to live while stationed at Kettering. Their first billet was a single room in the home of a local Kettering woman. The Red Cross paid the monthly rent, which included food. The room was fine, but the house was so dirty that it smelled. The landlady owned numerous pet cats and let them wander all over the house unattended. Consequently, the women found cat hair in everything, including their food! They were also served uncooked crêpes Suzette each morning for breakfast, and the women had to discretely find ingenious ways to dispose of them when the landlady was not looking. Plus, the landlady bathed but once a month and could not understand why her American boarders took one every night. She thought it was ridiculous and wasteful, so she turned the water off each evening after sundown.[155]

Not blessed with a strong constitution to begin with, Blanche soon developed food poisoning and spent an awful night throwing up in the toilet. Since the water had been turned off, Blanche could not flush or clean up until morning! It was a night she vividly remembered nearly 70 years later. That was the last straw. The women jointly asked the Red Cross to find them a new place to live in Kettering, and soon they were moved into a room rented out by Mr. & Mrs. (Stuart and Ethel) Mackay (pronounced "Macki"). The accommodations were smaller, so Blanche had to share a bed with Dottie, but the food was much better (and cooked!), the house was cleaner, and they all loved the landlady. Blanche had come to really admire the British and how they held up under the pressure of air raids and rationing without complaint, and Mrs. Mackay was a perfect example. She was obliging, courteous, and rarely complained about the war or the changes it had brought to her way of life. It was also obvious that she sincerely appreciated the Americans who had descended on her country and the importance of their service to the future of hers. Mrs. Mackay treated the women like her own children. She was wonderful. If one of the women got a cold, Mrs. Mackay would make the invalid stay in bed, make her special food, and bring it up to the sick room. She saw to it that the women had their boots on and something over their heads when they left each morning. She also went out of her way to try to keep the women from getting homesick.[156] Blanche and Mrs. Mackay became quite close during the six months that they shared a roof, and they remained in touch until well after the war ended.

While stationed at Kettering, the women were surrounded by thousands of American servicemen because of the numerous airfields located in and around Kettering. Earlier in the war, as part of the overall Lend-Lease Program discussed in Chapter 3, the British government had agreed to provide the United States government port and airfield facilities in return for military arms and supplies. Four American airfields, all part of the Eighth Air Force, had been built outside of Kettering and *The Maine* was assigned to all of them. They were 1) Molesworth, home of the B-17s that made up the 303rd Bombardment Group and located approximately 17 miles west of Kettering; 2) Harrington, home of the B-24s used for parachute drops by paratroopers behind enemy lines at night and located approximately eight miles to the west of Kettering; 3) Deenethorpe, home of the B-17s that made up the 401st Bombardment Group and located approximately 13 miles to the north of Kettering; and 4) Grafton Underwood, home of the B-17s that made up the 384th Bombardment Group and located under five miles to the northeast of Kettering and just north of the village of Grafton. The Grafton airfield was jokingly dubbed "Grafton Undermud" by the Americans serving there "because of the negative effects of the English weather of 'rain, rain, and more rain.'"[157]

Historians of World War II have uniformly credited the Eighth Air Force, along with British Bomber Command, as playing the lead role in "breaking the back" of the German air force, the Luftwaffe, and thereby clearing the skies over France and Germany, and in crippling German war industries during the last year of the war.[158] The units stationed at Molesworth, Harrington, Deenethorpe, and Grafton Underwood were key components of that distinguished war record.

Although each airfield had a Red Cross club (a permanent operation manned by Red Cross personnel who remained on the base day and night), and a few other clubmobiles stationed at and working out of Kettering such as *The Rhode Island*, Blanche, Dottie, and Lois spent about an equal amount of time at each airfield that they were assigned to. But because Blanche got to know the men at Molesworth the best, she made friends there and often spent what little free time she had at their air base.

Molesworth and the "Hell's Angels"

Molesworth, which took its name from a nearby village, was the home of the "Hell's Angels," and it was a typical Eighth Air Force bomber base. Located approximately 10 miles from Bedford, where Glenn Miller and his orchestra were stationed for a while, the air base

> … was surrounded by hay fields and contained within its spacious confines all the facilities and support units necessary to service the Group's four B-17 squadrons—the 358th, 359th, 360th and 427th. The Base also served as headquarters of the Eighth's 41st Combat Bomb Wing. … The first Eighth Air Force mission flown over Nazi-occupied territory had come from Molesworth in July of 1942. [Its] dominant feature was its triangle of three runways. … Ringing [them] in an irregular pattern were multiple taxiways joining 50 heavy bomber hardstands. The base's heart was a large "technical site" of buildings situated northeast of the runway triangle and adjacent to the central section of the main runway. The site contained the control tower, a huge J-type aircraft hangar, two

smaller T-2 hangers, and a complex of smaller structures east of these buildings that included ... Group HQ, Base Operations, officers and enlisted mess halls, and the buildings and barracks that belonged to the [different squadrons.][159]

The 303rd was one of the most famous bomb groups in the Eighth Air Force and had one of its most distinguished combat records.[160] It was named after its most famous B-17, "Hell's Angels," as that particular aircraft, and not the more well-known and celebrated "Memphis Belle," was the first heavy bomber in the Eighth Air Force to complete 25 missions. At the time, once a flight crew member completed 25 missions, they were eligible to return home. But the odds of reaching that magic number were a long shot at best and the men knew it. By the time Blanche arrived at Molesworth in August 1944, the 303rd's markings on its B-17s consisted of a red band framing a triangle C insignia on both tail and wing.[161]

During late 1942, all of 1943, and the first half of 1944, the Hell's Angels flew numerous missions over France and the Low Countries, as well as over German targets. In January 1944, the 303rd hit Oschersleben, Germany, after most of the Eighth Air Force and its fighter escort had aborted due to harsh weather. The devastating strike was the beginning of the end for the Luftwaffe, but it also cost the 303rd 10 aircraft and their crews. For this valuable contribution to the war effort, the men of the Group, both air and ground echelons, were awarded a Distinguished Unit Citation. In early March 1944, the Group participated in one of the first strikes on Berlin, and of course, the 303rd also played a part in the massive aerial support garnered for D-Day on June 6, 1944. In the later stages of the war, the 303rd struck industrial sites, transportation hubs, and oil refineries in Germany with increased efficiency and decreasing losses.

However, less than a week after *The Maine*'s arrival at Molesworth, the 303rd suffered one of its worst single days of the war when, on a mission to Wiesbaden, Germany, the Group was attacked on its return trip by the elite "Sturmgruppen," a special bomber-killer unit of the Luftwaffe. The Group lost nine planes that day with 24 men dead and 48 captured or missing.[162] Blanche vividly recalled the bleak and depressed atmosphere on the base that week and how the men each privately grappled with the loss in his own way. Although men from the newer crews talked about their experiences right after a mission, the men in the older crews generally did not. Instead, when they talked with the Red Cross girls, they would talk about where they were from, what they did before the war, sports, what they were going to do after the war, or about their sweethearts and family back home. The last part was often punctuated with the retrieval from their pockets of folded pictures of their loved ones. The Red Cross girls took their cue from the men and talked about whatever the men wanted to discuss. However, the men had little time to mourn fallen comrades, as they were in the air again and on another mission just three days later. "It was a telling demonstration not only of the 303rd's resiliency and recuperative powers, but also of the caliber of the men …"[163]

On those days when the Hell's Angels were going to fly a mission, the ground crews would be up and busy getting the planes fueled and ready to fly before sunup. Major Mel Schulstad, one of the first pilots in the Group, described it this way:

> When the ground crews got out to the hardstands, one of the first things they did was to start a portable gasoline engine. They used it to provide electrical power to the airplane and lighting to work. You'd hear the noise as a simple "putt-putt-putt" when the first engine started, and then soon it would be joined by others and grow until you heard this "hummmmm" coming in from the hardstands. To me there was always a terrible drama about it greater than the opening of Beethoven's Fifth, or the beginning of any symphony. When you heard that sound, you knew for sure that today men were going to die.[164]

On those days when a mission was on, Blanche and the other Red

Cross girls would often stand near the control tower and marvel at how the bombers from all the surrounding airfields would literally fill the sky as they waited for the other planes to become airborne and complete their formations. The noise was deafening, and it would take well over an hour for all the planes to arrange themselves in proper formation for the trip across the channel. The planes filled the sky, and it was an awe-inspiring scene that Blanche never forgot. Then, later in the day, Blanche, Dottie, and Lois would anxiously wait for the planes to return from their mission so that they could serve more coffee and doughnuts, this time to the exhausted and sometimes traumatized crewmen. Years later, Blanche vividly described how she stood on the tarmac when the B-17s returned to base, many shot up from flak and enemy fighters, and some crashing while trying to land. She also remembered how the crews would emerge from their planes, dirty, exhausted, and hungry, and how the doughnuts and hot coffee she offered them disappeared quickly.

In a letter home just a couple of weeks after the Wiesbaden mission, as Blanche tried to describe her activities to her parents without overly dramatizing them, she told them that

> ... sometimes we serve the fellows when they come back from a mission over Germany. Needless to say, I enjoy this the most. I say "enjoy," but what I really mean is the feeling of satisfaction one gets in knowing that you are on the spot and ready to give relief to weary, nervous fellows who are anxious to talk about all they have just been through. The hardest part for me is watching planes come in with one wing [shot up] or damaged in some other way and [having to watch] them crash land.[165]

Helplessly standing by and watching the planes break apart and sometimes explode and burn, the ambulances and ground crews rushing to the scene to try to save lives, and the faces of the men involved, was heart-wrenching. It also brought back painful memories for Blanche of her husband's death two years earlier, and how she envisioned his death in her nightmares. As another Red Cross volunteer vividly remembered it,

> You could see the entire range of human emotions in the faces and conduct of the fliers who had just returned. Some of them were dog-tired, others were elated. One of them would want to tell us everything that had happened ..., another wouldn't talk at all. ... We had to adapt ourselves to each new emotion as it came along. It was taxing on the nerves and spirit, and it took it out of us. Then, too, we had to brace ourselves against the fact that some of the boys to whom we had become devoted sometimes didn't come back at all.[166]

That last part was particularly difficult for Blanche as she had gotten to know some of the lost crews personally, knew their backgrounds, knew their plans for after the war, and knew that there were sweethearts and family members back home waiting for them to return. Naturally, she felt a kinship with the lost crews' loved ones.

Along with that letter to her parents, Blanche enclosed her first pictures from the ETO. They were taken by a photographer who was working with journalist and author Ernie Pyle, a roving Scripps Howard war correspondent.[167] The two men visited Molesworth and Blanche and the crew of *The Maine* had their pictures taken with Pyle's "short snorter." A short snorter was paper currency, usually an American one-dollar bill, that the owner would have people sign and state who they had flown with or who they had met. American airmen also often listed the bombing missions they had participated in and the dates. If someone signed your short snorter and later you could not produce it upon request, you owed him a dollar or a drink (i.e., "a short snort"). Given the number of flights he had been on and the number of people he had met on his travels, Ernie Pyle reportedly had one of the longest short snorters of the war.

Perhaps Pyle had the men of the 303rd in mind when he wrote

about the time he was around a bunch of pilots after they had returned safely from their first mission.

> They were so excited they were practically unintelligible. Their eyes were bloodshot, they were red-faced with excitement, and they were so terrifically stimulated they couldn't quiet down. Life had never been more wonderful. They told the same story of their day's adventure over and over two dozen times before bedtime. One boy couldn't eat his supper. Another one couldn't get to sleep. The older boys listened patiently. They had been that way not so long before. They knew that battle maturity would come quickly.[168]

A Temporary Infatuation

Shortly after her arrival at Molesworth in August 1944, Blanche attended her first dance at the officers' club on base. The officers routinely invited the Red Cross girls to their dances as American women were in demand. Surprisingly, considering that she was still wearing her wedding ring and was still quietly grieving for Les, she met, danced with, and quickly became "rather fond" of one of the pilots. He was Major Melvin Lewis "Mel" Schulstad Jr. of Reynolds, North Dakota. He was one of the 303rd's original cadre of pilots and had already completed 30 combat missions. During those missions, he had barely missed death on numerous occasions. In fact, his original plane, a B-17 named "Beat Me," had gone down with all hands during a mission over the Lorient U-boat pens in January 1943. Mel wasn't flying that day, and thereby survived, because he had been grounded with the flu.[169] By the time Blanche met Mel, he was serving as the Assistant Group Operations Officer.

Blanche was immediately impressed by the awesome responsibilities Mel had, and by his charm, personality, education, ambition, and, most importantly, sex appeal. She remembered him as a "real gentleman" who had a knack with words. There was an immediate chemistry between the two of them, and Mel seemed to fall for

Blanche right off. So, they quickly established a routine of going out twice a week and attending dances at the officers' club on weekends. Since Blanche worked at other neighboring airfields too, on days that he had asked her out, Mel would fly to the base where Blanche was working and fly her back to Molesworth. Often, after the dance was over, Mel would take Blanche to the officers' mess and fix her a late-night breakfast before taking her back to Kettering in the General's car. So, he could cook too! It was all very impressive and a bit overwhelming, and Blanche could not help but be dazzled.[170]

The first time Mel took Blanche to the officers' club, Mel purchased the drinks. Knowing that Blanche was a teetotaler, he brought back grapefruit juice for her—which was fine as far as she was concerned. But Mel had not bothered to tell her that her drink had gin in it too. It was the first time she got tipsy and the first time she experienced a bit of a hangover the next morning. However, predictably, she got used to the stuff, in moderation of course, and that is how she finally got over the strict habit of her youth of avoiding anything alcoholic. When she was young, neither her parents nor her siblings drank alcohol, nor did any of her close friends in high school or college. It was just another example of the sheltered atmosphere she had grown up in.

Blanche and Mel really enjoyed each other's company. Sometimes he would take her up into the base's control tower and allow her to make routine field announcements over the loudspeaker system. The men on base got a real kick out of her occasionally stumbling over technical words or when she went off script. Then once, while Mel and other officers were playing poker in the officers' club, a common pastime, Blanche came in the club and the men demanded that she join them. Since she refused to gamble, the men demanded that they play for clothes instead of money. Blanche reluctantly agreed but only to a single hand. She lost, of course, because the men made sure of it. Blanche obligingly stood up, as the men whooped and hollered, and she did a little dance mimicking a striptease. But instead of taking off an article of clothing, she pulled out several hairpins and threw them on the table. The men immediately cried foul, but Blanche just smiled and walked away.

Since Mel was serving as the Assistant Group Operations Officer, he recommended to his superiors how many planes were needed from each squadron for the next mission, and where they should be assigned. Naturally, the squadron leaders knew this and usually did their best to stay on Mel's good side. Discussions among squadron leaders could became fierce arguments and even get personal considering what was at stake. For example, when Mel would inform a squadron officer that a certain number of planes and crews were needed for the next mission, the squadron officer would sometimes complain that the request wasn't possible because of battle damage or whatever, then the two officers would go round and round until the matter was resolved.[171] Blanche knew that Mel carried "terrific responsibilities" for one so young, so she found herself somewhat "mothering him," and of course, when he was on a mission, she was always "anxiously awaiting his return."[172]

Obviously, Blanche had begun to really like Mel, and at one point, she even began to believe that she was falling in love with him, but that feeling was tempered by the realization that many of the men on the base disliked and even feared him. At first, she could not understand it. It was not consistent with his personality and gentlemanly behavior toward her. However, the mystery was solved one night on the dance floor at the officers' club. Mel had been called away, as he often was since he was always "on call" because of his operational responsibilities, and a young officer came up to Blanche and asked her to dance. She accepted, and while they were dancing, they chatted. When the officer asked Blanche if she had come to the dance with someone, and she responded by telling him that she was there with Major Schulstad, the officer abruptly stopped dancing, turned around, and walked away without a word. Blanche was dumbstruck.

When Blanche asked other officers at the dance for an explanation, most of them did not seem surprised but refused to answer. Finally, one officer pulled Blanche aside and quietly informed her that the Major had made it clear that if anyone danced with his date that that officer might find himself assigned to the next mission—whether it was his turn or not! Blanche was appalled. When she confronted Mel with the accusation, he passed it off as an exaggeration, but he didn't specifically deny it either. Although it could have been an empty threat on his part, one he simply used to ward off unwelcome social competition, it certainly explained why some of the men disliked and feared him. So that evening turned out to be their last date. The infatuation was over, and Blanche refused to go out with him again. However, they did manage to remain cordial.

After the break-up, Mel continued to pursue Blanche for a while, but after she left Kettering, he turned his attention elsewhere. He started dating an American nurse and they were married in May 1945. Consistent with his ambition, his career also continued to advance. He became the Group Operations Officer for the Hell's Angels, and for his distinguished combat service, he received the Distinguished Flying Cross with two oak leaf clusters, as well as the Air Medal with five oak leaf clusters.[173] After the war Mel remained with the Air Force, and, ironically, in the early 1950s, he was assigned as a staff officer to help implement a military assistance plan designed to rebuild the Luftwaffe and West Germany's military-industrial infrastructure. He retired as a full Colonel in 1965. During his retirement, he became active in "promoting professionalism in counseling for alcoholics," and became the founding president of the National Association of Alcoholism and Drug Addiction Counselors. As a recovering alcoholic, Mel was known for his "compassion and empathy" toward others struggling with addiction.[174] All in all, Mel Schulstad had a long, remarkable, and highly distinguished career.

A Close Call

During the fall of 1944, Blanche, Dottie, and Lois had fallen into a comfortable routine of visiting all four airfields on a weekly basis. Most of the men they interacted with were well-behaved. As clubmobiler Mary Metcalfe Rexford remembered it,

Some sexual innuendos [were always] present, but they were rarely explicit. And the [GI] who stepped out of line with his remarks was usually chastised by his buddies, not by us. We ... were respected. Even though we were surrounded by men, men who had been separated from their wives and sweethearts for months and years, we felt perfectly safe.[175]

But that was when the women were with large groups of men and when such self-policing worked. In those circumstances the women had learned how to "sing slightly bawdy songs, respond to off-color jokes, deflect a sexual advance," and yet remain respected. The officers and GIs loved them for it and jointly protected them.[176] It was when the women were alone with one or two men that problems could arise. In fact, Blanche experienced her first overt sexual assault while serving in England, and the perpetrator was an American GI.

While attached to the Eighth Air Force, the Red Cross girls did not just attend dances at the officers' clubs, they also went out of their way to attend enlisted men's dances when possible. They thought that it was important to do so for GI morale. So, on the night that an enlisted men's dance was to occur, the Army would send trucks to pick up the Red Cross girls at their billets and take them to and from the dance. Since there were not enough American women to go around, the Army would also pick up local English girls who wanted to attend. Upon the conclusion of one such dance, somehow Blanche and one of the English girls attending managed to miss their arranged ride back to Kettering. As Blanche tried to arrange another ride, the English girl told Blanche that she had already lined up a ride. According to the English girl, two of her "friends" (American GIs) had volunteered to drive them back to town. Although reluctant at first, since Blanche really didn't know any of them, she hesitantly agreed.

Just as Blanche had feared, halfway back to Kettering the GIs pulled their truck off the main road and onto a dark, secluded side road and parked. Immediately, prearranged no doubt, the driver started making love with the English girl in the front seat (with the girl's full consent). Taking his cue from the driver, the other GI pulled Blanche into the back of the truck and started attacking her. Although he was twice her size, somehow Blanche fought him off, broke free, climbed out the back of the truck and ran toward the main road. It was pitch-black outside, however, and Blanche could hardly make out her surroundings, but somehow, she ran into a local farmer who was out checking on his animals. She pleaded with the farmer to assist her, but he said and did nothing—he was reluctant to get involved or confront the American servicemen.

By then the GI had caught up with Blanche and forcibly pulled her back to the truck, but to keep her from screaming he promised to desist from his attack. Evidently, her violent reaction scared him. He knew if Blanche reported the incident to his commanding officer it could result in an immediate court martial. So, the disgusted GIs finally agreed to take Blanche back to Kettering. On the way back, Blanche sat quietly in the back shaking and did her best to collect herself. It had been a terrifying experience, but she never reported it to the Army or to the Red Cross. She did not want to become the focus of a military investigation and court martial or draw unwelcome attention to herself or to the Red Cross. But she knew she had been extremely lucky and silently vowed to be more careful in the future.

When discussing the incident decades later, Blanche admitted that she had often thought that she had made the wrong decision, that she should have filed a formal complaint with the Army. However, she also admitted that, at the time, she was too scared and upset to do so. Yet she could not help but wonder how many other women might have experienced a similar attack by that same GI. Based on the journals, autobiographies, letters, and oral interviews of other Red Cross girls, one would think that such things rarely if ever happened, but Blanche was not so sure.

Chapter 8

"Hey, small fry, did you get that load of gravel we sent?"

A Typical Day on The Maine

While stationed in Kettering, Blanche, Dottie, and Lois were routinely on their own and received little direct supervision from London. A typical day for the women would begin at around seven in the morning. They would awaken, take turns in the bathroom, get dressed, eat breakfast, and hopefully be ready to leave when their driver, Ted Scott, arrived to pick them up in *The Maine* at around eight o'clock. Ted would then drive the women to whichever air base they were to serve that day, and he would often pick up stray GIs along the way who were hitching a ride back to their base (especially on Sundays after a weekend leave).

Upon their arrival at the airfield, Ted would find a power source to hook up *The Maine*'s power cord, usually at or near the local Red Cross club, base mess hall, or Nissen hut near a hangar where there were outdoor plugs.[177] Another necessity was finding a water source for making the coffee and doughnut mix. Once that task was completed, they would often sit through briefings with "the fellows," serve them coffee and doughnuts just before they took off, and "sweat it out" until they returned. When the planes landed, the women would serve fruit juice and sandwiches to the exhausted crews. At night, the women would sometimes take hot coffee and doughnuts to the ground crews working on the planes and getting them ready for the next mission. That was a cold job.

To avoid boredom and to ensure that they equally shared the work, the women often rotated the specific jobs to be performed each day. That meant that one day Blanche might be making doughnuts, or "sinkers" as they were affectionately known by the GIs (the toughest job in her opinion), or fetching water and making the coffee, or setting up the back of the clubmobile and setting out the trays of chewing gum and cigarettes, or, later, doing what the women referred to as "jeeping"—taking a jeep or weapons carrier, always driven by an accommodating GI, to remote areas of the base where isolated pockets of men were working so as to serve them doughnuts and coffee.[178]

The "doughnut making" was always a challenge. The women developed an adversarial relationship with their doughnut machine, as it was on the one hand essential to their operation, but on the other hand highly temperamental, difficult to operate, and downright dangerous at times. Getting burned was always a risk. The women had to heat the grease inside the machine to 425 degrees Fahrenheit and carefully maintain that temperature throughout the doughnut-making process. (During the war, several Red Cross girls were severely burned while performing this process.) Meanwhile, they had to retrieve hot water from the mess hall and stir it in with the premeasured doughnut mix to make the thick dough. "If the water was not warm enough, the dough ended up as greasy doughnuts; if it was too hot, they wouldn't hold together. Getting the correct ... temperature for the water was a constant challenge ..."[179] Plus, the machine always emitted a certain amount of smoke, and although the clubmobile had a bantam flue for such purposes, the air often became hot, smoky, and suffocating. Even keeping the back door of the clubmobile open did not always help.[180]

In isolation, this process was challenging enough. But GIs always wanted to "help" and only managed to get in the way. This is how Blanche described one challenging day: First, she got a scale out and arranged the trays to receive hot doughnuts, then she got ready to mix and measure the flour. At that key moment, some GI Joe would appear and want to mix the flour. Next, a second GI would insist on measuring the flour for her, and in the process spill it from one end of the clubmobile to the other. By the time they are finished, flour is on the ceiling, on the walls, and in Blanche's hair. Finally, after Blanche regains control of the situation, she makes the dough and begins making the doughnuts. Then a third GI loudly complains, "Why don't you get some good records on this clubmobile?" Nevertheless, he finally finds one to his liking and then insists that Blanche dance with him right then and there. So, the second GI takes over the task of placing the dough into the machine and, failing to measure the dough properly, makes doughnuts the size of jeep tires. These misshapen sinkers the women jokingly refer to as "4 Fs"[181] (i.e., rejects).

After making hundreds of doughnuts and dozens of urns of coffee, the women either start serving on the spot or find the most strategic place to park the clubmobile where the men are preparing to take off on a bombing mission or are returning from one, or where the ground crew is hard at work. Then the women open for business. They open the side panels of the clubmobile, thereby creating a serving shelf, and begin distributing doughnuts and coffee to the men—many of whom had already started lining up alongside the clubmobile, being attracted by the aroma of hot coffee and the unmistakable smell of fresh doughnuts.[182] Although that smell attracted the men, the women serving the "sinkers" came to loathe it. Sometimes the smell was so overpowering that it became sickening. It permeated their clothes, their hair, and everything around them.

The immediate impact the appearance of a clubmobile had on air base operations was humorously described by Blanche in one of her letters home. She explained that once *The Maine* was hooked up to a power source and water obtained, and the coffee and doughnuts were made, the girls would turn on the outside speaker, hunt for "a good hot tune," place the record on the Victrola, "and blast the peaceful atmosphere of the field with the 'Java Jive.' Soon the clubmobile became jammed with GIs and officers. Blanche jokingly, but not altogether inaccurately, noted that the war had to cease temporarily because officers couldn't get their clerks at headquarters to answer their phone because the clerks were in the clubmobile. The food in the mess hall kitchen is being burned because the kitchen staff are talking to Dottie, and all transportation ceases because the fellows at the motor pool are fighting over who is going to be the lucky fellow to drive Lois around to the remote corners of the field with doughnuts and coffee."[183]

Once the initial chaos dies down, Blanche tries to settle down for a few quiet moments, only to be met with the familiar refrain, "How about a date shorty?" She diplomatically explains to the GI that she is all "dated up" for about the next three weeks but reminds him that she plans on attending the base dance on Thursday and promises to see him there. At around midday, Dottie finishes making more coffee and comes in to relieve Blanche so she can walk to the mess hall and get some "chow." Without fail, as soon as Blanche enters the mess hall, a GI sees her and yells out so everyone can hear him, "Hi, Kansas City!" or "Well, there's shorty!" or "Hey, small fry, did you get that load of gravel we sent?" The gravel, of course, was to fill up the hole Blanche was always standing in. Once she gets her food and is ready to sit down, the pushing and jostling starts as the GIs fight over the right to sit near her.

After lunch, Blanche returns to the clubmobile to make more doughnuts, as the men never seem to get enough of them, and to get things cleaned up and ready for a second round of serving. While Blanche is busy doing so, a GI insists on arranging the tray of chocolate candy and cigarettes. And, of course, "he eats more than he gets in the serving container." Then the women open the side of the clubmobile again, usually at around 2:30 p.m., and start serving to yet another lengthy line of men. On a normal day, they would serve about 2,000 doughnuts and about 60 gallons of coffee!

Naturally, while the women were serving as fast as they could, a GI would insist that they step outside for a moment to have their picture taken. After finally running out of coffee and doughnuts, the women would close shop, chase the GIs out from the back of the clubmobile, and start for home. This usually took place at around 5:00 p.m., unless a mission was on, and the planes had not yet returned. By the end of the day the women were thoroughly "worn out and hungry."[184]

If the women got back to Kettering at a decent hour, they would take a bath and eat dinner before "the fellows" started to arrive. The clubmobile girls and their dates or other male friends would either attend a base dance, go to a picture show or a local pub, or play games at the boarding house until about 11:30 p.m. when the Liberty run (base transportation) went back to the field and the men had to leave. They were long and exhausting days, and often Blanche had to skip the activities after dinner and simply retire or risk not being able to properly function the next day.

The work they did daily met the traditional mid-20th century definition of "women's work," in that "they cooked, cleaned up, and waited on men. Yet [they] did essential war service that included demanding physical labor and at stressful emotional costs. Their jobs required sophisticated organizational skills and superb interpersonal relations. … Their experience, maturity, and education gave them a self-awareness and understanding of the job they were doing."[185] It was simple, yet strenuous, manual labor that was far below the women's educational achievements, but given the circumstances and the overall mission, it was incredibly rewarding work for Blanche and the other clubmobilers. They knew that they were helping the men's morale and that they were giving the men a little taste of home every time they interacted with them.

It has been asserted that raw physical strength and hardiness were more important for those who served on a clubmobile than for staff working in other ARC departments. "The daily work required [the] women to perform tasks such as loading flour bags, carrying coffee urns, stocking the vehicles with supplies, preparing donuts and coffee in massive amounts for hours at a time." Given these demanding and strenuous duties, the clubmobilers generally needed more physical strength than Red Cross staff working in the established clubs.[186] Obviously, Blanche was not physically well-suited for clubmobile service, but she persevered and refused to allow her physical limitations to interfere with her duties. As if the weekly routine was not hard enough, Blanche also volunteered to play the organ each Sunday morning during the military chaplain's religious services for the men on base.

A Dirty Little Secret

During World War II the American military was still racially segregated. This was accomplished by creating separate African American units and then primarily assigning them behind the lines in service and support functions. The Army also enforced the strict separation of the races at American military facilities, including mess halls, barracks, and entertainment venues such as USO clubs. As the American military redeployed into Great Britain, it tried to export these restrictive racial policies and practices into the ETO under the guise of military discipline and efficiency.[187]

When the American military presence in Great Britain reached its apex in early 1944, however, and the number of African American GIs there exceeded 130,000, strict enforcement of these policies became difficult and controversial. The African American press and political leaders back home were constantly pointing out the "similarities between the racist policies of the Axis powers and the discrimination suffered by Black service men and women." They "urged African Americans to embrace the 'Double V' campaign—victory against the Axis and victory at home over racial discrimination."[188]

These criticisms were also directed at the military's support organizations such as the USO and the ARC. Publicly, and to avoid such criticism and maintain broad-based financial and volunteer support, the Red Cross announced that American service members, regardless of race, were always "welcome at all American Red Cross clubs, canteens or recreation centers." But, at the same time, in an effort to cover all its bases, it noted that, since the Army usually concentrated its African American troops in certain limited geographical areas, the Red Cross would hire "colored male and female personnel" to staff the facilities located in those specific areas.[189] This was disingenuous and hypocritical, as it ensured the segregation of the races at Red Cross clubs. It also reflected a belief, fostered by years of racist dogma, that allowing white women to directly serve African American GIs was dangerous. The actual practices of the Red Cross in Great Britain were far from egalitarian. Blanche, familiar with the Red Cross's public announcements regarding equal treatment for all, soon discovered the hard way the organization's real unwritten policies.

Sometime in late October 1944, Blanche, Dottie, and Lois were asked to serve coffee and doughnuts to a company of African American soldiers billeted separately at a nearby air base. Before they started to serve the company, Lois, as the captain of the clubmobile, told Blanche and Dottie that they needed to keep the back door of *The Maine* closed to keep the men from entering. Blanche thought that that instruction was inappropriate and contrary to explicit Red Cross policy, but she was too busy at the time to protest. She and Dottie had already opened the side panels of the clubmobile and were in the process of serving the men their coffee and doughnuts.

As always, the women were chatting with the men as they went by in line. As the rush finally subsided, Blanche started talking to a handsome, well-spoken junior officer, and in the process discovered that he had attended Princeton University.[190] Their conversation soon turned to dancing and the sad fact that Blanche had never learned how to "jitterbug" (the most recent dance craze). The young officer graciously offered to teach Blanche the new dance. Excitedly, and without giving it a second thought, Blanche put jitterbug music on the Victrola and headed out the back door to dance with the officer. The other men loved it and gathered around the

dancers and shouted their encouragement. Although Blanche did
not remember the officer's name, she did remember that he "was a
wonderful dancer and a good teacher," and soon she was getting
the hang of it. She was delighted.

Lois, however, was furious. Failing to get a firm commitment
from Blanche never to do such a thing again, Lois reported the
incident to the Red Cross headquarters in London. Within days,
Blanche was ordered back to London to report to her supervisors in
the Clubmobile Department. Her supervisors asserted that by
Blanche leaving the clubmobile and dancing with an African American soldier she had "endangered the other Red Cross girls."
Blanche thought that that assertion was ridiculous, but out of defer-
ence to her supervisors she remained silent. Then the supervisors
went too far. They warned Blanche that if she ever did something
like that again they would dismiss her from the Red Cross and
immediately send her home. They also ordered her to always remain
in the clubmobile while serving African American soldiers, and to
never allow them into the back of the clubmobile to read newspapers and magazines, etc. like other American GIs. Thus, Blanche
finally realized that Lois had been following the real, behind-the-
scenes, unwritten racial policies of the Red Cross.[191]

Blanche was flabbergasted! After slowly collecting herself and
carefully weighing her words, she calmly and succinctly pointed out
to her supervisors that, "While performing my Red Cross duties I
have often had to dance with white soldiers that were uncouth,
unclean, and uneducated, and who I would never voluntarily socialize with in my civilian life. Nevertheless, I do so because it is my job
and my duty. Those GIs are risking their lives for their country, and
they deserve my attention just like the officers do." Then Blanche
pointed out that the African American soldiers were also risking
their lives for their country and deserve no less. Finally, she noted
that the officer she had danced with had attended Princeton and
was "every bit a gentleman."

Nevertheless, her supervisors were unconvinced and reiterated
their threat to send her home if she ever did something like that

again. Now, a bit angry, Blanche stood up and informed her supervisors that, while performing her official duties, if another African American GI asked her to dance, she would do so regardless of what they thought. With that unequivocal and unambiguous declaration of defiance, the meeting was quickly terminated, and Blanche returned to Kettering fearing that she would soon be sent home and wondering how she would explain her termination to her family and friends.[192]

Either Blanche's supervisors had been bluffing, or the issue was referred to top ARC leadership for a final decision. But, either way, because of Blanche's firm response and openly defiant attitude, it was decided that the ARC could not risk dismissing her (as it might have created negative publicity if she were to talk to the press). Instead, they solved the problem by never asking her clubmobile to serve African American soldiers again. Naturally, Blanche was relieved that she was not being sent home, but she was deeply disappointed with the Red Cross and with her captain, Lois Stone—and their relationship never recovered. Blanche was not a social crusader, and she was often a bit naive about the human interactions and relationships going on around her, but she had a keen sense of what was right and what was wrong. Once she determined what she perceived to be the right course of action, she rarely wavered.

Blanche never forgot that young officer either, or the fact that he took the time to teach her how to jitterbug—a talent she used repeatedly to interact with and entertain GIs during the rest of the war. Clubmobiler B.J. Olewiler had experienced the same phenomenon regarding "jitterbugging." She noted that the dance "had become a real dividing line separating eighteen-year-olds [the average GI] from twenty-eight-year-olds [the average Red Cross girl]." GIs would often ask B.J., "Do you jitterbug?" and it bothered her that she could not comply. She noted that the jitterbug had "become the dance of the moment, without my noticing that my type of dancing was [now] passé."[193] Thus, learning how to jitterbug like the 18-year-old GIs quickly became a required job skill for all clubmobile girls.

New Responsibilities and New Crewmates

In November 1944, not long after the incident involving the African
American GIs, Lois Stone left Kettering and prepared for a reassignment to France. Stephanie J. Jackson of Binghamton, New York,
took Lois's place on the crew of The Maine. Stephanie was a petite,
sociable, attractive brunette, who seemed to really take to her clubmobile duties and got along with just about everybody. Her parents
were first-generation Lithuanian immigrants, and she was fluent in
several languages.

With Lois's departure, Blanche automatically became the "captain" of the clubmobile, but although the designation carried more
responsibility and more pay (equivalent to a captain's pay), it did not
carry the same importance in the Red Cross as it did in the Army.
The woman on the clubmobile with the most experience and senior-
ity automatically became the captain. The duties of the clubmobile
captain included supervising the services provided by the crew,
coordinating supplies, acting as the clubmobile's liaison with local
military brass and the Red Cross field supervisor assigned to the
area, looking out for the crew's welfare, and maintaining all
required records and reports—and all accomplished with little
administrative support or oversight from London.

In late December, to Blanche's sincere regret, Dottie Barrett was
also reassigned. Blanche really liked Dottie and was sorry to see her
leave. But Elizabeth "Libby" Harnies of Pittsburgh, Pennsylvania,
soon arrived to take Dottie's place. Libby was an outgoing, athletic,
vivacious young woman with auburn hair, who had come from a
wealthy Pittsburgh family. Her parents were well-educated first-generation English transplants, and her father was the president of a
Pittsburgh insurance company. Libby had had a privileged upbringing and, thus, had never had to learn to do her own washing, ironing, cleaning, or cooking. Those things had always been done for
her by the family's domestic staff, so adjusting to the life and strenuous work of a clubmobile girl was difficult for Libby at first, but she
was determined to learn. She quickly became a valued member of

The Maine and became Blanche's and Stephanie's favorite Red Cross colleague. In fact, Libby was the only clubmobile girl Blanche stayed in touch with decades after the war ended. When the weather permitted (as it rained a lot in the Midlands that November), and on the rare days that they had a day off, Blanche, Stephanie, and Libby would take long walks from town to town to take in the beauty of the English countryside. Each village was like taking a step back in time, with their little shops and cottages, thatched roofs, medieval churches, and the ever-present village pub, and each town seemed untouched by war—at least on the outside.

Blanche, Stephanie, and Libby made up the new crew of *The Maine* from December 1944 to late February 1945. However, they regularly collaborated with other Red Cross girls who were assigned to the permanent base clubs, such as Zephyr Boyajian of Forest Hills, New York, who was a second-generation American from Armenia, and Sarah Cofer Lenzen of Chicago, Illinois, who was one of the few clubmobile girls in the area who was married.

Christmas in the ETO

Just nine days before Christmas 1944, on the morning of December 16, the last major German offensive of the Western front began along the border between Germany, Luxembourg, and Belgium in the dense, cold, forbidden forests of the Ardennes. The offensive, and the Allied response, came to be known as the Battle of the Bulge. "Aimed at splitting the Allied armies in half and recapturing Antwerp, the Allies' most vital supply port …, it achieved total strategic and tactical surprise and was launched in poor weather … which, as Hitler had calculated, neutralized Allied air power."[194] Ultimately, however, the Allies organized a devastating counteroffensive on multiple fronts which lasted well into the new year and resulted in a resounding Allied victory.

As the holiday season approached, the 303rd suffered its worst single day of the war from ground flak during a mission over Merseburg, Germany. It lost four B-17s, and another 31 planes sustained major damage but managed to get their crews back to base.[195] During the month of December, the 303rd flew 16 additional missions over Germany.[196] "The Eighth made the ultimate maximum effort to support the ground troops during the Battle of the Bulge …, even ordering aircraft to fly which were not at their home bases after the previous day's mission. A record 2,046 heavy bombers were dispatched, together with 853 fighters."[197]

While the 303rd flew their missions over Belgium and Germany, Blanche prepared for her first Christmas away from home and family. Her maternal aunt had sent her a miniature Christmas tree and Blanche set it up in her room at Mrs. Mackay's boarding house. In a letter home just before Christmas, Blanche admitted that she had only sent them one package, as it was "impossible to buy anything [in England]," and she thanked them for sending her a "hat, socks, sweaters, blouse and gloves." She admitted that, as the notorious English winter moved into the Kettering area, those gifts were "life savers." She then described how she and her crewmates had prepared for Christmas. They had "managed to get a small Christmas tree and a few Christmas wreaths …" and build "something that look[ed] like a fireplace in the clubmobile." She even made stockings for each airfield that they regularly visited and hung them at the makeshift fireplace. They also managed to borrow a small reed organ and Blanche organized a choir at one of the airfields. A few GIs traveled around with the clubmobile girls and sang Christmas carols wherever they went. One of the GIs even agreed to play Santa Claus and wear Libby Harnies' long red flannel underwear as part of his Old Saint Nick costume.[198] On Christmas Eve, Blanche sent her parents a Western Union telegram wishing them a Merry Christmas and then attended church at a local parish.

The next day, Christmas Day 1944, the Hell's Angels held their annual Christmas Party for local children.[199] This was the only Christmas that Blanche spent overseas, and it was, in her opinion, "miserable!" She yearned for home. After all, the holiday season meant family and her family, and the families of the millions of American GIs, was on the other side of the Atlantic. However, trying to make the best of it, Blanche and the other Red Cross girls spent Christmas with the officers and men stationed at Molesworth at their holiday party. The women were picked up in the morning by Air Corps personnel and driven to the base in style. They spent the day decorating the officers' club with whatever they could find, attended a nondenominational religious service, and spent the evening singing songs with the officers and toasting the season. But as they did so, a thick fog moved in and it was too heavy for the cars to safely return to Kettering, since it was during the Battle of the Bulge and the trucks could not use their headlights. Thus, the clubmobile girls were forced to spend the night on the base. As there were no segregated accommodations available for women, Blanche, Stephanie, and Libby had to spend the night in sleeping bags on the concrete floor of the storeroom in the club. Blanche remembered that they "nearly froze to death!"

The fog had not lifted by morning, but by then Blanche was dog-tired and had had enough. Therefore, she put her pride aside and called her former boyfriend, Major Mel Schulstad, and asked him for help in getting them home. After the Major confirmed her story (to make sure that they had not spent the night with some of his men, a premise that Blanche found personally insulting), he had his personal car and driver take them back to Kettering—fog and insult notwithstanding.

It was several weeks after Christmas when Blanche finally received another holiday package from her parents. It included a homemade record of her parents and their friends wishing her a Merry Christmas and Happy New Year, and a recording of her mother reading an appropriate poem and her father playing the piano and singing "My Bonnie Lies Over the Ocean." Blanche cried when she finally had a chance to hear it.

As the new year rolled around, the Hell's Angels flew no less than 16 missions over Germany and one over Belgium during the month of January, and then 17 more missions in February.[200] *The Maine* pitched in too. It drove to Molesworth and to the other airfields day and night and served the ground crews who were working overtime to repair and maintain the planes so that they would be ready for the next mission. If a plane returned to the base shot up and damaged, the ground crew would start working on it instantly and continue to work until the plane was ready to fly. The ground crew did not even stop for their meals, so the women would take them hot coffee and doughnuts to tide them over.[201]

On January 21, 1945, Blanche celebrated her 27th birthday, and between the 22nd and the 25th, the women of *The Maine* hosted an "open house," from "15.00 hrs. to 17.00 hrs." each night at a different airfield. The invitation they distributed in advance played on their clubmobile's name and a little American history to create a catchy flier that hopefully attracted the appropriate attention from the GIs. It was addressed to "… all Yankee-Doodle-Dandies!!" and declared that they should "Remember the Maine" and come out and have some "fun and music" with them on the appointed day.[202] The invitation was signed by "the three Yankee-Doodle Bugs and their English boyfriend." Their English "boyfriend," of course, was their clubmobile driver, Ted Scott. The 303rd's Commanding Officer, Col. William S. Raper, and the other officers of the Hell's Angels returned the favor by inviting the women to a base dance at the officers' club on February 10, 1945.[203] It was one of the last dances Blanche was able to attend at Molesworth, as a new assignment and new challenges were just around the corner.

Chapter 9

"We would not have traded our right to drive for anything."

Clubmobiles on the Continent

For the better part of a year prior to D-Day (the Normandy Invasion of June 1944), the American Red Cross in London had been preparing for its own move to the continent. Where the boys went, the Red Cross was determined to follow, including its highly successful clubmobile program.[204] General Dwight D. Eisenhower had specifically asked ARC Commissioner Harvey Gibson to make sure that clubmobile services were going to be available to American troops on the continent as soon as it was safe to do so. The General was of the opinion, and Gibson agreed, that the clubmobile program was perfectly suited for continuing to deliver "morale support to the highly mobile invasion force."[205]

It was clear early in the planning process, however, that the Green Liners, those big, long, converted London buses that had been ideal for the flat English countryside, were ill-suited for the narrow, combat-scarred, often bombed-out and muddy roads of the continent. Thus, it was obvious to Gibson and his staff that the next phase of clubmobile service was going to require a new, smaller, and redesigned vehicle. Since they would be constantly on the move, following the advancing American forces wherever they went, and no longer able to rely on a single supply and maintenance depot, keeping the clubmobiles supplied and operating was going to be a huge challenge. Careful logistical planning by the Red Cross was clearly required.

It was finally decided that close to 100 two-and-a-half-ton American GMC 6×6 trucks, or "Jimmys" as they were affectionately called, had to be obtained and converted into smaller and nimbler clubmobiles. The Jimmy was a U.S. Army cargo truck, the original "Deuce and a Half," and it came in many variants, including open or closed cabs, with a long or short wheelbase, as well as over a score of specialized models (including the new converted clubmobile).

The clubmobile model had a higher clearance than the other models so that the women could stand in the rear of the truck. The sides were also modified to fold down to provide serving space for the women just like with the Green Liners. Naturally, each truck was equipped with a doughnut machine, coffee urns, a sink, attachments for hooking up running water, a water heater, and a portable field range. Like its larger predecessor, the GMC trucks contained a small back room filled with books, a phonograph and speaker, and folding bunks for the women to sleep on when necessary.[206]

The ARC also obtained a smaller number of English Bedford QL trucks, which was a series originally produced by Bedford Manufacturing for use by the British armed forces. They were high, squarish, two-ton jobs (like a moving van) with an open cab on both sides. They also had side panels in the back that lifted so the women could serve hot coffee and fresh doughnuts to the troops directly from the truck just like the GMCs and Green Liners. Each clubmobile was normally staffed by three women who were responsible for driving, preparing, and serving the doughnuts and coffee, and doing just about everything else. However, the Bedford clubmobiles only had a small kitchen and they did not have room for a lounge in the back.

Finally, the ARC obtained scores of American Dodge WC-62 trucks, a medium range, six-wheel-drive utility vehicle produced by the Chrysler Corporation under the Dodge brand. The military version was nicknamed the "Beep." The ARC version was constructed with a specialized rear chassis that was converted into what the ARC dubbed its "cinemobile." Each cinemobile was crewed by two women who drove, maintained it, and operated its film projector and screen (designed to show American movies to the GIs). The crew also sang, danced, and played a piano that was stored in the back of the truck. The left-hand side and the rear of the truck folded down to form the stage needed to perform the entertainment or show the movies. Why Blanche was not assigned to a cinemobile on the continent, given her musical talents, was always a source of wonder to her. But she was content with the assignments she received. She was where she wanted to be and performing services that she believed the men wanted and appreciated.

These new redesigned clubmobiles and their crews were to solely operate on the European continent, or the ARC's designated "Zone V." The new clubmobiles were organized into nine "groups," each consisting of eight clubmobiles, one cinemobile, one or two jeeps used as staff cars for field communication, and up to three or four Hillmans and other supply trucks and trailers used for transporting and delivering supplies.[207] The English Hillman was a specialized vehicle manufactured by The Hillman Motor Car Company, a British automobile manufacturer based in Ryton-on-Dunsmore, near Coventry, England. Its best-known version was called the "Tilly," a British Army utility truck. The Hillmans were small and "notoriously unreliable," which caused problems for all who utilized them. Naturally, all the vehicles in the group were painted Army gray or light gray.

These nine groups were each given organizational designations using one of the first 12 letters of the alphabet, A through L (except for the letters I and J which were excluded for some reason). Each one of these groups had approximately 32 or 33 persons assigned to it, including the 26 women who crewed the eight clubmobiles and one cinemobile, three or four drivers, a female group captain who oversaw the activities of the crews, and a male field supervisor who acted as a liaison with the Army's G-1 branch (Special Services) and who carefully planned the itineraries of each clubmobile.[208] Each clubmobile group also had several GIs assigned to it who were electricians and responsible for running and keeping in working order the doughnut machines and the two generators that provided electricity.[209] Each group traveled with the rear echelon of the Army Corps it was assigned to—usually serving troops at rest a few miles behind the front lines. This approach was continued in each country liberated and well into Germany itself. Camilla Moss of New York City was the overall field representative for the northern sector of the ETO, and she served as the liaison officer between Red Cross headquarters in London (and later in Paris) and the American military.[210]

The clubmobiles on the continent were not exclusively named for American states or major cities like the ones in Great Britain, but sported symbolic, patriotic, or place names, or even proper names of famous Americans that would appeal to American soldiers—names such as *The Southern Belle, The Golden State,* and *The Kit Carson.*[211] *The Daniel Boone* of Group B was the first to land on the beaches of Normandy in mid-July 1944, and it served 75,000 doughnuts by the end of its first week of operation![212] By the end of July, five more clubmobile groups arrived in France, and, by mid-August 1944, all nine groups were in France and were wandering the country back roads as they closely trailed behind their assigned U.S. military units. The ARC divided up the nine clubmobile groups between Gen. Courtney H. Hodges's First Army to the north and Gen. George S. Patton's Third Army to the south.[213]

Although exact numbers are hard to come by, only about 400 American women ended up serving on clubmobiles in France, Belgium, Holland, Luxembourg, Austria, and Germany during the final year of the war.[214]

Reassignment to the Continent

After six months in the English Midlands, Blanche received orders to report to London for a new assignment. She was, of course, sad to be leaving Mrs. Mackay and the men of the Eighth Air Force, but she was excited about the prospects for a new challenge. After making her final farewell, she took a train to London and reported to Red Cross headquarters. Blanche had suspected that she would be sent to the continent, as that is where most of the women were being sent, but of course, there was no guarantee. Upon her arrival at the ARC headquarters in London, Miss Cook informed Blanche that she would be heading for France, and Blanche was delighted. She knew that by going to France she was being given a unique opportunity to serve as near as possible to the front lines, and that is what she wanted.

From her lodgings in London, using her new stationery appropriately entitled, in script, "Babble from Blanche," she wrote her last letter to her parents from England on February 19, 1945. Although given the prevailing military censorship rules that she could not provide her parents details concerning her new assignment, she did inform them that they should not expect any long, newsy letters from her for the near future because she was "going to be very busy from now on." Nevertheless, she assured them that she was safe and "having a perfectly wonderful time," and of course, she promised to "take very good care" of herself, as she was always trying to allay her parents' worst fears.

Also arriving in London for reassignment to France, although at separate times and coming in from different directions, were nearly 30 other Red Cross girls, most of whom Blanche had already met at least in passing. She had met them either during their initial training in Washington, D.C., their train trip from Washington, D.C. to New York City, their voyage across the Atlantic on *The Queen*, or while serving in Scotland and England. They included Aileen "Andy" Anderson of Kansas City, Kansas; Josephine "Jo" Banichar of Leechburg, Pennsylvania; Bette Brigham of Palatine Bridge, New York; Marge Calhoun of Bellevue, Washington; Peggy Evans of Swearingen, Texas; Nancy Fiske of Montclair, New Jersey; Polly Haskins of Jackson Springs, North Carolina; Mary Haynsworth of Greenville, South Carolina; Marge Hillman of Macon, Georgia;

Beth McCoy of Lebanon, Ohio; Margaret Morrison of Watertown, New York; Nancy Nicholas of Long Island, New York; Lindsay Rand of Rye, New York; Mary Read of Pelham Manor, New York; Eloise Reilly of Westport, Connecticut; and Elizabeth "Liz" Richardson of Mishawaka, Indiana.[215]

In preparation for her new assignment, Blanche and the other women who had been serving on the Green Liners, at least those who already knew how to drive, were given additional training. This was deemed necessary because once the women were deployed on the continent and assigned to a smaller GMC, Dodge, or Bedford truck, they were going to be without their English drivers. Instead, they were going to have to drive the vehicles themselves and, no doubt, under extremely rough and sometimes dangerous conditions. Most of the women wanted to drive the American trucks because of the obvious advantage of having the steering wheel on the left and the fact that they would be easier to maintain and service.

The instructors were English and all male, and in an age when jokes about women drivers were pervasive, one wonders what the instructors thought of their new assignment and the female students they were to teach. As another clubmobiler observed, "For these men, ... teaching women to drive was a distinct cross between a reward and a punishment. At first, they seemed unable to decide whether it was sheer heaven to be in the company of an American woman ... or sheer hell to be teaching her to drive. In the end, they responded with typical rivalry, each wanting to show that his charge could outdo the others."[216]

Once the training started, the instructor went over the function and workings of each major feature of the truck, including the ignition key, lights, mirrors, steering wheel, brakes, and stick shift. Next, the women were taken for a drive in the country and shown how to double-clutch without stripping the gears. Double clutching entailed depressing the clutch once to take the truck out of gear, releasing it, and then depressing it again before moving the stick shift into the next gear level. It had to be done quickly and seamlessly to avoid slowing down, especially when traveling up a steep hill. The women were also taught how to put the truck into a lower gear when descending a hill instead of solely relying on the brakes. This helped conserve the brakes from undue wear.

After the instructor showed the women what he could by demonstration, the women were asked to get behind the wheel and display their newfound skills. The double-clutching was the hardest part for most of the women, but although a bit rusty, Blanche took to it immediately. She had experience driving trucks for her father's poultry and egg business back in Kansas City. The challenge for her, however, was getting used to the clutch on an English vehicle and driving from the right side.

The last part of their training included the basics of vehicle repair and maintenance, which entailed opening the truck's hood, or "bonnet" as the English called it, and learning about the generator, distributor, fan belt, fuel lines, and air cleaner, and how to maintain the proper water level in the radiator as well as putting chains on the tires for winter weather. Clubmobiler Mary Metcalfe remembered that they spent a "day lying (very comfortably) under the truck while listening to a lecture on the transmission, transfer case, differential, pillar box, velocity joints, and the thirty-six points for greasing the chassis."[217] That was the easy part. The hard part for Blanche, given her small stature and limited physical strength, was learning to change a tire. Using the crowbar to initially loosen dirty or rusty lug nuts and lifting the huge truck tire while manipulating it off the wheel was impossible for Blanche. The instructor finally gave up and simply muttered under his breath that she had better hope that she had someone with her to help if she ever had to change a tire in the field.

During her few days in London, Blanche was able to visit friends and do some more sightseeing. The highlight of her brief time in London was successfully meeting up with her brother-in-law, Newell Barnes, Les's older brother, at London's famous Sherry's Tea House.

Newell was in the U.S. Navy and stationed in England at the time. Given the limitations of communication and censorship rules during wartime, finding an old friend or relative in the same place and at the same time as yourself was extremely difficult, and Blanche failed often. Therefore, meeting up with Newell was a special treat. She had always liked her brother-in-law, and it was a pleasure to converse with someone who had known her husband so well, since Blanche sometimes felt isolated in her grief, as she was surrounded by people who had never known him.

The rest of Blanche's week in London was spent preparing for the trip across the channel. This entailed the assembly of the equipment needed for the new assignment. Since her footlocker had to be left behind (to be shipped over later), all she was taking with her was one barrack bag and one musette bag, a bedroll and sleeping bag, her battle dress, GI raincoats, blankets, etc. In preparing for the harsh French winters, she noted with disgust that her old winter clothes were too tight on her. When she wore her oversize battle dress she did not even notice, but when she wore slacks, it was obvious that she had gained weight—no doubt from eating too many Red Cross sinkers.

The "Boat Train" to France

Once it was time to depart, the 30 or so Red Cross girls who had assembled for the crossing were split up into smaller groups and sent across the channel from different ports during the weekend of February 24 and 25, often with a handful of American WACs, GIs, and British and French military personnel. First, they assembled at Victoria Station and took trains to either Newhaven or Dover for embarkation. Blanche was directed to Dover, a major ferry port in Kent in southeast England, and only 21 miles from France across the Strait of Dover, which is the narrowest point between England and France. At Dover, Blanche and her compatriots were processed for departure and then boarded a small cross-channel ferry or "boat train," which had only resumed service the week before.

The boat's accommodations were Spartan, but it was only a two-hour journey to France. As the boat left port, Blanche looked back toward the English shore and beheld the beautiful and majestic White Cliffs of Dover for the first time, and she was overcome with the sensation that one chapter of her life was closing and a new one was beginning. Ever since she was a young girl and had begun studying the "Great Masters," Blanche had dreamed of traveling to France and Germany and visiting the homes and churches of the most famous composers of Western classical music. Of course, she had not envisioned attempting to do so during a global world war, but, nevertheless, she was determined to try to track them down if the opportunity presented itself. She was successful some of the time.

On the other side of the channel lay the little war-damaged town of Dieppe, in Picardy, a French seaport at the mouth of the River Arques. It had only been in Allied hands since early September. That is where Blanche and the other women landed, and after a few hours of waiting, they boarded a train for Paris. Clubmobiler Liz Richardson was impressed "with the cleanliness of the carriages … and … the dining car," and the quality of the food and drink they were able to procure on the train. The train followed a route past Beauvais, France, "through calm rural countryside strangely reminiscent of home." Liz also noted that "[t]he destruction of the towns was different than that of England, the difference between bombing—and artillery plus house-to-house fighting."[218]

Paris and a New Clubmobile

Naturally, all the women were excited at the prospect of visiting Paris, which had been liberated by the Allies in August 1944, and they were all glued to the train's windows as they entered the outskirts of the city. When the Eiffel Tower finally came into view, Blanche was awestruck. She had finally made it to the "City of Lights!" Their accommodation would not disappoint either—in fact, it was luxurious compared to what they had become used to in

England. The women were assigned spacious rooms in the Normandy Hotel, which had been taken over by the Red Cross for use
by its female personnel and women military officers. It had been
previously occupied by German officers and was located at 7 Rue de
l'Échelle. Like the other large hotels near the Louvre and the Tuileries Garden, the Normandy Hotel had been built in 1877 to cater
to tourists arriving in Paris after disembarking in Normandy.
Although not strictly tourists, the Red Cross girls had every inten-
tion of making the most of their brief stay in the French capital.

After reporting in at the Red Cross's Continental Headquarters,
located at 12 Boulevard de la Madeleine, about three blocks north
of the Place de la Concorde and the Tuileries Garden, the women
broke up into small groups and began their sightseeing in earnest.
Even the overcast skies could not dampen Blanche's enthusiasm for
the beautiful, wide boulevards; numerous street vendors; opulent,
well-stocked stores (that did not require rationing coupons!); spec-
tacular French architecture; and the overall ambience of the French
capital. Naturally, they also visited the main Red Cross Club in
Paris, also referred to as "Rainbow Corner" just like the main club
in London had been, and they ate at an "elegant restaurant" near
the Place de l'Opéra, with which the Red Cross had a billing
arrangement. Consequently, the Red Cross girls were required to
eat there unless they wanted to pay for their own meals.[219] Unfortunately, the women had to pay for their own liquor, but that did not
bother Blanche in the least as she rarely drank.

For Blanche, the highlights of her first visit to Paris, besides the
Eiffel Tower, were her visits to the Champs-Élysées, the Arc de Tri-
omphe, the Louvre, the Tuileries Garden, the Place de la Concorde,
and Notre-Dame Cathedral. To get around the city, the women
used the famous Paris underground which was always jam-packed
with people, and Blanche found her knowledge of the French lan-
guage inadequate for the tasks at hand. The most startling sight for
Blanche were the street toilets located on corners all over the city.
They were metal walls folded around each other to create an

entrance and inside area for two toilets. But besides the ever-present smell emanating from them, Blanche was taken aback by the fact that everyone could see the feet of the occupants—men and women alike. She made sure she never had to use one of the contraptions.

While in Paris, Blanche was delighted when she ran into Dottie Barrett, her fellow clubmobile crew member from Kettering, who was also in Paris for reassignment. It was a wonderful reunion for both women after a three-month separation. When they finally returned to Red Cross headquarters a few days later to receive their new marching orders, Blanche and Dottie were pleased to be sent in the same direction. Some of the women were sent to Le Havre, some to Rouen, and some were sent to the clubmobile groups (wherever they happened to be) as replacements. Blanche and Dottie were teamed up with four other Red Cross girls, including Dorothy "Dottie" Fargo of Illinois, and Eloise Reilly of Connecticut, and given two English Bedford clubmobiles. The women were not being assigned to one of the established clubmobile groups as replacements; instead, they were going to operate as independent rangers, which was why they were stuck with the less reliable Bedfords versus GMC clubmobiles. For the near future, they would be operating out of a small geographical area around Rouen.

Even though Blanche's new clubmobile was much smaller than *The Maine,* Blanche was excited about being able to drive it and, for her and her crew, to be essentially on their own. As clubmobiler B.J. Olewiler admitted, "We would not have traded our right to drive for anything. It was a precious manifestation of usefulness and independence, and something more; to see a woman driving a truck was so unusual in those days, that it was always a source of conversation and amusement to the men which meant we were getting a good start on our job without any more effort than it took to drive up to the outfit."[220] The hardest part about driving the English Bedford in France was the fact that, being an English manufactured truck, the steering wheel was on the right side of the vehicle and traffic in

France was on the right side of the road. That made the new driver, grappling with traffic coming from the other direction, a bit nervous at first. However, Blanche adjusted to the Bedford clubmobile quickly and, therefore, did most of the driving over the next few months.

Chapter 10

"Hey, look, a real, live American girl!"

Rouen, France

In the dead of winter, February 27, 1945, Blanche, Dottie Barrett, Dottie Fargo, Eloise Reilly, and two other Red Cross girls climbed into their English Bedford clubmobiles and headed for Rouen. Given her proficiency behind the wheel, Blanche was chosen to drive one of the trucks. What they saw on their way was sobering and a bit disconcerting. Everything was "a complete wreck." The roads were covered with the remains of German tanks, trucks, and equipment, and everywhere they looked there was evidence of hard fighting. Thankfully, most of the dead bodies and dead animals had been removed.

Using maps provided by the Red Cross, the women drove to an area outside of Rouen where they were billeted in a three-story 17th-century French château. When they drove up to the château, they were impressed by its size and apparent grandeur, but their enthusiasm quickly faded once they unpacked their belongings and made their way inside. Almost all the furniture had been stolen or wrecked, there were small holes in the walls and floors (and in places that presented a danger if the women wandered about at night without sufficient light), and there was no indoor plumbing or functioning well. That meant they had no water and that they had to use a smelly indoor privy (a hole going down the entire building to the basement) for a makeshift bathroom.

The absence of water meant that the women had to take turns driving over 50 miles (round trip) every three or four evenings to obtain fresh water from an Army depot. It was hazardous duty as they were driving at night with only slits for headlights (required by black-out orders) and dodging other large vehicles on narrow French roads. If that was not bad enough, the women had been cautioned not to veer off the roads under any circumstances since they might run over unexploded mines! Blanche found it particularly difficult to move out of the way of tank carriers and large vehicles while also avoiding moving too far off the road. Plus, drawing upon the training the Red Cross had given her before she left England, Blanche, often with the help of an obliging GI, found herself changing a flat tire caused by shrapnel and other debris. "Flat tires are a regular thing [here] … Also broken springs are not uncommon as all the roads are badly torn up."[221] Since all the beds were gone at the château and only cots with straw mattresses were provided (which were really uncomfortable), the women used their sleeping bags over the mattresses as a makeshift bed. Blanche did not even do that since she was allergic to straw. It was a Spartan existence to be sure.

Shortly after arriving, the women drove into Rouen and visited the Red Cross Club there to meet up with their ARC field representative and receive their orders. Before the war, Rouen had been a charming medieval city laced with historic buildings, cobblestone streets, and timbered commercial building façades. However, in April 1944, the British bombed the city, leaving over 700 French civilians dead. Over a month later, on May 30, 1944, just before the D-Day invasion, Allied bombers hit the city again. That bombing took a heavy toll on many of Rouen's historic buildings, including the famous Notre-Dame Cathedral and the Rouen Palais de Justice.

Nearly 1,500 civilians died and more than 40,000 were left homeless when a large part of the left bank was destroyed. These attacks were designed to slow down the quick movement of German reinforcements and the movement of vital supplies to German ground forces defending Normandy.[222] Blanche was struck by the stark contrast between Rouen and Paris. Paris had certainly suffered some damage during the war, but nothing compared to Rouen. It really saddened her, and for the first time, Blanche had to come to grips with the reality of the devastating effect the Allies' bombing campaign had on civilian targets.

The Cigarette Camps

The ARC assigned Blanche and the other women the task of working the reception and replacement camps that were providing temporary housing and services to thousands of American servicemen. The camps also served as depots for the stream of supplies being forwarded to the front. There were nine of these camps, or replacement depots ("Repo Depots"), established by the U.S. Army and located in what the Army designated as the "Red Horse" staging area—roughly the surrounding area between Le Havre (on the eastern side of the Bay of the Seine, opposite Cherbourg) and Rouen. The camps were primarily named after popular American cigarettes for security reasons. They were Camp Chesterfield, Camp Herbert Tareyton, Camp Lucky Strike, Camp Old Gold, Camp Pall Mall, Camp Philip Morris, Camp Twenty Grand, as well as Camp Wings and Camp Home Run. By naming the camps in this fashion, without a reference to geographical location, the Army hoped that the enemy would not know exactly where they were located. Germans and their spies "eavesdropping or listening to radio traffic would hopefully think that cigarettes were being discussed …" instead of replacement camps.[223] It is estimated that nearly three million American troops either entered or left the European continent through these camps between 1944 and 1946.

Over the next month and a half, Blanche worked at six or seven of these camps, but the only ones she remembered by name were Camp Old Gold and Camp Twenty Grand. Camp Old Gold was located outside Ourville and at top capacity housed about 35,000 men. Camp Twenty Grand was located outside of Duclair and had a capacity of 20,000 men. She remembered the camps as primitive, treeless, stark places—nothing more than sprawling tent cities with few basic conveniences.

In March 1945, the men temporarily housed at these camps were destined to be the replacements for the killed and wounded in the American divisions bloodied during the Battle of the Bulge. None of the men were meant to be at the camps for long, so that is why the camps were as primitive as they were. The men were housed in thousands of six-man pyramidal canvas tents lined up row after row, with typical Army precision, as far as the eye could see. Since the camps had been constructed in a hurry, the tents had few modern conveniences and were exposed to the winter weather, which, in March 1945, consisted of constant cold, wind, and rain. As a consequence, trench foot and the flu ran rampant and some soldiers began referring to the camps as "pneumonia holes."[224] Although, originally, the tents in the camps were erected on bare dirt floors and their stoves scarcely provided sufficient heat during the cold winter months, by the time Blanche arrived in March 1945, most of the tents had been provided wood floors and doors which helped keep some of the wind and rain out. Recreational facilities had also been built by then and the camps were wired for electricity. However, the men did not have bathing facilities.

The opportunity to take a hot bath or shower was nonexistent for the men at the camps, and rare for the Red Cross girls. The only place available for the women to shower was the Red Cross Club in Rouen or private facilities. Instead, they would try to take a sponge bath each night. That made staying clean difficult, as it rained constantly, and the resulting mud was everywhere. The mud also made driving the clubmobile on the unpaved French roads difficult, and of course, the mud got into everything—their hair, on their clothes and boots, inside the truck, and in the living areas of their château. It was particularly rough for Blanche and Dottie, considering Dottie's privileged background and Blanche's health concerns. It meant that by the end of the day they were dirty and exhausted. Nevertheless, Blanche was enjoying every minute of it, as she explained to her parents in another letter home:

> [I] am really roughing it now, but [I] am in a place that is definitely out of danger so please don't worry. This is really proving to be fun. Our equipment consists of a bedroll and barracks bag. The rest of our things we had to leave behind. This bedroll is a pretty important piece of equipment as it is all we have to sleep on, or I should say in. We have taken over an old French Chateau that the Germans had requisitioned. There is next to nothing in it and it shows evidence of the fact that the Americans literally forced the Germans to evacuate it. We do not have running water but carry our water in our helmets or buckets. These are also used to wash in. Baths are unheard of. … We do manage to get our clothes washed, but a pressed blouse is out of the question. Here we use Army trucks for clubmobiles and drive them ourselves. We have one we call "Huckleberry Duck." It really gets around.[225]

What Blanche was enjoying was the opportunity to interact with and help with the morale of thousands of young (most of them were only 18 or 19 years old), homesick boys facing an unknown future. Unlike in England, where the clubmobilers often made the coffee and doughnuts in their vehicles, in France, because of the smaller size of the trucks and the substantial increase in the number of men served each day, the Red Cross had set up a "Doughnut Factory" outside of Rouen. Clubmobiler Jane Stottler of Drexel Hill, Pennsylvania, was in charge and oversaw 20 French men and women hired by the ARC to make hundreds of urns of coffee and 14,000 doughnuts daily during two long shifts, one during the day and one during the evening. Each clubmobile crew would drive to the factory each morning, and before heading to their assigned camp, they would load up with urns of coffee and boxes of doughnuts.[226]

When the clubmobilers first drove into a cigarette camp and set up their operation at the camp crossroad, the GIs would immediately start lining up with their canteen cups in hand. They kept coming for hours, and the women just kept working, smiling, and chatting with the men the entire time. The women tried never to allow the men to see how tired and worn out they were. They knew that each man was someone's son, brother, father, husband, or sweetheart, and that they were there to try to brighten his day. For the women it was a sacred trust that they took seriously, and the men obviously appreciated it. The men would often remark that they could not believe that the women were there voluntarily, and that they willingly endured such horrible conditions just to serve GIs hot coffee and a few doughnuts.

In the evenings, officers would regularly come to call at the château and drink, play cards, and talk with the women until late. One evening, Dottie and Blanche, exhausted as usual, went to bed right after dinner (they shared a room) to get enough sleep to be able to function the next day. The other clubmobile girls, however, with more energy and endurance, stayed up and entertained some Army officers in their living room. After the women and officers had all been drinking for several hours, the men got, what one of the women referred to as, "a little too friendly." So, the women began gently trying to get the officers to leave, but with no success.

Listening from their bedroom, Blanche and Dottie found the whole thing humorous, and they were impressed by the ingenuity shown by the other clubmobilers. The women convinced the officers to stand up and in unison sing a popular little ditty of the day, the "Hokey Pokey," and, importantly, to act out the words. "You put your right foot in, you take your right foot out, you put your right foot in and shake it all about." But as the men performed the required steps, the women slowly maneuvered them toward the door and right into the hall. By this stage in the war, the women had become experts at fending off the constant advances they had to deal with daily and were quick enough on their feet to diplomatically remove themselves from difficult social situations without offending.

On the other hand, given her religious and sheltered parochial background, Blanche was often clueless when it came to subtle sexual innuendo, which sometimes proved annoying to her fellow, and more worldly, clubmobilers. A perfect example was when a GI asked Blanche one day if he could paint a name on one of the other clubmobiles. The ARC had not taken the time to name the Bedfords the women were using. Thinking that a name for the clubmobile was appropriate, Blanche agreed. When the GI asked her what name she wanted to use to christen her clubmobile with, she thought about it for a second, and thinking of the rivers of mud they all had to deal with and the difficulty the women had staying clean, she said, "The Little Horrors." The GI, probably with a smirk, duly painted the new name on the clubmobile. From then on, the women became the butt of GI jokes. The other women were not amused and initially were upset with Blanche, until they realized, to their utter amazement, that Blanche sincerely had no idea what a "whore" was! It was not the first or the last time Blanche's naivete got her in trouble with her fellow clubmobilers.

While stationed outside of Rouen, Blanche and the other women also had the unique and memorable opportunity to hear Gen. George S. Patton Jr., the commander of the Third U.S. Army, address his troops and give them a little pep talk before they headed off for the front lines. Although Blanche was fully aware of the General's bombastic and salty reputation, and his often-repeated adage that he didn't want his men to die for their country, but he wanted them to make damn sure that the other poor bastard died for his country, she was unaware of how his speeches were laced with "colorful" words rarely spoken in polite society or in front of women. In addition, the General's gestures, and vivid description of how he wanted each man to use his bayonet to "gut" every "German bas-tard" he came across was extremely shocking to Blanche. The General either did not know that women were present or did not care, and it was a "performance" (and that was exactly what it was) that Blanche never forgot.

"Women Drivers!"

On one occasion, Blanche, Dottie Barrett, and another clubmobile girl were directed to serve coffee and doughnuts to the 13th Armored Division, known as the "Black Cats." At the time, the 13th was performing occupation duty, but come April, they would be sent to Hamburg and attached to the Third Army.[227] After watching Blanche drive her Bedford clubmobile up to their bivouac, the men of the 13th decided that it would be great fun to teach Blanche how to drive one of their Sherman tanks. As usual, she was game. So, excitedly, Blanche climbed into one of the tanks and sat in the driver's seat. After one of the GIs gave her quick instructions, Dottie Barrett got in and stood behind Blanche in the turret and laid her feet on top of Blanche's shoulders. Since Dottie could see where they were headed and Blanche could not, Dottie was instructed to give Blanche directions by using her feet. Gently pushing down on Blanche's right shoulder meant Blanche should turn the tank to the right, and pushing on her left shoulder meant the opposite direction. With those simple instructions, the women were off.

Even though the tank was out in an open field with few obstructions to contend with, the GIs watching the demonstration could not resist running for cover in all directions and yelling at their fellow tankers, "Watch out, women drivers!" When Blanche and Dottie were finished driving their Sherman, and thankfully without mishap, the men made them their official tank "sweethearts" and they all posed for pictures. The men really enjoyed the visit.[228] The enthusiastic reception the women received from the tankers was hardly unusual. As historian James H. Madison explained in his excellent book about clubmobiler Elizabeth "Liz" Richardson,

For many American GIs, the mere sight of the Red Cross girls was so unusual and special that it immediately lifted their spirits. They would yell out, "Hey, look, a real, live American girl!" It didn't matter where in the States the girls were from, the main thing was that they were female, they spoke English and they were American. It wasn't just their small numbers that made the Red Cross girls special. They knew the GIs' slang, had the right "American look," knew the current music and could dance to all of it, knew how to receive and return a wisecrack or tell a joke, and they knew how to talk about baseball, Glenn Miller and apple pie ...[229]

A Little Spy Ring

In late March 1945, Blanche, Dottie Barrett, and some of the other Red Cross girls in their group were given a weekend pass, and they decided to drive to Paris. The other women remained in Paris and went shopping and did additional sightseeing, but Blanche decided to travel to the Palace at Versailles, the former royal residence of the kings of France and located about 12 miles west of Paris. She spent an entire afternoon touring the palace and its grounds. The palace conservators had hired young women who could speak English fluently to serve as guides for any American or English servicemen who wished to tour the palace, and one of these young women, by the name of Rose Marie, offered to give Blanche a tour and provide her some of the history of the structure and its furnishings. The tour did not disappoint. Blanche found the Hall of Mirrors breathtaking and the gardens around the palace stunning.

Throughout the afternoon Rose Marie was attentive and friendly. So much so that when the tour ended, she invited Blanche to have dinner with her and her parents at their apartment in Paris. Thinking that the opportunity to get to know a few locals and have a real home-cooked French meal sounded too good to pass up, Blanche accepted.

That evening, Blanche found Rose Marie's apartment. It was not just a one-room apartment like Blanche had envisioned; it was an upstairs suite in a building located on one of Paris's many long and lovely tree-lined boulevards. Upon Blanche's arrival, Rose Marie greeted her warmly, introduced Blanche to her parents, fetched refreshments, and proceeded to tell Blanche the history of the area, of the building, and of the apartment. Rose Marie claimed that the apartment was either owned by, or used to be owned by, the famous French singer and movie star Maurice Chevalier. Chevalier was best known for his trademark boater hat and tuxedo, and his popular songs of the 1930s. He also made a splash in Hollywood with hit movies such as *The Big Pond, The Love Parade, Love Me Tonight,* and *The Merry Widow.* After the war he had perhaps his biggest success with the movie *Gigi,* and the signature song that went with it, "Thank Heaven for Little Girls."[230]

Not surprisingly, the apartment was fabulous, and Blanche was duly impressed. The dinner was fabulous too. It consisted of an outstanding five-course French meal with expensive wine—all of which made Blanche more than a little suspicious. She and the other Red Cross girls had been told that the French civilians had just been through four years of occupation and rationing, and if invited to one of their homes, the women should always offer to bring food along. When Blanche had done so, Rose Marie appeared insulted and promptly declined Blanche's kind offer. Surprisingly, obtaining food was not a problem for Rose Marie and her parents. Blanche became even more suspicious when they kept pushing more wine on her and asking her about her role with the Red Cross, about the cigarette camps and the American Army in and around Rouen, the number of troops stationed at each camp, and where they were headed, etc. The whole evening seemed strange and a bit contrived.

During their initial Red Cross training and on numerous occasions thereafter, Blanche and the other clubmobilers had been warned against openly talking about military matters with nonmilitary personnel and about the potential harm such information could have on the Allies' war effort. "Loose lips sink ships" was more than a catchy phrase; it was a succinct warning that enemy spies could be anywhere and that even little pieces of information from multiple sources could allow the enemy to piece together vital military information that could cost American lives. Plus, the Red Cross knew that clubmobile personnel were logical targets for spies, as the women spent all their time conversing with GIs and, as a result, often knew more about what was going on in multiple sectors than the frontline troops did. Given her suspicions, Blanche drank little that evening, which was not unusual for her anyway, and kept her responses general. She also claimed, sometimes truthfully, not to know the answers to her hosts' questions.

When the evening was over, Blanche thanked Rose Marie and her parents for a wonderful evening and departed. However, because of the unusual questions asked by her hosts, and the rumors then circulating about Maurice Chevalier—that he was a collaborator—before leaving Paris, Blanche reported the evening's discussion to Red Cross headquarters. Red Cross officials no doubt contacted the U.S. Army's Counter Intelligence Corps, because Blanche was later told that the matter had been investigated and that Rose Marie and her parents were, indeed, German spies. But Blanche never learned what became of them.

The Parisian Black Market

When Blanche met up with the other clubmobilers, they were disappointed with their weekend shopping. The stores simply did not have everything the women were hoping to obtain, especially cosmetics. Although it was wartime and the women spent most of their time in their dirty "battle dress" uniforms, that did not mean that they did not want to continue to look as good as they could. That included using lipstick to remind themselves that they were still women and that they could still look attractive. During the war, even after the liberation of Paris, basic cosmetics were hard to find. Almost all the ingredients used to make cosmetics were being used primarily for war materials.

During the German occupation, Parisians had been subjected to the imposition of restrictive rationing. Ultimately, bread, sugar, milk, butter, eggs, cheese, oil, meat, coffee, chocolate, produce, shoes, textiles, and tobacco, as well as coal (a winter necessity), were rationed. French civilians were issued rationing cards based on a German classification system that used the civilians' ages, occupations, and perceived nutritional needs to determine what each civilian received. What food was allowed by the Germans, however, was of low nutritional value. It was an intentional policy designed to strip France of its assets for the benefit of the German war effort and German civilians.[231]

Naturally, Parisians found rationing extremely difficult to abide by and soon an underground Black Market developed that provided Parisians almost everything they needed—but, of course, for a hefty price. This was particularly important during the harsh winter months when coal was vital for warming homes. After Paris's liberation by the Allies in August 1944, the Black Market system became even more widespread than before. As the Germans withdrew from Paris, they did a thorough job of looting Paris boutiques of "women's lingerie, lipstick, and perfume."[232] But even with an expanded Black Market system, by the spring of 1945 most Parisians were living on the edge.

The Red Cross girls discovered how it all worked. Through an accommodating shopkeeper, they were informed that if they came back to his shop after closing time, he would meet them in the back alley and sell them the cosmetics they were asking for. The shopkeeper was part of hundreds of neighborhood Black Market trading groups who refused to sell rationed goods for the prices officially set by the government, and instead sold them on the sly for inflated prices.[233]

Figuring that there was safety in numbers, the women returned to the shop after the sun went down and successfully purchased what they wanted. Blanche found it exciting. In fact, her entire weekend in Paris had been incredibly exciting and enlightening. As one wag observed after a similar visit to Paris, "I now know the difference between Britain, France, and the United States. The British obey all laws, the French obey no laws, [and] the Americans obey only the good laws."[234]

A few weeks later, Blanche wrote to her parents and mentioned that she had been to Paris for a few days' rest. She admitted that she had had a wonderful time and conveyed her impression of Paris and how it compared to the United States and England.

> Paris is certainly beautiful and comes the nearest to being like home of anything I have seen since I left the States. ... Everything in England reminds one of the gay nineties [but] without the gaiety. Both England and France are still run on the remains of the old Feudal system. ... There is little middle class. London of course, is like any large city except it is about 100 years behind America. Paris is up to date and beautiful.

Finally, probably stemming from her recent experience with the Paris Black Market, she astutely observed that "If one had the money, one could buy anything [there] ..."[235]

Plates II

Blanche hard at work making donuts inside *The Maine* at an airfield near Kettering, England, fall 1944. Notice the coffee cups below carefully stored for travel.

Blanche serving coffee and donuts through the side panels of *The Maine,* at an airfield outside of Kettering, England, September 1944. Note the two large coffee urns on either side of her.

(L to R) Captain Lois Stone, Blanche, and Zephyr Boyajian with Dutch Schultz, Ingvald Iverson, and Marion Niemantsat at the Molesworth Airfield, near Kettering, England, October 1944.

(L to R) Clubmobile driver Ted Scott, Libby Harnies, Stephanie Jackson, and Sarah Cofer Lenzen with *The Maine*, November 1944, at the Molesworth Airfield, near Kettering, England.

*Open House will be held on the American
Red Cross Clubmobile, Maine,
from 15.00 hrs. to 17.00 hrs.*

on *Monday, Tuesday, Wednesday, Thursday,
January 22 to 25*

at *all the fields*

*Stephanie, Libby and Blanche cordially invite you
to attend*

An "Open House" invitation, January 1945, from the crew of *The Maine* to the Air Corps personnel at the airfields outside of Kettering, England. *(Author's family photo.)*

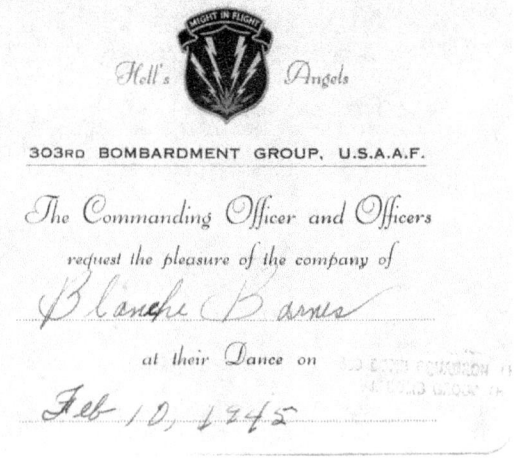

Hell's Angels

303RD BOMBARDMENT GROUP, U.S.A.A.F.

*The Commanding Officer and Officers
request the pleasure of the company of*

Blanche Barnes

at their Dance on

Feb 10, 1945

Blanche's invitation to a dance at the Molesworth Airfield from the officers of the 303rd Bombardment Group, February 1945. By the end of the month Blanche was reassigned to duty in France.

The "Boat Train" to Paris. This is the way Blanche made her way across the English Channel to France in February 1945. *(Imperial War Museum, #D 24240.)*

Camp Twenty Grand, one of the Cigarette Camps outside Rouen, France, March 1945. The men have already been served their coffee and doughnuts and are getting ready to dance with Blanche.

Blanche with the men of the 13th Armored Division, "The Black Cats," outside of Rouen, France, March 1945. This is a good example of how the clubmobile girls were always surrounded by scores of GIs wherever they went.

"Watch out, women drivers!" Blanche with GIs from the 13th Armored Division and the Sherman tank she had just successfully driven, France, March 1945.

Blanche and Eloise Reilly with GIs somewhere in France, March 1945. When coffee cups were unavailable, the men used whatever they had available.

The Ludendorff Bridge after its collapse and the two U.S. Army pontoon bridges at Remagen, Germany, March 1945. Blanche blocked all traffic on one of these pontoon bridges when her clubmobile's brakes locked up. *(Operation 2021/Alamy.)*

Dottie Fargo and Blanche somewhere in Germany, April 1945. Initially, they worked well together, but their relationship became strained by war's end.

Blanche and Dottie Fargo dancing with GIs behind their clubmobile *Yankee Doodle*, somewhere in Germany, spring 1945. Dancing with the GIs was a regular occurrence wherever the clubmobile girls went.

Blanche in front of Lt. George Gangwere's jeep, September 1945, Regensburg, Germany. For the first time in three years Blanche was not wearing her wedding ring.

Blanche preparing to fly to Paris from Regensburg, Germany, September 1945. This picture was taken by Lt. George Gangwere, and Blanche was already certain that she had found the right man.

A view of Regensburg, Germany, from the spot along the Danube
River where Lt. George Gangwere and Blanche had their picnics. St.
Peter's Cathedral is in the distance on the far right. George bought
the painting from a local German artist, and it hung in George and
Blanche's living room for their entire marriage.

Oct. 2, 1945

Dear George,

Since you gave me stationery, envelopes and all, guess I'll have to write to you before I write to anyone else. I had 24 letters waiting for me when I returned yesterday. Among them was your letter with the pictures. Thank you again for them.

Believe it or not but I do miss you. Didn't even have a movie to go to tonight. Decided to get into bed and write letters. My room is nice and warm, heated by steam. I filled the bath-tub with hot water and swished it around a lot. It does a beautiful job of heating.

My trip to Paris wasn't too pleasant, but I did make it all in one day. Johnson, the driver of the jeep, was certainly nice. He drove me

The first page of one of Blanche's letters to Lt. George Gangwere, dated October 2, 1945. George had given her the stationery to make sure that she would write to him after she left Regensburg.

Blanche Barnes and Capt. George H. Gangwere outside her parents' house in southwest Kansas City, Missouri, the day after they became engaged, January 22, 1946. They were happily married for nearly 57 years.

Chapter 11

"It seems almost impossible that I have actually lived through so many experiences in the last three years ..."

On to the Third Reich

Near the end of March 1945, as the Allied armies on the western front continued moving east into the heart of Germany and the winter weather began to lift, Blanche was given new orders. To Blanche's sincere regret her good friend Dottie Barrett was assigned somewhere else. Unfortunately, they never saw each other again.

Before leaving the Rouen area, Blanche took the opportunity to visit Le Havre. It is a major seaport in Normandy and located on the right bank of the Seine estuary, about 53 miles west of Rouen.[236] In September 1944, almost three quarters of Le Havre was destroyed during a week of British bombing raids that preceded the capture of the city. As a result, between 1,500 and 2,000 French civilians were killed, and it took decades for the city to rebuild and recover from the shock.[237] Blanche was dumbfounded and saddened by what she saw. "[It] must have been beautiful at one time, but one certainly wouldn't be able to tell it now," she admitted to her parents in a letter home.[238]

After her trip to Le Havre, Blanche was grouped together with another clubmobiler, Dorothy "Dottie" Fargo, of Glencoe, Illinois, whom Blanche was already acquainted with through their joint work in and around the Cigarette Camps. However, it was an odd pairing as the two women could not have been more different. Although both women were Midwesterners and similar in age, Blanche was petite, physically challenged, shy, silently religious, and an introvert. Dottie, on the other hand, was strong, almost masculine-like, loud, assertive, and an extrovert. Whereas Blanche had little interest in dating, chasing men was Dottie's primary social pursuit. Other Red Cross girls derisively referred to Dottie, behind her back of course, as the "Fargo Express," but Blanche did her best to get along with her and initially Dottie reciprocated. Although mismatched, in the beginning, the women successfully worked together as a team.

The ARC gave Blanche and Dottie another English Bedford to use as their clubmobile, and this one the women christened *The Yankee Doodle*. Then they were ordered to proceed to Bad Neuenahr, Germany, and serve as an independent ranger crew. Bad Neuenahr was and still is a small town located to the north of the Rhineland-Palatinate and just south of Bonn, which had been captured by the U.S. Army at the beginning of the month. Bad Neuenahr lies in the Ahr Valley on the left bank of the Rhine River, over 750 kilometers (466 miles) from Rouen. While stationed there, the women would work with different units of the Fifteenth U.S. Army Group. Although the European war was in its final six weeks, traveling through conquered territory was still a dangerous proposition, so the women had to be careful to follow the exact route outlined by the Red Cross and sanctioned by the U.S. Army, to remain out of harm's way.

The route Blanche and Dottie took was a tortuous one, often over rough and damaged roads, and through or around bombed-out crossroads. However, the first part of their trip was well-traveled and easy. They took the famous "Red Ball Express" to Versailles, and from there east to Sommesous, France. The Red Ball Express was the famed truck convoy road system that had been used by the Allies in 1944 to supply its advancing armies in central France until the port facilities at Antwerp, Belgium, were captured and made available for resupply.[239] At Sommesous, the women were told to head north into Luxembourg (being careful to remain south of Belgium), and then drive on toward the northeast into recently captured portions of northwest Germany (while remaining on the west side of the Rhine River). It took the women three to four days to complete the trip without major mishap. It took that long partially because of the roads, and partially because they were constantly stopping to hand out coffee and doughnuts to stray GIs whom they met along the way.

Blanche and Dottie Fargo were stationed at Bad Neuenahr for six weeks, and they were billeted in a confiscated building in town. At night Blanche could look out her window and see and hear the explosions and flashes of artillery fire off in the distance to the north in the Ruhr Pocket. She was finally within miles of the front lines and that realization was both exhilarating and a bit scary. Surprisingly, her first impression of Germany was generally favorable. Germany was obviously wealthier than France, Belgium, or Luxembourg, and industrially it was far superior to its neighbors. The German people were hardworking, better educated, and more progressive than their neighbors, and they obviously took real pride in their homes, roads, and businesses. Everything was laid out in a systematic and organized manner compared to France. But, like its neighbors, German cities, towns, railroads, roads, and bridges had suffered heavily from Allied bombing. Nevertheless, most German civilians, at least in the areas Blanche visited, did not appear to be openly hostile toward Allied soldiers or Allied support personnel like the Red Cross. That was probably because the German people knew the end of the war was near and they uniformly preferred to be occupied by the Americans or British versus the Russians, and there was a noticeable lack of avid Nazis present.[240] Most of the fanatical Nazis around Bad Neuenahr were either dead, in hiding, or had fled to another area.

During every workday, while stationed at Bad Neuenahr, Blanche and Dottie climbed into their clubmobile; cleaned the back of the truck thoroughly; made sure they had sufficient supplies of kerosene, flour, coffee, etc. for the day's work; and then ventured forth in a never-ending quest to find and serve the different military units in the area. When they first arrived at a camp where the men were bivouacked, the women would try to find an electrical source or a portable generator to hook up the clubmobile. Then they proceeded to make thousands of doughnuts on their built-in doughnut-making machine, heat gallons of water, and brew numerous 50-cup urns of coffee—which was replenished throughout the day.

Since inside bathroom facilities were nonexistent in the field, after their arrival, accommodating GIs would dig a mini latrine with a tarp around it for the women's use. But, when serving units stationed in a town, the Army would allow the Red Cross girls to use the unit's latrine. Sometimes that meant an outdoor latrine with canvas walls but often without a roof. The local commander would station MPs nearby to ensure that the Red Cross girls had privacy. The canvas walls were helpful for that purpose but were of little help with the surrounding buildings. Once, while Blanche was using one of these outside latrines in the center of a town, GIs happened to be on the roof of a nearby bombed-out building, and they could easily see right down into the latrine. By the time Blanche discovered her mistake, it was too late; or, as Blanche delicately put it, she "was already at the point of no return."

Once these preliminaries were accomplished, the women would begin serving an endless line of hungry GIs. Unlike in England, the number of GIs involved was often overwhelming. Even if they were only serving a portion of a U.S. Army division, such as a brigade, they could still end up serving two to three thousand men in one afternoon.[241] It was truly exhausting work, and yet highly rewarding. Blanche knew that they were making a substantial contribution to the overall morale of the men. The presence of American women, coupled with the distinctive aroma of American coffee and doughnuts, always managed to attract large crowds of GIs. Although often battle weary and exhausted, "[T]he spirit and morale of the soldiers were excellent. ... So many of the soldiers looked like boys, but they were indeed men ... for they had endured so much hardship." Being that close to the front, the clubmobile girls "... also saw much of the horrors of war, for every day, as [they] went to and from camp, [they] passed piles of [dead German soldiers]. ... And the stench of death was sickening."[242]

The clubmobile crews assigned to such forward areas in the spring of 1945, and especially the clubmobile rangers like Blanche and Dottie, were basically "on their own." The Red Cross knew where they were stationed, of course, what they were supposed to be doing, and which Army units they were supposed to be attached to, but that was about it. Day-to-day contact and direction were rare. Plus, traveling in recently captured German territory was dangerous. As a U.S. Army study acknowledged after the war,

> Due to their mission, clubmobiles necessarily worked with forward troops, and the security of these units was one of continuing concern to commanders. When en route to and from serving troops, it was the practice to provide guards and guides.[243]

Another clubmobiler, who had also been attached to the Fifteenth Army Group in 1944, described her experience in a forward area this way:

> [W]e operated as best we could without interference or concern from anyone ... [But] it was a thrill to be welcomed with whoops of delight ... [a]nd even more of a thrill to be welcomed by the ones we went out to serve on their well-deserved pullback periods, especially if it were their first time to see us. ... [S]o many of those we served are no longer with us because we concentrated on the infantry as we should have, because they are the ones who really did the fighting.[244]

Being that far north in Germany in the month of April meant that sunset came early each day. So, Blanche and Dottie often found themselves driving back to Bad Neuenahr in the dark and on narrow, damaged roads that they were not familiar with. Sometimes they had to travel miles to do so, and always without headlights (which they were prohibited from using). It could be a nerve-racking experience, and getting a flat tire while driving over the debris-strewn roads was always a possibility. Consequently, the women often chose to sleep in their truck and spend the night with the unit they had been serving earlier in the day, and then move on to another unit the next morning. While on the road, the women would often run into all sorts of military vehicles filled with GIs.

> They [would slow] down at the sight of the [clubmobile]. Amazed GIs, dusty, tired, nerves high-geared from battle strain, clambered down to listen to the latest swing records and gulp down a hasty cup of coffee. An incongruous scene, laughter, song, and merriment, dimming the sharp crack of ack-ack and mellowing the grim boom of the 155-mm guns thundering in the distance![245]

There was little doubt concerning the importance the Army placed on having clubmobile service for its frontline troops or how much the men loved it.

A Trigger-Happy Sentry

One evening when Blanche and Dottie decided to spend the night with a field unit to avoid the long trek home, Blanche volunteered to take coffee and doughnuts to the sentries guarding the camp's perimeter. Before going on duty, the sentries had been notified of her intentions, but that had been hours before. When Blanche finally set out on her care mission it was already dark, and the moon offered little assistance in illuminating her way since the path was surrounded by trees and dense underbrush.

For days the sentries had been trading potshots with German snipers, and everyone was concerned about German infiltrators. Consequently, the sentries were understandably nervous and on edge. In order to avoid "friendly fire" casualties, if someone approached their perimeter, the sentries were trained to call out "Halt!" and immediately demand the daily password such as "applesauce" or "dipsy doodle."[246] If the password was not promptly given, the sentries were ordered to open fire. Naturally, Blanche had been given the day's password and was prepared to use it. But as she approached the sentries' supposed location, no one yelled out a demand to halt. Instead, Blanche suddenly felt the rush of cold air pass her face, as if an insect had just flown by, which was quickly followed by the sharp and distinctive report of an American Garand M1 rifle. She knew instantly what had happened. A nervous sentry had shot at her without yelling "Halt!" or demanding the required password.

Blanche's knees almost buckled, and she instinctively yelled out the required password, "horse feathers," and, as calmly as she could muster, begged the hidden sentry to "please don't shoot again!" Even after the embarrassed trigger-happy soldier apologized for his failure to follow protocol and instructed Blanche to come forward without fear, Blanche found it difficult at first. A cold shiver ran down her body and her hands began to shake. It had been a narrow escape; and although the bullet missed its mark, it had been a nerve-racking experience.

Later that evening, back in the safety of her tent, Blanche quietly pondered how a sheltered midwestern girl who, prior to joining the Red Cross, had never been east of Chicago, now found herself halfway around the world in the middle of a great world war, and how she had almost lost her life for a doughnut.

A General's Nightmare

On one of Blanche's daily forays to a forward Army field unit, this time east of Bad Neuenahr, she had to cross one of several

temporary Army pontoon bridges built over the Rhine River at
Remagen—upstream from where the infamous Ludendorff Bridge
had stood just weeks before. The bridge had been captured intact
by American forces on March 7, 1945, and had been successfully
held against spirited German counterattacks and air strikes. Cap-
turing the bridge allowed the flow of troops and supplies across the
river for 10 vital days. Although the bridge ultimately collapsed
from the damage it had sustained, killing 28 American GIs and
injuring nearly 100 more in the process, by the time it did so five
American divisions had crossed to the east side of the Rhine.[247] The
establishment of a bridgehead across the river was a major psychological and tactical success for the Allies, and probably advanced by
weeks the Allies' planned crossing of the river and subsequent move
east toward the German heartland.

Even before the bridge collapsed, several pontoon bridges had
been built downstream under constant enemy fire, by the U.S. Army
Engineering Corps, to assist with the heavy flow of troops and supplies moving to the east. The first one, started on March 10, was
built by American engineers using inflatable rafts, and reinforced
with pneumatic floats topped with a steel platform and hooked
together side-by-side. Over the top of the steel platform were laid
two metal tracks with lips on either side and a space between both
tracks. Then a second pontoon bridge was constructed, allowing
traffic to flow continuously in both directions. When completed,
the first pontoon bridge was 969 feet long and weighed over 25 tons.
It was "the longest floating bridge ever constructed by the Corps of
Engineers under fire."[248] Driving across a pontoon bridge in a clubmobile was always an "exasperating" experience. The driver had to
carefully line up the clubmobile's six large tires and, with the help
of a crewmate looking out the window on the other side, keep the
tires online with the narrow lane across the bridge. This was no
mean task, especially if the clubmobile was towing a generator.[249]

On this day Blanche was on her own. Dottie was ill and had
remained behind. As Blanche took *The Yankee Doodle* across the
single-lane pontoon bridge toward the east bank, carefully

ensuring that the truck's wheels remained within the metal tracks, her brakes suddenly locked up! She could not believe it. Locked brakes occurred from time to time because they got overheated or parts were damaged or broken, but this time it happened in the middle of a pontoon bridge across one of Germany's largest rivers. It was horrible timing, and nothing Blanche or anyone else did could get the truck's brakes unlocked. Soon numerous agitated officers and MPs rushed to the scene to find out what was holding up the vital flow of troops and supplies across the river and on to the front lines, but faced with the locked-up clubmobile, none of them had a solution. The only thing they could do was send for a mechanic who knew how to deal with the brakes of a British-made vehicle and wait.

Wishing to lighten the mood and with nothing else to do, Blanche decided to get the clubmobile's Victrola out of its compartment in the back and place it on the clubmobile's front fender. Once she hooked it up to the clubmobile's loudspeakers she put on a record, or as she put it "a real hot one," and proceeded to jitterbug with the GIs milling about. The GIs thought it was great; but it had to be a general's nightmare. If General George Patton had been present, he probably would have ordered his men to push the club-mobile into the river so that the troops and supply trucks could get on with the war. Luckily for Blanche and *The Yankee Doodle*, no one thought of it or felt that they had the authority to order such a drastic solution. But it was an incongruous sight—scores of trucks stacked up behind a single Red Cross clubmobile stopped dead in its tracks, and a handful of GIs and a lone "Donut Doll" jitterbugging in the middle of a pontoon bridge in the middle of a war zone.

Piloting a B-17 Flying Fortress

One clubmobiler rightly observed that the Red Cross was, to her mind, "the most privileged group on the continent."[250] Unlike the military, the Red Cross had a liberal leave policy and most of the women took full advantage of it. Consequently, Blanche saw much of war-torn Europe as the limits of transportation and time would allow. In late April, as the war in the ETO began to approach its inevitable end, Blanche requested and received a five-day furlough. She decided to return to England to visit her friends in and around Kettering. To get there she took a train to Dieppe, another "boat train" across the English Channel to Paddington, and two trains (one to London and another to Kettering).

Upon Blanche's arrival in Kettering, her first stop was a brief visit with her former landlady, Mrs. Mackay. During their conversation, Mrs. Mackay mentioned the passing of U.S. President Franklin D. Roosevelt several weeks before and how Vice President Harry S. Truman had become the new American president. Knowing that Blanche was from Missouri, Mrs. Mackay asked Blanche whether she was proud that someone from her home state was now in the Oval Office. Somewhat embarrassed, Blanche admitted that she was anything but happy with Truman's elevation, and that, in fact, she was sincerely concerned.

Up until 1939, Kansas City government had been controlled by a corrupt political machine run by Boss Tom Pendergast, and Pendergast had been responsible for helping elect Harry Truman to successive public offices including the U.S. Senate. Furthermore, Truman had refused to publicly distance himself from Pendergast after the Boss's conviction and imprisonment for income tax evasion. Truman, as the newly elected Vice President, had even attended Pendergast's funeral in early 1945, the only public official to do so. Thus, Blanche and her parents were convinced that Truman was a crook. It was only years later that Blanche began to change her opinion of President Truman.[251]

Of course, Blanche spent most of her furlough visiting the "Hell's Angels" at Molesworth, including her old flame, Major Mel Schulstad, and Mel and the other men went out of their way to entertain her. When it was time for her to return to Germany, Major Schulstad graciously arranged a car to pick her up at her billet in Kettering and drive her back to Molesworth where a B-17 was waiting for

her. Its crew flew Blanche to another airfield where she was transferred to a second B-17 that was scheduled to fly to Paris.[252] Blanche
was thrilled. She thought the B-17 was the most beautiful plane she
had ever seen. As one Eighth Air Force pilot described it:

> One look at the B-17, silver and elegant and indomitable-look-
> ing on the tarmac, bristling with armature, that massive reas-
> suring tail fin crowning its splendid architecture, and the
> world started all over again. … [T]hat airplane was that stu-
> pendous to behold …[253]

Although Blanche had been inside a B-17 on numerous occasions
while stationed in Kettering, she had never flown in one. Once airborne, and since the plane was flying low enough that oxygen masks
were not necessary, Blanche systematically wandered about taking
some movie film and taking in all aspects of the plane's operations.
The crew let her talk on the radio, sit in the bombardier's seat in the
Plexiglas nose section, walk back to the waist gunners' stations and
bomb bay, and do whatever she wanted to do. It was an exhilarating
experience, and the pilot and crew could not have been more
accommodating. Blanche basically "had a blast."

As the plane cleared the English shoreline and headed out over
the English Channel, the pilot, knowing that Blanche was also a
pilot, offered to let her fly the plane! Blanche jumped at the opportunity. She sat down in the copilot's seat, took over the controls, and
flew the plane across the channel. The cockpit offered an amazing
view, and the plane's controls were surprisingly light and easy to
handle. Blanche had no difficulty maintaining her altitude and
bearing. Some of the members of the crew, especially the copilot,
were not amused at this turn of events. The copilot did not think a
female should fly a plane, especially a large bomber like the B-17.
Apparently, he wasn't familiar with the WASPs whose members were
trained pilots who tested and ferried military aircraft, as well as
helped train other pilots for the military, thus freeing them up for
combat service.[254] Blanche didn't care. She had been told all her life

that she could not do certain things because of her sex, her small stature, or because of her health concerns, and she had become adept at ignoring such opinions and diving ahead regardless. Flying that plane was an experience she never forgot, and 68 years later she took another ride on a B-17, the Aluminum Avenger, when it visited the Kansas City area. The crew placed Blanche right behind the pilots so that she could relive that initial flight.

Attacked in Paris

Upon landing in Paris, a car was waiting for Blanche to take her to her hotel in the city, again courtesy of Major Schulstad. He had really gone all out for her, and she appreciated it, but she still had no interest in renewing their romantic relationship. She had completely moved on from that brief chapter in her life.

When Blanche arrived at her hotel, she had another thrill. A married member of her church back in Kansas City, whom Blanche had also known in high school and was currently serving as a chaplain in the U.S. Army, had arrived in Paris and checked in to the same hotel just a few minutes before she did. His name was George Waldon, and after they both got settled in, they spent the rest of the day and evening together "talking like a couple of magpies" about their families, mutual acquaintances, home, etc.

Later, George insisted on taking Blanche out to dinner, and while they were leaving their hotel for a local restaurant, his French secretary suddenly appeared out of nowhere and physically attacked Blanche! The secretary had talked Waldon into bringing her along on his trip to Paris so she could visit her aunt. But, as he discovered later, to his regret, she did not have an aunt in Paris. She just wanted to go to Paris with him in the hope of striking up a romantic relationship with the good pastor. Since arriving in Paris, she had been following him everywhere he went. When she saw him leaving the hotel with another woman, she flew into a jealous rage and attacked Blanche—pulling at Blanche's hair, tearing at her clothes, and trying to scratch her face before Waldon and another GI could pull her off a shocked and badly shaken Blanche. After his secretary finally departed the scene, Waldon, who was deeply embarrassed, explained the situation and profusely apologized for his secretary's ill behavior. Blanche quickly recovered and took it in stride, and they thoroughly enjoyed their remaining evening together.

By the end of the war in Europe, it had been three years since Blanche and Les had been married, and nearly a year since she had joined the Red Cross. In thinking about it, Blanche could hardly believe all the things she had lived through and experienced during those three short years. She had lived through a North Atlantic Ocean crossing in sub-infested waters, German buzz bomb attacks, being shot at by a trigger-happy sentry, and even being attacked by a jealous secretary. Plus, she had learned to drive a 2½ ton truck, drive a Sherman tank, and fly a B-17. She had also seen the horrendous effects of war firsthand, and that caused her perspective to profoundly change. She had gained a new understanding of America's place in the world and what total war felt and looked like. It had been a maturing experience and had instilled in her a new respect for America's war effort, for the American GIs fighting the war, and for the European civilians who suffered the consequences of war. She admitted to her parents that she had "… a chance to see firsthand everything that has happened over here. … [And] it is an experience that I shall never forget, and I hope I will be capable of learning something from [it all]. … It seems almost impossible that I have actually lived through so many experiences in the last three years …"[255]

Chapter 12

*"I am doing something that I believe in
with all my heart and soul."*

The Death of Hitler and V-E Day

On the last day of April 1945, as advancing Russian forces moved closer toward the Führer bunker in the center of Berlin, Adolf Hitler and his new wife of one day, Eva Braun, committed suicide. Before he died, however, Hitler appointed Grand Admiral Karl Dönitz as the new Reich President. It was a hollow bequest to be sure. Dönitz's new government was forced to accept unconditional surrender only a week later. Thus, the Third Reich officially died, and the Allied occupation of Germany began.[256] When Blanche and those around her heard of Hitler's death, they did not know if it was true and, if it was, whether Hitler had been killed, assassinated, or committed suicide. Naturally, they hoped it was true, and that his death meant that the war in Europe was almost over.

During that first week of May, while Blanche and Dottie were working at yet another field unit outside of Bad Neuenahr, a young infantry first lieutenant from Girard, Ohio, who had been recently reassigned to the Fifteenth Army Group, noticed Blanche from afar. He instantly liked what he saw and intended to find a way to introduce himself to the pretty, petite, auburn-haired clubmobile girl, but he didn't get the chance. They were both too busy for the right moment to present itself, and by the next day, the young lieutenant had been sent back to the Third Army. But as fate would have it, a month later they would see each other again, and the young lieutenant would make sure that he did not miss a second opportunity to introduce himself to the "cute little Red Cross girl" he had first laid eyes on at Bad Neuenahr.[257]

Lost in the Hinterland

Several days before the war in Europe officially ended on May 8, 1945, Blanche and Dottie received orders from Red Cross headquarters in Paris to leave Bad Neuenahr and link up with clubmobile Group K, which was attached to XII Corps headquarters somewhere in southeastern Germany. Before leaving, the women were given a different clubmobile. To their delight their new clubmobile was a GMC truck, which was larger, sturdier, more reliable, and easier to repair compared to the Bedford. Plus, it was easier to drive since it was American-built and had the steering wheel on the left side. The women were also granted a much-needed two-week furlough, so they decided to do a little sightseeing while they searched for the XII Corps.

As they prepared to depart, Blanche and Dottie were advised to remain on the west side of the Rhine River as long as they could, since that part of Germany had been under Allied control longer than the east side and was viewed by the Red Cross as safer. So instead of crossing the Rhine at Remagen, they headed toward Koblenz, which was located at the junction of the Rhine and Mosel Rivers and approximately 35 miles southeast of Bad Neuenahr. Koblenz had served as the command center for German Army Group B and had been heavily bombed during the last year of the war, leaving the heart of the city in ruins. Plus, during mid-March 1945, Koblenz was the scene of heavy street-to-street fighting between the German defenders and the U.S. 87th Infantry Division.[258] When Blanche and Dottie arrived in the city, many of the streets were still blocked with rubble and the buildings, if still standing, were mostly bombed-out shells. In a letter home, Blanche referred to the city as a "regular ghost town" where syphilis had begun to spread, and the people were lice infected and starving. It was a sobering and horrible sight to behold.[259]

Moving on, the women continued south to Mannheim, approximately 110 miles away along rough, often damaged, roads, only to find a similar scene of destruction. Located at the confluence of the Rhine and Neckar Rivers, Mannheim had also been pulverized by Allied bombing. The center of the city had been destroyed and thousands of civilians had been killed.[260] It was a heart-wrenching scene of devastation, and it was obvious to Blanche that Mannheim's citizens were in a desperate state. By May most of them had emerged from their places of refuge, only to find that their homes and businesses had been damaged, looted, or destroyed. Furthermore, water and food supplies were extremely limited, and medical care was nonexistent. Anticipating these conditions, the American military had sent in special units to help reestablish order, clear roads of debris, and provide civilians food, water, and other necessities. But that process had only just begun.

It was at Mannheim that the women decided to cross over to the east side of the Rhine so that they could start heading east to where they believed XII Corps headquarters was located. Although the bridge at Mannheim had been destroyed by the retreating Germans, U.S. Army engineers had built a temporary treadway pontoon bridge linking Ludwigshafen with Mannheim. It was dubbed the Gar Davidson Bridge by the GIs, in honor of the engineers' commanding officer. The bridge was approximately 893 feet in length.[261] Although the engineers knew their craft, the makeshift bridge was anything but a stable platform. The women held their breath as they guided their clubmobile across the river and felt the pontoon bridge dip in places from the truck's weight. But they made it without mishap, and the brakes on their GMC clubmobile did not lock up halfway across the bridge like they had at Remagen the month before.

Heidelberg was only about 14 miles southeast of Mannheim and, unlike Koblenz and Mannheim, was almost completely intact, having been spared from Allied aerial bombing raids. When the women arrived in Heidelberg, they decide to spend three or four days sightseeing at Dottie's insistence. They visited the University of Heidelberg, the Heidelberg Castle, and the Church of the Holy Spirit or "Heiliggeistkirche." They also drove outside of town to a Nazi amphitheater, which had been built in 1935 as part of Joseph Goebbels's (the Nazi Minister of Propaganda) "Thingspiel" movement. This was his plan to build thousands of outdoor amphitheaters, often in areas of historical significance, where thousands of German citizens would assemble and hear propaganda presentations made by the government. These specially constructed theaters were called "Thingstätte." However, only about 45 of them were built. When the Heidelberg theater was opened, "20,000 people turned out to hear Goebbels himself."[262]

While visiting the theater, the women came across a German citizen, Herr Wedde, training his pet eagle. Although the Army and the Red Cross had strict nonfraternization rules in effect at the time, Blanche's curiosity got the best of her, and she ended up conversing with the man about the eagle. She even took 8mm film of the two of them. Herr Wedde informed Blanche that he intended to present the eagle, when trained, to General Dwight D. Eisenhower, the Allies' Supreme Commander, as a present! He failed to disclose how he planned to meet the General to do so, or why he thought the General would want an eagle. In the man's mind, no doubt, it was meant to be a symbolic gesture of friendship.

From Heidelberg the women should have driven directly toward Munich, about 213 miles east by southeast of Heidelberg, but instead they headed south. Although they thought they are heading in the right direction, unbeknownst to them they were using a German map printed in English and specifically designed to confuse the Allies. It is unlikely to have confused the American military, but it completely befuddled Blanche and Dottie. All along the way they were also regularly stopping to feed hungry (and sometimes lost) American soldiers by handing out their extra K-rations and collect the soldiers' letters and cards (to be mailed later).

After wandering German back roads for days, the women finally arrived at the Austrian border north of Innsbruck. That is when they finally realized that they were lost and that their German map was worthless. Thankfully, they were able to procure a new map from American MPs and head back to the northeast toward Bad Tölz, Germany. That is where, they had been told, the Third Army had recently moved its headquarters. Since they had no idea where the XII Corps was, they figured that someone at Third Army headquarters would be able to point them in the right direction. At that point it had already taken them over three weeks to travel about 360 miles, and they were anxious to finally link up with the XII Corps.

When they reached Bad Tölz, which is located on the Isar River at the foothills of the Bavarian Alps, Blanche and Dottie were directed to Third Army headquarters, which was housed in a gigantic building that used to be a Waffen-SS troop barracks. After reporting in, a special services officer found the women a place to stay for the night. They also promptly received an invitation to join Third Army officers for dinner that evening. Once Blanche and Dottie cleaned up and changed clothes, they found the officers' mess and discovered that they had been seated at the General's table. There was not anything particularly unusual about this, since American officers always liked to include American women at their mess when possible, and the generals were always first in line. Most clubmobile girls returned to the U.S. after the war able to tell family and friends about the top brass they had dined with at one time or another. Apparently, the generals were no different than the GIs. The inclusion of "real American girls" always made for a more enjoyable repast and more interesting and entertaining conversation.

This evening General George S. Patton, the commander of the Third Army, was not present. He had recently left to attend a

Memorial Day commemoration at a Nuremberg military cemetery.[263] However, to Blanche's sincere delight, General Omar N.
Bradley, Commander of the Fifteenth Army Group (of which the
Third Army was a part), was present and was sitting at the head of
the table. Although Blanche and the General were not sitting next
to each other, they were close enough to converse and she found
him to be quiet, polite, and unassuming—exactly like what she
expected from someone from her native state. Bradley was certainly
a different personality from the loud, vulgar, and bombastic
Patton.

At the appropriate moment, Blanche asked another officer
about the whereabouts of the XII Corps and was duly informed that
Corps headquarters was headed for Regensburg, Germany, to the
northeast. So, the very next day, after mapping out their route using
a reliable American map, Blanche and Dottie left Bad Tölz and
headed for Munich. Munich was only about 20 miles north. It was
the fourth largest city in Germany at the time, and once had served
as the capital of Bavaria and the center of the Weimar Republic.
The city had been occupied by American forces, with little resis-
tance, just weeks before. By the time Blanche and Dottie arrived in
the city, it was mostly in ruins and its population had disappeared
into the countryside or were dead. Everywhere Blanche and Dottie
went, they saw evidence of the Allies' carpet-bombing campaign.
The city had been bombed on numerous occasions by both the British and Americans, resulting in nearly 90 percent of the old section
of the city being destroyed and more than 6,600 people killed and
15,800 wounded.[264] Nearly every street in the center of the city had
impact craters, and "splintered boards and scattered glass ... strewn
over the sidewalks. Roofs cratered. Windows and doors gone. Hunks
of concrete piled up. Church steeples destroyed."[265] Once again, it
was a sad and sobering experience for the American women.

After leaving Munich, Blanche and Dottie continued toward
Regensburg, about 150 miles to the northeast. Soon after leaving
Munich, the women drove past the Dachau Concentration Camp,
which was the first camp created by the Nazi government in 1933.

When American forces approached the camp in late April, the German SS attempted to evacuate at least 25,000 of the prisoners by forcing them to march to the south or by transporting them in overcrowded freight cars. "During these so-called death marches, the Germans shot anyone who could no longer continue; many also died of starvation, hypothermia, or exhaustion." When American forces arrived at the camp on April 29, "they found more than 30 railroad cars filled with bodies …, all in an advanced state of decomposition."[266] When Blanche and Dottie drove by the camp, the inmates were still housed there but were being fed and cared for by the U.S. Army. The women did not attempt to enter the camp, however, and Blanche never regretted their decision. She did not think she could have managed it, as she had heard stories of the horror of it all from GIs who had been there.

To the north of Dachau, the women ran right into a large formation of German soldiers. The Germans still had all their weapons, and the women were convinced that they were about to be captured. So, they frantically searched for their identification cards—which would confirm their status as officers. But the Germans paid no attention to them, and Blanche and Dottie drove right on by and on to Regensburg. Luckily, the German soldiers were a part of a regular army group, and not an SS contingent, or the soldiers' reactions may have been vastly different.

Strained Relations

During the women's time billeted at Bad Neuenahr, Dottie Fargo had been going out with one officer after another and becoming annoyed that Blanche was not interested in joining in her extracurricular activities. It began to place a strain on their relationship. For example, one evening Dottie had asked Blanche to leave their rooms for the evening so that Dottie could privately "entertain" her date. On another occasion, without discussing it with Blanche first, Dottie set Blanche and herself up for a double date with two officers. At first Blanche declined, but Dottie was so insistent that

Blanche finally acquiesced to maintain harmony, but when their dates arrived, Blanche was shocked to discover that their so-called date was to take place in their bedrooms. When Blanche refused to go to bed with her date, Dottie and the men were furious with her. In their minds, Blanche was a prude and a bore. To Blanche, such conduct was against her religious beliefs and morally unacceptable. Over the next month the relationship between Dottie and Blanche continued to deteriorate.

Plus, during the later part of April, Dottie became constantly ill, and Blanche had to perform Dottie's duties as well as her own. It was hard enough on Blanche to physically perform her own responsibilities, but constantly covering for Dottie created a physical strain on Blanche and it started to impact her health. Slowly but surely, Blanche was becoming exhausted and, of course, highly frustrated.

Since leaving Bad Neuenahr, Dottie was sick most mornings. Blanche could not understand it. She certainly was sympathetic with anyone dealing with illness, as she had had to deal with illness her entire life, but she was doing all the work and when she suggested that they stop to find a local doctor and determine what was wrong, Dottie would angrily refuse without explanation. This just made Blanche more upset and perplexed. Dottie did not bother to confide in Blanche probably because she thought that Blanche was too straitlaced and, therefore, too judgmental to understand or be sympathetic to her situation, and Blanche was too naive to figure it out on her own. Thus, it was a perfect situation designed to create tension, animosity, and misunderstanding. By the time the women reached their destination, their relationship had soured. Blanche kept her frustration to herself, but Dottie did not.

With the assistance of another clubmobile girl stationed at Regensburg, Dottie quietly found a local German doctor and he quietly solved her problem. Plus, she told the other clubmobile girls of Group K how horrible Blanche had been to her during their month-long trek across Germany. Without bothering to get

Blanche's side of the story, the other clubmobile girls simply accepted Dottie's version of events. Blanche already had a reputation for being a "Goody Two-shoes," so it was easy for the other women to believe Dottie's story. Thus, a handful of the women even refused to talk to Blanche unless they absolutely had to. Naturally, it bothered Blanche, but she never attempted to correct the situation as she decided that she did not have any desire to become friends with the other women stationed at Regensburg anyway. She did not fit in, and she knew it, and she accepted the situation and got on with her job. She did her best to maintain a business-like relationship with Dottie and the other clubmobilers, but it made working with Dottie over the next couple of months even more difficult.

Clubmobiler B.J. Olewiler explained these types of situations best when she wrote about the varied backgrounds clubmobile girls had and how it impacted their relationships:

> [W]e were all thrown into this thing from greatly differing backgrounds and environments. … Much more so than the Army where an outfit was largely from one section of the country. We had girls … from all over the states. And while diversity made for some interesting discoveries about the great differences based on which part of the U.S. you called home, it became apparent that the girl nurtured in the precise refinement of an Eastern girls' school found it difficult to relate immediately to the girl who had grown up in the Southwest learning to drive a tractor. And the girl who had come from a midwestern puritanical community did not understand that the questionable oaths punctuating a southern girl's conversation were not an indication of complete moral laxity.[267]

In a letter to her parents written right after arriving at Regensburg, Blanche underscored this unique social dynamic.

It seems that for a long time now I have not been able to cope with [my] social life. ... I just don't fit in. ... Then I met Les and was deliriously happy ... because he didn't drink, he liked church life, and ... he was very intelligent (a combination hard to find these days). ... Now I am doing something that I believe in with all my heart and soul. I love every minute of my job and wouldn't do anything else for anything in the world, but when it comes to [my] social life, again, I am a complete flop. Why? Because I don't drink and smoke, and believe you me, I am practically an oddity for a museum.[268]

What Blanche did not mention in her letter home was the issue of sex, which was revealing. That was a subject Blanche never discussed with her parents. What little Blanche had learned about the subject prior to her marriage to Les had come from her female friends in college. Blanche was simply too shy, too naive, and too straitlaced to fit in with the more worldly women all around her. It was one of the factors as to why Blanche made so few close friends while she was overseas.

Regensburg and a New Beginning

Blanche and Dottie arrived at Regensburg on either the 1st or the 2nd of June 1945, just a few days after the XII Corps had transferred its headquarters to the city. Unlike Cologne, Koblenz, and many other German cities, the center of Regensburg had escaped from heavy Allied bombing and was still basically intact. It was a midsized Bavarian city located at the confluence of the Danube and Regen Rivers, and its medieval German architecture and curving stone slab streets were stunning. People still come from all over the world to take in Regensburg's history and beauty.

The women's first stop was to check in with the leaders of Club-mobile Group K—Elma Ernst of Quincy, Illinois, and Mary Moore of Seattle, Washington. They directed Blanche and Dottie to the XII Corps' Special Services office. The first XII Corps soldier the women met was Major William A. McClung of Norfolk, Virginia, the head of Special Services, who, because of his position, would be primarily responsible for the women during their stay in Regensburg. Naturally, the women told the Major all about their run-in with the German soldiers on their way up from Heidelberg, and he jokingly told them that they should turn around and "go back out there and bring them in and be the first Red Cross girls to capture a German Army!" The women sensibly declined the offer. The Major finally informed the ladies that the Germans were just looking for American units to surrender to, the German soldiers were flocking west toward American lines in the hope of avoiding the Soviet Army.

Major McClung assigned the women rooms at the historic Bischofshof Hotel in the center of the old section of the city. The Bischofshof was the west wing of a four-section building complex that had been built between the 12th and 15th centuries as part of a bishop's palace and adjoining courtyard. It had been built on Roman foundations and on an old monastic compound.[269] Before its modernization after the war, the hotel only had one bathroom per floor and the Army had placed all visiting women (Red Cross girls, entertainers, nurses, etc.) on a single floor for privacy. So, bathroom access presented some logistical problems for the women. One morning the line for the bathroom stretched all the way down the hall. While waiting her turn, Blanche casually turned around to say good morning to an older lady standing behind her. Blanche introduced herself and the lady, who was still in her bathrobe and slippers, hair a mess and without makeup, responded to Blanche's cheery greeting in a deep, sultry German accent and simply said, "Good morning, I'm Marlene Dietrich."[270] Suddenly, Blanche recognized the famous movie actress and entertainer, who was in town for a show, and was so stunned that she was speechless. Before being able to collect herself and say something further, the line surged forward and it was Blanche's turn in the bathroom, and Miss Dietrich patiently waited outside until Blanche was finished.[271] Even with only one bathroom, compared to sleeping in the back of a

clubmobile or in a sleeping bag on the ground, the accommodations at the Bischofshof were a substantial step up and the women
quickly settled in to their new surroundings.

The morning after Blanche's arrival in Regensburg, while she
was having breakfast at the officers' mess, Major McClung walked
up to the table and introduced his friend, 1st Lt. George H. Gangwere
Jr., of Girard, Ohio. The day before, after first meeting Blanche and
Dottie, Major McClung had told George about "the cute little red
head" that had just arrived in town, and once George saw Blanche
from across the officers' mess, he immediately realized that she was
the same clubmobile girl he had seen the month before at Bad
Neuenahr and had admired from afar. So, he asked the Major to do
the introductions.[272] After the Major had performed his duty, he
made a tactical retreat and left the field open for George. After a
little small talk, George got around to casually mentioning the
dance Special Services was hosting that evening at the officers' club.
He slyly asked Blanche, "Are you going to the dance tonight?" It was
his indirect way of asking her out, and somehow, she managed to
comprehend his meaning and quickly accept the invitation.
Although she had turned down many other offers for dates over the
past few years, she accepted George's invitation because "he was
extremely handsome, well-spoken, and well-mannered." Plus, after
a long month on the road, Blanche needed some entertainment
and thought a dance was just the ticket.

That same evening, George picked Blanche up at the Bischofshof
and they walked to the officers' club and slowly began the process
of getting to know one another. Years later Blanche admitted that at
first, she was not overly impressed with George, as he seemed
reserved and aloof. She was used to men giving her the full court
press when they were pursuing her. However, George carried himself extremely well, and at the dance she happily discovered that he
had a great sense of humor and was a good dancer. He was also
well-educated. He had received his bachelor's degree in economics
from the University of Michigan at Ann Arbor and had completed
one year of law school at Michigan before being drafted in 1941. He

intended to return to Ann Arbor after the war to complete his legal studies, and it was obvious to Blanche that he was a serious, ambitious, and highly intelligent young man who knew where he was going and how to get there. Suddenly, for the first time since her dating relationship with Mel Schulstad had ended the year before, she was finding herself thoroughly enjoying the company of a man. The fact that Blanche had been married before and was still wearing her wedding ring (although a widow), did not seem to bother George, although it played a part in his cautious approach.

As the dance progressed, Blanche carefully observed her date interacting with other officers and admitted that she was "bowled over" by how captains, majors, and even a few colonels freely conversed with him and carefully listened to his comments and opinions. They obviously respected him and did not treat him like just another lowly lieutenant, so Blanche decided then and there that, if given the opportunity, she wanted to get to know this handsome young lieutenant better. To her delight, George immediately followed up their first date with an invitation for lunch the next day. The lunch took place on a gently sloping riverbank on the far side of the ancient stone bridge that stretches over the Danube River. From the spot George had selected, the couple could see the towering spires of St. Peter's Cathedral in the distance. The church is the most recognizable landmark in Regensburg, and George could not have picked a more romantic setting. For their meal, such as it was, he had brought a bottle of French wine, cheese, crackers, and canned sardines, and the young couple sat on a blanket, enjoyed their repast and the beautiful June weather, and continued to get to know each other better. She told him about her upbringing in Kansas City, her time at Northwestern, a little more about Les and his premature death in 1942, and why she had joined the Red Cross. He told her about his upbringing in Girard, Ohio, a small suburb outside of Youngstown, why he picked law as a profession, and his current duties as a liaison officer with the XII Corps.

For the next two weeks, Blanche and George continued to have lunches together on the banks of the Danube, attend dances at the officers' club or plays at the Capitol Theater, go to movies at the Half Crown Theater, and take long walks through the old section of Regensburg. During this period, several of the Group K clubmobile girls privately pulled George aside and told him that they thought he could do a lot better than Blanche, but he understood the reasons for their comments and it only served to make him more interested.[273] So by the end of their brief time together at Regensburg, George was determined to keep in touch with Blanche and pursue the relationship after the war, and Blanche was pretty certain that she had finally met the right man. In fact, she took the momentous step of taking Les's wedding ring off her finger for the last time and tucking it away. She felt as if she was starting a new chapter in her life, and she was finally ready to embrace it.

Chapter 13

"Now that the war is over, I believe [that] I can contribute a little more to the world than coffee and doughnuts ..."

Passau, Germany

After spending several weeks providing coffee and doughnuts to XII Corps units stationed in and around Regensburg, Blanche and Dottie were teamed up with Elsie S. Yeager of Mount Vernon, Washington (a Canadian by birth), and the women were sent to Passau, Germany, for a month to provide clubmobile services to the 83rd Infantry Division, also known as "The Thunderbolt Division." Passau is about 74 miles southeast of Regensburg in Lower Bavaria and is known as the "City of Three Rivers," as it sits at the confluence of the Ilz, Danube, and Inn Rivers. Having Elsie added to *The Yankee Doodle*'s crew initially helped ease the tension between Blanche and Dottie, but it was still lurking under the surface.

When the women arrived at Passau, they were directed to the 83rd Division's Rest Center, which had been established in the historic Veste Oberhaus castle. The castle sits atop a small mountain called the "Georgsberg."[274] It was where the women were billeted during their stay in Passau, along with other Red Cross personnel, and it had been founded in 1219 and overlooked the town. For most of its history, the castle served as the stronghold of the Bishop of Passau. It is considered one of the largest and best-preserved former military fortresses in all of Europe.[275] During the 19th and early 20th centuries, the castle served as a state and military prison, and during the war, German and then American military forces utilized the castle for housing their troops.

To get to the front of the castle, the women had to take a narrow, winding, one-lane road, with trees on one side and a sheer cliff (and no railing) on the other, which ran up the front of the mountain. As usual, Blanche was driving, and she had to slowly make her way up the road given the size of their GMC clubmobile. Nearing the top, the women approached an old medieval stone arch that had to be passed to get into the castle courtyard and the buildings beyond. However, they soon discovered that the arch was too narrow for the clubmobile. It simply would not fit.

Upon inquiry, a nearby MP informed the women that the only other way into the castle complex was from the opposite side of the castle, which could only be approached by taking a different road located on the back side of the mountain. Since the road they had utilized was too narrow to turn the clubmobile around, Blanche had to back the truck down the mountain slowly and carefully to avoid a disaster.[276] It was a nerve-racking descent, and to make matters worse, for some odd reason, Dottie was furious with Blanche (as if Blanche should have known that there was an arch at the top of the road and that it would be too narrow for the clubmobile to drive through). As Dottie vented, and Blanche protested, Elsie said nothing and did her best to stay out of it, but it was not a good beginning to their stay in Passau.

After several hours, the women finally entered the castle's grounds by using the back entrance suggested by the MP. The castle was beautiful and gigantic, with a stunning view of the valley below. The rest center established at the castle was a "GI's dream" since uniform regulations were not enforced, and saluting was not required. The GIs housed there ate "civilian style while German fräuleins" waited on them, and they "drank beer at the Terrace Bar and danced there to the music of the Division and various local bands." Furthermore, the men got to sleep "between freshly laundered sheets," and enjoy the center's game rooms, movie theater, swimming pool, and volleyball, archery, tennis, and badminton courts. Plus, a Red Cross doughnut dugout was in the castle which provided coffee and doughnuts throughout the day.[277] Blanche, Dottie, and Elsie also were able to enjoy those services and facilities. So, it was a dream assignment, and that helped to soften the lingering tension between Blanche and Dottie.

Over the next few weeks, *The Yankee Doodle* served different units of the 83rd and provided them with their full panoply of services. *The Yankee Doodle* even drove to Austria to attend to units stationed across the border.[278] It was estimated that during their time at Passau the crew served an average of 1,000 men per day, and approximately 2,000 doughnuts and 90 gallons of coffee, along with cigarettes, candy, and gum.[279]

While at Passau, Blanche met and was strenuously pursued by a young GI, but she managed to politely wave off his advances, as her romantic interest was still centered on the young lieutenant back in Regensburg. She also was asked by the 83rd's Special Services officer to entertain GIs in the evening on the castle's grand piano. In return, and because of her obvious love of music, the officer gave Blanche an old lute that had been left behind in the castle when the Germans departed. It had been allegedly owned by an SS officer. Blanche loved it and taught herself how to play it, and luckily, she managed to get it shipped back to the United States. It has remained in her family ever since.

The Glenn Miller Orchestra

During the summer of 1945, USO entertainers routinely came to Passau to entertain the GIs stationed there. Some of the entertainers who visited the castle that summer were comedian and movie star Jack Benny, Swedish movie star Ingrid Bergman, comedian and movie star Bob Hope, actor Jerry Colonna, harmonica player and composer Larry Adler, and big band singer Martha Tilton.[280] While Blanche was staying at the castle, the Glenn Miller Band and Orchestra came to Passau to perform several concerts for the 83rd Infantry Division at the Passau Arena. They were completing six months on the continent and a year in Europe, and during that time, they had performed over 300 public appearances (concerts and dances), over 500 radio broadcasts, and entertained more than 600,000 American servicemen.[281]

The founder and conductor had been, of course, Major Glenn Miller. He was, perhaps, the most famous bandleader in America during the late 1930s and early 1940s. However, tragically, he had disappeared in a plane over the English Channel the December before. The remaining band members, who were also in the Army, were soldiering on without him and were still entertaining American troops throughout occupied Europe. The band, a 42-piece orchestra with a 19-piece swing band at its core, was made up of some of the best musicians from the classical and jazz fields and was known for its pre-war hits such as "Moonlight Serenade," "In the Mood," "A String of Pearls," "Sunrise Serenade," and "Tuxedo Junction."[282]

Blanche attended one of the band's concerts in Passau in late June, and later that night the band visited the Veste Oberhaus for a little R&R. Blanche, Dottie, and Elsie met the band members while serving them coffee and doughnuts. Several of the band members began talking to Blanche and they ended up engaging in a lengthy conversation about their mutual interests in music. Later, the men invited the women to join them for a swim in the castle pool. The ladies readily accepted, and when the women arrived at the pool at the designated hour, they were wearing the swimming suits they had brought with them from the states the year before. They quickly discovered, however, that the men had not had the same foresight. Instead, the men were all swimming in their boxer shorts. Dottie and Elsie did not hesitate and jumped right in. It took Blanche a few moments to assess the situation, but she finally decided to go with the flow and joined everyone in the pool. She remembered that everyone had a wonderful time that evening, and it had been a special treat for her—being able to socialize and converse with some of the best and most famous jazz and classical musicians of her era.[283]

Hitler's Yacht

While stationed at Passau, Blanche had occasion to meet Lt. Gen. Leonard T. Gerow, commander of the Fifteenth U.S. Army. Apparently, the general liked what he saw, which he made abundantly clear to Blanche. A few days later Blanche, Dottie, and Elsie received an invitation to join the general for dinner at the officers' mess at the general's command post in Passau. The other women were delighted, but Blanche did not want to go, as she was suspicious of the general's intentions, and she had no romantic interest in him whatsoever. Although Gerow was not unattractive for his age, he was 30 years older than Blanche, and most importantly, he was married. When a sergeant arrived in a jeep that evening to pick the women up, Blanche told the sergeant that she was not going. With that response the sergeant turned white and became almost frantic. He pleaded with Blanche to change her mind and said, "Oh, please, please, come with me. If I return without you, I am going to be in serious trouble." So, Blanche took pity on the poor GI and finally went along.

The dinner that night was not unenjoyable, as many other officers were present and the clubmobile girls received a lot of favorable attention, as they always did. Blanche also did her best to be cordial to General Gerow, who had insisted that she sit next to him at the dinner table. She knew that Gerow was held in high regard by American high command and was widely known to be an old friend of General Eisenhower's. However, many of his peers and officers who served under him considered him to be cold and detached. Gerow had served as the Chief of the War Plans Division on the War Department's General Staff prior to the war. After the war started, he became the commander of the 29th Infantry Division and later

of the V Corps. As such, he played a major part in the planning of
Operation Overlord, the invasion of continental Europe, and was
the first corps commander to step ashore on D-Day. He continued
in command through the Battle of Normandy and, in January 1945,
assumed command of the Fifteenth Army.[284]

When the evening was over and Blanche and the other women
were preparing to leave, the general pulled Blanche aside and
invited (demanded really) that she join him, as his personal guest,
for a cruise on Adolf Hitler's captured yacht. Not knowing how to
say no to a lieutenant general, Blanche reluctantly agreed but immediately formed a plan to ensure that she would not be alone with the
general. She told Dottie and Elsie that they had also been invited
and took them along for "protection." When the women all showed
up together at the designated dock in Passau the next morning, the
general was forced to accept the change in plans. The yacht they
cruised down the Danube on was probably the *Ostwind* (*East Wind*
in English). The *Ostwind* was one of two boats commissioned by
Adolf Hitler as an Olympic sailing vessel, although it never saw competition. Instead, during the war, it was used by German government and military officials. Although often referred to as Hitler's
yacht, there is no evidence that Hitler ever set foot on the ship.

When Blanche met Lt. General Gerow in Passau, the Fifteenth
Army consisted of a small staff and special troops assigned to gather
historical data on Allied operations during the war and serve as the
temporary custodian of valuable items of personal property seized
from the Germans, such as the *Ostwind*.[285] The sailboat, designed by
noted naval architect Heinrich Gruber, was 86 feet in length—sleek
and lovely. She had been meticulously constructed of mahogany
planking over a steel frame, with a teak, mahogany, rosewood, and
walnut finish throughout the interior.[286] It was a classic and beautiful sailing vessel, and it happened to be a beautiful summer day in
Bavaria, so Blanche and the women enjoyed themselves thoroughly.
The general, however, was a bit put out by being outmaneuvered by
a Red Cross girl. No similar invitations were forthcoming, which
was fine with Blanche.

A Return to Paris and a Possible Reassignment

In a letter to her brother and sister-in-law at this time, Blanche admitted that she was thinking of requesting a change of assignment with the Red Cross. She felt that now that the war was over, she could, perhaps, "contribute a little more to the world than coffee and doughnuts ..."[287] What she had in mind was a transfer to a club in a major city, such as Paris, or to a military hospital where she could use her musical talents to entertain GIs. To achieve that goal, she requested and obtained a pass to return to Paris and to make her request directly with Red Cross clubmobile leadership. She also saw a transfer to a new assignment as a means of effectively removing herself from the stress she was feeling from constantly navigating her way around difficult social situations. She knew that she didn't fit in with her crew or the other Group K women; in particular, her relationship with Dottie was still strained and likely to remain so.[288] A transfer seemed like just the thing.

The Red Cross officials in Paris were not opposed to Blanche's request, as many Red Cross volunteers, especially the ones who had already been overseas for more than 24 months, were leaving for home in the summer of 1945. Thus, many vacancies in the field structure were opening. Plus, at the time, clubmobile leadership was thinking about who might be reassigned to the Pacific Theater of Operations. So before agreeing to reassign Blanche, they insisted that she see a heart specialist and receive his recommendation relating to her continued service; her first visit with the specialist was inconclusive. But one of the highlights of her visit was playing the pipe organ in the Chapel at the Sorbonne, located in the Latin Quarter of Paris. Sorbonne University dates from the middle of the 13th century. The Chapel was rebuilt in the 17th century on the orders of Cardinal de Richelieu, and its pipe organ was constructed in 1825.[289] Given its history, having the opportunity to play the organ at the Sorbonne was a real treat for Blanche.

While in Paris, Blanche also ran into her old clubmobile crewmate from Kettering, Libby Harnies, and they had a wonderful reunion. While doing so, they decided to try to obtain leaves at the same time and return together to visit old friends at Kettering. Blanche also did something that she had never done before. She called George Gangwere at Regensburg to let him know where she was and what she was doing (in case he was trying to contact her at Passau). They had been writing to each other, but in her entire dating history, going all the way back to high school, Blanche had never done anything that could even remotely be considered forward when it came to men. So, her calling George and letting him know where she was and what she was doing was an absolute first. It underscored how seriously she was taking their budding relationship.

Underscoring the affect that a young, attractive American woman had on GIs serving overseas during World War II, while Blanche was in Paris, she innocently created quite a scene at a local Parisian movie theater. Blanche had decided to go out for the evening by herself in her civilian dress. Since she was on leave, she could properly do so, and being in civilian dress helped ensure a certain level of anonymity while frequenting public places. Since the movie was being presented in English, not surprisingly, the theater was packed with American servicemen, and since Blanche was in civilian dress, the GIs did not notice her at first.

After paying for her ticket, Blanche attempted to enter the theater and find a seat on her own—not realizing the local protocol for such things. A French usher immediately stopped her and demanded that she allow him to show her to a seat. She reluctantly agreed but did not realize that it was the French custom to tip the ushers after they had done so. When Blanche sat down and failed to tip the usher, he immediately became quite irate. Apparently, the usher did not believe that the tip was discretionary. He even began to curse Blanche, in his native tongue of course, and she had no idea what he was saying. He made such a scene that she finally stood up to protest. "I'm sorry. I do not know what you are saying. I am an American and I do not speak French."

When the GIs heard her declaration and turned and took one look at Blanche, the place went wild. The catcalls, whistles, and humorous pickup lines became so loud that the projectionist had to stop the movie! One gallant serviceman came to Blanche's rescue, tipped the irate usher, and then told him to get lost. Other GIs started joining in and yelling at the usher to back off. Wisely, the usher made an immediate retreat, and once everyone had settled down, the projectionist continued the movie. Blanche was, of course, totally embarrassed, but she was also a bit amused. A Red Cross girl unintentionally causing a scene in a public place was not an unusual occurrence, and having a theater full of GIs come to her rescue was, in her estimation, well worth the temporary embarrassment.

V-J Day and the End of the War

On August 6, 1945, the United States dropped its first atomic bomb on Japan at Hiroshima, but the Japanese government refused to surrender. So, three days later, a second bomb was dropped on Nagasaki. Finally, through the direct intervention of the Japanese Emperor, the Japanese government sued for peace. President Harry S. Truman announced Japan's unconditional surrender on August 14, and the surrender documents were officially signed on September 2 on the deck of the battleship USS *Missouri* while anchored in Tokyo Bay. World War II had officially come to an end.

Just after President Truman's historic announcement, Blanche and Libby Harnies enjoyed a one-week furlough together. They took a boat train back to England and were staying with Mrs. Mackay, their former landlady, at Kettering. In a letter home that month, Blanche admitted that while she was stationed in England, Mrs. Mackay had been like a mother to her.[290] Libby seemingly felt the same way. It broke Blanche's heart to lose touch with Mrs. Mackay after the war, but apparently Mrs. Mackay followed through on her plans to move away from Kettering.

Unbeknownst to Blanche, while she and Libby were in England, George Gangwere obtained a furlough of his own and flew to Paris looking for Blanche. But he was a few days late. By then she was in

England, and by the time Blanche returned to Paris, George had already flown on to Cannes (near Monaco) on the French Riviera for some R&R with friends.

Back to Regensburg

In September, the Red Cross sent Blanche to see another heart specialist and he did not recommend that she be sent to the Pacific Theater. With that issue decided, the Red Cross offered Blanche several temporary assignments or the option to return home. By then, returning home was exactly what Blanche wanted.[291] However, until arrangements could be made for her departure, Blanche requested that she remain attached to Group K so as to return to the Regensburg area and hopefully be near George. The Red Cross agreed, and for the last two weeks in September, Blanche and George found themselves together again and free to continue their courtship. Dances in the evenings, picnics on the shore of the Danube, long walks through the stately medieval streets of Regensburg, and bridge games with friends took up their free time during those few delightful weeks.

In July, at the request of his friend Major McClung, George was transferred from his liaison duties to Special Services. Although it was supposed to be a temporary assignment, when McClung suddenly received orders to return home, George took over as the Corps' Special Services Officer (SSO). As such, his new responsibilities included taking care of the needs of the Red Cross girls assigned to the Corps (a responsibility he enjoyed); the scheduling, publicizing, and handling of all administrative details for the USO shows in the area; and handling the showing of all 16 and 35mm films presented for the GIs' entertainment, etc. His SSO duties meant that he was also responsible for the care and feeding of all USO performers and the preparations for their public performances. As mentioned before, during the fall of 1945, the list of USO performers visiting the XII Corps area included such all-star actors and entertainers as Bing Crosby, Bob Hope, Jack Benny,

Marlene Dietrich, Jerry Colonna, Ingrid Bergman, Billy Rose, Larry Adler, and Martha Tilton.[292]

Given Blanche's musical background and George's total lack of it, she proved to be a vital resource as he attempted to perform his new SSO responsibilities. A perfect example was when George was making the arrangements for a piano concert at the officers' club being hosted by the Corps commander. The pianist the general had procured for the event was none other than Wladyslaw Szpilman, the Polish ex-patriot freshly released from a Nazi prison camp. His autobiography, *The Pianist*, was made into a successful motion picture of the same title in 2002. Knowing nothing about music or pianos, George had arranged to have an old upright piano set up in the officers' club for Mr. Szpilman's performance.

When Blanche realized what George was planning, she immediately stepped in and convinced him that an old upright piano simply would not do. She convinced him that he had to find a grand piano and make sure that it was properly tuned. George wisely deferred to her advice and procured a grand piano from a local hotel and used German POWs to have it taken to the officers' club. Then he found someone to properly tune it. The concert went off without a hitch. In other words, Blanche saved George from a lot of embarrassment, and he sincerely appreciated it. He also appreciated that when he organized a day tour of the historic buildings and Roman ruins of Regensburg for local GIs, Blanche was the only one to show up and take the tour.

Going Home!

At the beginning of October 1945, Blanche hugged and kissed George goodbye and left Regensburg and, failing to procure a flight, took a rough and uncomfortable jeep ride back to Paris. From that point on the letters between Blanche and George became increasingly frequent and warm. In her first letter to George, using stationery and envelopes he had given her before she left Regensburg, written on her first night in Paris, she cautiously tells him that she misses him already, how much their past two weeks together had meant to her, and sends her "love."

> Dear George, Since you gave me stationery, envelopes and all, guess I'll have to write to you before I write to anyone else. … Believe it or not I do miss you. Didn't even have a movie to go to tonight. Decided to get into bed and write letters [instead]. … I can't tell you how much the past two weeks have meant to me. I had a wonderful time, thanks to you. Give my regards to [all] and my love to … (three guesses). Blanche.[293]

While in Paris waiting for arrangements to be made for her trip home, Blanche tried to arrange a flight to Accra so she could visit the military cemetery where Les Barnes was buried. But, when that plan fell through, she obtained a plane ride to Dinant, Belgium, and did a little sightseeing. After also visiting Mouscron, Brussels, and Antwerp, all in just a few days, Blanche hitched a plane ride back to Paris with the crew of General Gerow's Douglas C-47 transport aircraft. The General was not present.

When she got back to Paris, the Red Cross had finished making the final arrangements for her departure, so Blanche turned in her Army equipment, which included her steel helmet and liner; canteen and cover; cup; mess kit; knife, fork, and spoon; gas mask (which thankfully she never used); blankets; bedroll; sleeping bag; and protective clothing.[294] Next, she took a train to Le Havre and awaited transportation back to the States. While at Le Havre, she got talked into going to a party with an Army officer and ended up having to fight him off all evening. She discouraged him by telling him that she was engaged, and amazingly, the news made its way through the Army pipeline all the way to George in Regensburg! However, George dismissed it as nonsense. By then he was totally confident of his standing with Blanche.

Nevertheless, in her last letter to George before leaving for the states and mailed from Le Havre, Blanche danced around the exact status of their relationship, but subtly attempted to make her intentions clear.

> George, Since I won't get any more mail from you until I get home, and since I do not know your new address, … I am going to write to you without hearing from you. Is that all right? … I am still in Le Havre but will sail about the 17th if everything goes as planned. … Am certainly sorry I didn't manage to get you on the phone the first day [that] I called. I did try hard. I would have loved to have seen you again, and, whether I like to admit it or not, I have missed you a great deal. It was very nice talking to you on the phone. I hope for your sake that the 90th Division doesn't take too long getting to the States. Am wondering about a lot of things … As ever, Blanche[295]

George finally let her know his feelings in a letter that didn't make its way to Blanche until she was already back in Kansas City. He admitted to her, in his own cryptic style, that after their brief time together she somehow had become closer to him than anyone else in his life, and that he "wouldn't be surprised if it would stay that way …"[296]

The ship that was to take Blanche home was the SS *Mariposa*, and on October 17, it departed Le Havre for Boston Harbor. The Mariposa was a luxury ocean liner launched in 1932 as one of four ships in the famous Matson Line's "White Fleet." The passage was slow and unremarkable, and the passengers disembarked at Lynn, Massachusetts, on October 24. In a few days, the Red Cross personnel took a train to New York City where they were processed and formally discharged from the ARC. Finally, from New York City, Blanche took another train back to Missouri.

On the long train trip home, Blanche had time to contemplate her service in Europe, the close calls, the people she had met, the places she had seen, and the lessons she had learned. Overall, it had been all she could have hoped for and more. She also thought about what was next, and that's where George came in. She was not sure that he felt as strongly about her as she did about him, but she hoped that he did. One comforting realization was that she would not have to worry about money for a while. One of the benefits of Red Cross service was its overseas pay—a clubmobile captain like Blanche was making $175 a month by 1945, or around $3,036 today. So, after 15 months of overseas service, Blanche had saved enough money to help her start a new after-war life. She had no idea what would come next, but she was confident that she would find her way.

When Blanche arrived in Kansas City, her parents met her at Union Station and were delighted that she had returned to them, safe and sound. Thus, Blanche officially returned to civilian life—older, more mature, and a lot wiser than when the war had started four years earlier. She and the millions of other Americans that made up what has been termed as America's "Greatest Generation" had grown up during two of the most traumatic events in American history, the Great Depression and World War II, and those milestones left an indelible mark.

Blanche's experiences, of course, paled in comparison to what the men of the Eighth Air Force or the GIs on the front lines had endured, but for a woman of the 1940s, it had been utterly unique. For Blanche, World War II transformed her from a naive, sheltered, parochial midwestern girl, to a grown woman with a better understanding of the world and her place in it, but without losing her faith in God or her faith in mankind in the process. Most importantly, it had helped her finally move past her personal grief and obtain a new purpose in life. Her Red Cross service had been the capstone of that transformation and had instilled in her a deep pride in what she had accomplished. As she said years later when reflecting on her Red Cross service, "I take a great deal of satisfaction in knowing that I contributed to the war effort by making the lives of thousands of GIs a little less burdensome and a little less lonely."

Epilogue

It has been estimated that between 1943 and VE Day in May 1945, Red Cross clubmobile girls served millions of doughnuts to American servicemen in England, Scotland, Ireland, Wales, France, Belgium, Luxembourg, Holland, Switzerland, Germany, Austria, and Czechoslovakia. They also served hundreds of thousands more in North Africa, Italy, and during the years of the American European occupation.[297] As described by historian George Korson, in the process,

> Red Cross clubmobile girls had one of the most extraordinary experiences of the war, performing an unprecedented service with enthusiasm and a contempt for personal danger that had the whole Army tossing its helmets into the air. They had a ringside seat at one of the greatest dramas of all time, moving with more freedom than many soldiers.[298]

It was a time that Blanche would never forget. On the other hand, she rarely talked about her World War II service in social settings. Perhaps it was because she never felt that she had done anything extraordinary compared to the millions of men who put their lives on the line for their country during the war. She was justly proud of her service, but to her it did not compare with what the GIs had accomplished and endured. When forced to talk about her wartime experiences, like many of her generation, she often responded with a clinical lack of emotion and a frustrating lack of detail unless drawn out by a determined interviewer. However, she had an incredible memory when prodded.

Because of her background and personality, Blanche developed few close friendships with other clubmobile girls and, in fact, often found herself on the outside of their social network. However, she had, from the very beginning, a strong sense of loyalty to the Red Cross and its mission, and to the American GIs it was serving. It was her way of trying, in the only way open to her, to honor her husband's memory and to give meaning to his sacrifice, as well as her personal loss. In later years, it was her family and her music that provided her with the greatest personal satisfaction and pride. The war was just a short tragic interlude to the rest of her life, but it had forged in her a level of independence, determination, and self-confidence that she had lacked before the war, and it helped her deal with and overcome barriers placed in her path later in life.

In one of her final letters home, Blanche briefly summed up her Red Cross service and her hope for the future:

> This job with the Red Cross proved to be a 24 hour one at times, and if it hadn't been so interesting and self-satisfying I am not sure that I would not have been able to stick it out. ... I have certainly managed to see some of the world, and I must say [that] Germany is the most beautiful country of them all. ... Gosh, I'm anxious to [get back to you and] ... back to my music. I have missed it but wouldn't have done anything else for the world.[299]

Several months after Blanche arrived home, George Gangwere returned home too, and, within weeks of his arrival, he took a train to Kansas City to ask Blanche to marry him. She accepted without reservation, and they were married in June 1946. Subsequently, George completed his legal studies at the University of Michigan and the couple settled in Kansas City where he became a partner, and later the senior partner, in a local law firm and served for 17 years as the Chief Counsel for the National Collegiate Athletic

Association, specializing in sports and constitutional law. They raised three children together and were married for 57 years before George's death in 2003.

As planned, Blanche continued to ensure that music played a key part in her life. Her professional music career included serving as children's choir director at a local Methodist church, and later as the organist for the Independence Boulevard Christian Church in the northeast area of Kansas City, the same church she had grown up in. When her public performing days were over, she did not retire from music. She authored three internationally recognized reference books on music history covering the Late Roman, Gothic, and Renaissance Periods. Her books can be found in libraries and universities throughout the United States and Western Europe. In addition, in anticipation of the building of a new performing arts center in Kansas City (named the Kauffman Center for the Performing Arts), Blanche and other local organists formed a committee that successfully lobbied for the inclusion of a concert pipe organ in the center's main concert hall. She can be seen on YouTube playing Johann Sebastian Bach's "Toccata and Fugue in D minor," when she was 94 years old, on the Kauffman Center's gigantic Casavant organ, Opus 3875, and absolutely nailing it. Blanche was also the composer of numerous musical compositions for the pipe organ, all of which are now in the Library of Congress. Blanche died in 2019, at the age of 101, after living a long, full, and highly productive life.

Although much of what the American Red Cross, and the clubmobile girls in particular, accomplished during World War II has been forgotten by the average American, in 2012 the United States Senate took note and passed Senate Resolution 471, "Commending the Efforts of the Women of the American Red Cross Clubmobiles for Exemplary Service During the Second World War," and appropriately commemorated their service:

Whereas, during the Second World War, the American Red Cross was charged by the United States Armed Forces with providing recreational services to the soldiers serving in the war;

Whereas Harvey Gibson, the Red Cross Commissioner to Great Britain during the war, conceived of the Clubmobiles in 1942 as a means of providing hot coffee, fresh doughnuts, and a vital connection to home to thousands of servicemen at dozens of airfields, bases, and camps throughout Great Britain during the buildup to D-Day;

Whereas thousands of young women, from every State in the United States, volunteered to serve in the Clubmobiles, and were chosen after a rigorous interview process in which less than 20 percent of applicants were selected;

Whereas, less than 1 month after the invasion of Normandy, France, in June 1944, 80 Clubmobiles and 320 American Red Cross volunteers crossed the English Channel and began providing coffee, doughnuts, and a friendly smile to servicemen fighting on the front lines;

Whereas the Clubmobile volunteers saw service across Europe in France, Belgium, Italy, Luxembourg, and Germany, and later in the Far East, touching the lives of hundreds of thousands of United States servicemen until victory was achieved;

Whereas, during the war, the American Red Cross purchased enough flour to produce more than 1,500,000,000 doughnuts, many served from the windows of a Clubmobile;

Whereas a visit from a Clubmobile, which could serve gallons of coffee and hundreds of doughnuts every minute, was often the most significant morale boost available to servicemen at war;

Whereas 52 women of the American Red Cross, some of whom served on the Clubmobiles, perished during the war as a result of their service; and

Whereas 70 years have passed since the Clubmobiles were founded, and only a few women who served in the Clubmobiles remain to share their stories:

Now, therefore, be it Resolved, That the Senate—

(1) Commends the exemplary and courageous service and sacrifice of each of the patriotic women of the United States who served in the American Red Cross Clubmobiles during the Second World War;

(2) Honors the Clubmobile women who lost their lives during the Second World War;[300]

(3) Calls upon historians of the Second World War to recognize and describe the service of the Clubmobiles, and to not let this important piece of United States history be lost; and

(4) Urges the American Red Cross to publicly commemorate the stories of the Clubmobiles and the amazing women who served in them.[301]

Endnotes

Prologue

1   Unless otherwise indicated, Blanche Gregory Barnes Gangwere's personal story, opinions, observations, and recollections are all drawn from oral interviews conducted by the author between 1978 and 2018, and from her wartime correspondence, diary, photographs, 8mm film, and scrapbooks in the possession of the author (cited under her married name "Barnes"). The author has reproduced her correspondence as originally written; however, he has omitted words, letters, and information that is repetitive or of little relevance to the story. People, place names, technical terms, foreign words, and slang are identified and explained only when helpful to the understanding of the overall context of the story.

2   George Korson, *At His Side: The Story of the American Red Cross Overseas in World War II* (New York: Coward-McCann, Inc., 1945), 283.

3   The General Board, U.S. Army, "Study and Report of the Organization and Operations of the American National Red Cross Activities in European Theater of Operations." Washington, D.C., 1946, 17.

4   Charles B. MacDonald, *A Time for Trumpets: The Untold Story of the Battle of the Bulge* (New York: William Morrow & Company, Inc., 1985), 224–26.

Chapter 1

5   Barnes, Personal story, opinions, observations, and recollections.

6   Kansas City, Missouri, Office of Civilian Defense, *Bulletin No. 7* of the Civilian Defense Speakers Section, Public Relations Division, March 3, 1942, 2.

7   *Kansas City Times* and *Kansas City Star*, 1 and 3 April 1942.

8   Blanche's father, Charles Henry Gregory (1882–1948), was a direct lineal descendant of the Elder William Brewster (ca. 1566–1644), a passenger on the Mayflower in 1620 and the religious leader of the Pilgrims. See www.ancestry.com, "The Gangwere_Gregory Family Tree" (2024).

9   Hans Christian "Pop" Feil (1879–1972) was the organist and choir director at Independence Boulevard Christian Church, Kansas City, Missouri, from 1916 until his death. He also taught organ, piano, and voice to scores of students, and the pipe organ as an adjunct at the University of Kansas City (MO). His wife, a gifted soloist, was Margaret McGilvary Feil (1883–1963). As a young man Pop attended Elmhurst College in Elmhurst, Illinois, and studied organ with the great Alexandre Guilmant at the prestigious "Schola Cantorum" in Paris, France. Guilmant had studied with Belgian organ virtuoso Jacques-Nicolas Lemmens in Brussels and was trained in the great Bach organ tradition. Pop had a fluid and immaculate playing style and technique. Over the years Pop wrote a great deal of music. Most of it was composed for organ, or for church choirs and soloists. He also wrote two pieces for violin. But, his largest and most popular composition was his *Easter Fantasy*, which is a cantata in three parts *(The Crucifixion, The Resurrection,* and *The Ascension)* "for Soli, Chorus and Instrumental Accompaniment or Orchestra." See Ernst Christopher Krohn, *A Century of Missouri Music* (St. Louis, MO: Privately printed, 1924), 48, 61, 108; and the "Hans Christian Feil Collection" at the Miller Nichols Library, University of Missouri-Kansas City.

10   Henry A. Bowman, "Should Soldiers Marry?," *American Magazine,* August 1942, 47.

11   Doris Weatherford, *American Women and World War II* (New York: Facts on File, Inc., 1990), 249.

12   Barnes, Personal story, opinions, observations, and recollections.

13   Blanche Barnes, *Scrapbook for 2nd Lt. Leslie C. Barnes, U.S. Army Air Forces,* 1942. In the possession of the author.

14   See the church's website at https://www.ibcckc.org/ourhistory (2024). Independence Boulevard Christian Church is located at the corner of Gladstone and Linwood Boulevards, Kansas City, Missouri. In the decades between the world wars, it was one of the largest and most influential churches in the city. Many of the city's business elite were members. In fact, the church edifice was built through the financial benevolence of local lumber baron Robert A. Long (1850–

1934). He also personally procured and paid for two expensive pipe organs. The sanctuary's organ, the instrument that Blanche Gregory Barnes learned to play the organ on, was a four-manual Austin with fifty-three ranks (or over 4,500 pipes), which, at the time, was one of the largest pipe organs in the Midwest.

15   Stewart Halsey Ross, *Strategic Bombing by the United States in World War II, The Myths and the Facts* (Jefferson, NC: McFarland and Company, 2003), 126–29. The Norden bombsight measured an aircraft's ground speed and course without the need for complicated and time-consuming in-flight procedures and mathematics. This allowed the Army Air Corps to conduct daytime strategic bombing from high altitudes with improved precision. The bombsight had a primitive but effective mechanical computer that constantly calculated the bomb's trajectory based on flight conditions, which in turn allowed the bombsight to react quickly and accurately to changes in the wind speed or other atmospheric conditions.

Naturally, the bombsight was operated by the bombardier who provided it with vital information such as wind speed, the plane's air speed, flight path, altitude, and angle of drift. This is what Les Barnes was trained to do at the Air Corps Training Center in Albuquerque. In addition, the redesigned and improved Norden was connected to the aircraft's autopilot. This was a huge advancement as it allowed the pilot to turn the autopilot on as the plane approached the target, effectively taking human error out of the final approach. Meanwhile, the bombardier could make minor adjustments to the flight path during the final few minutes of a bomb run without turning the autopilot off.

To protect the secrecy of the Norden bombsight, the military had established strict protocols regarding its use. Prior to a mission, the device was loaded onto the host bomber under an armed guard and placed in a secure area of the plane just before takeoff. It was removed as soon as the plane landed. In-flight and prior to the bomb run, the bombardier checked the bombsight out of its guarded area, took it out of the carrying case, mounted it in the nose of the plane, and turned it on. The last step was programming the bomb's actual time of descent and glide path and setting the target under the horizontal crosshair of the bombsight. Should the plane be shot down, the bombardier would be responsible for destroying the bombsight so it would not fall into enemy hands. Les, along with all the bombardiers using the Norden, took a special oath to protect the bombsight with his life if necessary. The oath read as follows:

> Mindful of the secret trust about to be placed in me by my Commander in Chief, the President of the United States, by whose direction I have been chosen for bombardier training … and mindful of the fact that I am to become guardian of one of my country's most priceless military assets, the American bombsight … I do here, in the presence of Almighty God, swear by the Bombardier's Code of Honor to keep inviolate the secrecy of any and all confidential information revealed to me, and further to uphold the honor and integrity of the Army Air Forces, if need be, with my life itself.

16   Barnes, *Scrapbook for 2nd Lt. Leslie C. Barnes.*

17   Anthony Atwood, "A State of War: Florida from 1939 to 1945" (Florida International University Theses and Dissertations, 2012), 8.

18   Graham M. Simons, *Consolidated B-24 Liberator* (Barnsley, England: Pen & Sword Books, Ltd., 2012), 70; Paul Eden, ed., *The Encyclopedia of Aircraft of World War II* (London: Amber Books Ltd., 2017), 80–81; and "The Consolidated B-24 Liberator," The National World War II Museum, date retrieved: 18 June 2024 20:34 UTC, permanent link: https://www.nationalww2museum.org/visit/museum-campus/us-freedom-pavilion/warbirds/consolidated-b-24-liberator.

19   Stephen E. Ambrose, *The Wild Blue: The Men and Boys Who Flew the B-24s Over Germany* (New York: Touchstone, 2002), 21–22.

20   Wikipedia, The Free Encyclopedia, "John R. Kane," date of last revision: 30 December 2023 22:59 UTC, date retrieved: 18 June 2024 20:31 UTC, permanent link: https://en.wikipedia.org/w/index.php?title=John_R._Kane&oldid=1192714744, page version ID: 1192714744.

21   Atwood, "A State of War," 9.

22   Joseph Freitus and Anne Freitus, *Florida: The War Years, 1938–1945* (Niceville, FL: Wind Canyon Publishing, Inc., 1998), 27.

23   M.L. Shettle Jr., *Florida's Army Air Fields of World War II* (Roswell, GA: Schaertel Publishing, 2009), 137.

24   Freitus and Freitus, *Florida: The War Years*, 18.

Chapter 2

25   U.S. Census Bureau, *The Sixteenth United States Census, Florida, 1940*, Table 31, 124.

26   Atwood, "A State of War," 61–62.

27   Atwood, 74–75.

28   Wesley Frank Craven and James Lea Cate, eds., *The Army Air Forces in World War II, Volume VII* (Chicago: University of Chicago Press, 1948), 47 and Map 1.

29   Barnes, *Scrapbook for 2nd Lt. Leslie C. Barnes.*

30   Barnes.

31   Barnes.

32   Weatherford, *American Women and World War II*, 298.

33   Barnes, *Scrapbook for 2nd Lt. Leslie C. Barnes.*

34   Barnes. The author of the letter, Lt. John Raymond Burger (1917–1973), was also a bombardier and was awarded the Distinguished Flying Cross in 1943 for his part in the raid on Naples Harbor in December 1942. He survived the war and was honorably discharged in 1946 with the rank of major.

35   Barnes.

36   Barnes.

37   Craven and Cate, *The Army Air Forces in WWII, Volume VI*, 586.

38   Christopher Shores and Giovanni Massimello, *The History of the Mediterranean Air War, 1940–1945, Volume II, North African Desert, February 1942–March 1943* (London: Grub Street Publishing, 2014), U.S. Casualties for Thursday, July 23, 1942, B-24D, #41-11814, 288; and U.S. Army Air Forces, Accident Report #43-7-24-505 (October 29, 1942), retrieved from AAIR Aviation Archaeological Investigation & Research, https://www.aviationarchaeology.com/. The report indicates that the *Rose Bud* broke up in flight from either a lightning strike or tornado-strength winds. It did not crash into a mountain as reported by 2nd Lt. Burger. The wreckage of the plane fell near the village of Fallah, near Lake Chad (which is over 100 miles from the nearest mountains). Les Barnes's body was one of only four of the eleven crew members that was initially identified since the other bodies were burned beyond recognition. Les was identified by his dog tags. The others were identified later by personal items and dental records. All members of the crew were initially buried at the crash site but were later moved to permanent resting places in Africa and the United States. At his mother's request, Les's body was re-interred at the North African American Cemetery in Tunis, Tunisia (Plot G, Row 9, Grave 13).

39   Craven and Cate, *The Army Air Forces in WWII, Volume VI*, 587.

40   Craven and Cate, 334.

41   Barnes, *Scrapbook for 2nd Lt. Leslie C. Barnes.*

Chapter 3

42   American Red Cross, "Our History," date retrieved: 18 June 2024
     20:26 UTC, permanent link: https://www.redcross.org/content/dam
     /redcross/National/history-full-history.pdf.

43   Harvey Dow Gibson, *Harvey D. Gibson: An Autobiography* (North
     Conway, NH: The Reporter Press, 1951), 342–43; and *World War II
     and the American Red Cross,* an American Red Cross publication, 1–3.

44   Marjorie Lee Morgan, ed., *The Clubmobile: The ARC in the Storm, A
     Personal History of and by the Clubmobilers in the European Theatre of War
     During World War II* (St. Petersburg, FL: Hazlett Printing & Publishing,
     Inc., 1982), 14.

45   Gibson, *An Autobiography,* 342.

46   Gibson, 346–47.

47   Gibson, 339–40.

48   Wikipedia, The Free Encyclopedia, "Harvey Dow Gibson," date of
     last revision: 19 September 2022 06:17 UTC, date retrieved: 18 June
     2024 20:21 UTC, permanent link: https://en.wikipedia.org/w/index
     .php?title=Harvey_Dow_Gibson&oldid=1111081872, page version ID:
     1111081872.

49   Gibson, *An Autobiography,* 340.

50   Gibson, 344.

51   Gibson, 345.

52   Gibson, 341–42.

53   Juliet Gardiner, *Overpaid, Oversexed, and Over Here: The American GI in
     World War II Britain* (New York: Abbeville Press, 1992), 105–6.

54   Gibson, *An Autobiography,* 343.

55   Gibson, 355–56.

56   Gibson, 346–57.

57   Gibson, 350; and Morgan, *The Clubmobile,* 14.

58   Morgan, 18; and Korson, *At His Side,* 267.

59   Gibson, *An Autobiography,* 361.

60   Gardiner, *Overpaid, Oversexed, and Over Here,* 105–6.

61   Gibson, *An Autobiography,* 361; and Korson, *At His Side,* 267.

62   Gibson, *An Autobiography,* 350–51.

63   Gibson, 349.

64   Julia A. Ramsey, "'Girls' in Name Only: A Study of American Red
     Cross Volunteers on the Frontlines of World War II" (Auburn, AL:
     Master's Thesis, Auburn University, 2011), 55; and Gibson, *An
     Autobiography,* 352.

65   Oscar Whitelaw Rexford, *Battlestars & Doughnuts: World War II Clubmobile Experiences of Mary Metcalfe Rexford* (St. Louis: The Patrice Press, 1989), 3.

66   Ramsey, "'Girls' in Name Only," 43.

67   Ramsey, 5.

68   Ramsey, 21.

69   Ramsey, 5.

70   Morgan, *The Clubmobile*, 15–17.

71   Korson, *At His Side*, 267.

72   Ramsey, "'Girls' in Name Only," 27.

73   Korson, *At His Side*, 121.

Chapter 4

74   Barnes, Personal story, opinions, observations, and recollections.

75   Henry W. Holden with Lori Griffith, *Ladybirds: The Untold Story of Women Pilots in America* (Mt. Freedom, NJ: Black Hawk Publishing Co., 1991), 65.

76   Wikipedia, The Free Encyclopedia, "Jacqueline Cochran," date of last revision: 29 September 2018 16:03 UTC, date retrieved: 18 June 2024 20:06 UTC, permanent link: https://en.wikipedia.org/w/index.php?title=Jacqueline_Cochran&oldid=861729321, page version ID: 861729321.

77   Wikipedia, The Free Encyclopedia, "Women Airforce Service Pilots," date of last revision: 24 September 2018 02:10 UTC, date retrieved: 18 June 2024 20:09 UTC, permanent link: https://en.wikipedia.org/w/index.php?title=Women_Airforce_Service_Pilots&oldid=860934948, page version ID: 860934948; and Leslie Haynsworth and David Toomey, *Amelia Earhart's Daughters: The Wild and Glorious Story of American Women Aviators from World War II to the Dawn of the Space Age* (New York: William Morrow Paperbacks, 2000), 141.

78   Shannon Collins, "WASPs Were Pioneers for Female Pilots of Today, Tomorrow," March 2, 2016, Department of Defense News Features, Defense Media Activity, date retrieved: 18 June 2024 20:18 UTC, permanent link: https://www.defense.gov/News/News-Stories/Article/Article/684700/wasps-were-pioneers-for-female-pilots-of-today-tomorrow/.

79   U.S. Department of Commerce, Economics and Statistics Administration, Bureau of the Census, *Statistical Abstract of the United States*, Number 65, Chapter 5 (Washington, D.C.: June 1944).

80   Holden and Griffith, *Ladybirds*, 75.

81   Wikipedia, The Free Encyclopedia, "Chicago Executive Airport," date of last revision: 24 January 2019 16:21 UTC, date retrieved: 18 June 2024 20:47 UTC, permanent link: https://en.wikipedia.org/w /index.php?title=Chicago_Executive_Airport&oldid=879979306, page version ID: 879979306.

82   Wikipedia, The Free Encyclopedia, "Piper J-3 Cub," date of last revision: 19 September 2018 23:22 UTC, date retrieved: 18 June 2024 20:50 UTC, permanent link: https://en.wikipedia.org/w/index. php?title=Piper_J-3_Cub&oldid=860334154, page version ID: 860334154; and Rod Simpson, *Airlife's World Aircraft: The Complete Reference to Civil, Military and Light Aircraft* (Marlborough, UK: Crowood Press, 2001), 429.

83   "Why Planes Take Off Into the Wind," One Monroe Aerospace, April 26, 2017, date retrieved: 18 June 2024 20:59 UTC, permanent link: https://monroeaerospace.com/blog/why-planes-take-off-into-the -wind/.

84   Deborah G. Douglas, *U.S. Women in Aviation, 1940–1985*, Smithsonian Studies in Air and Space, Number 7, Table 4 (Washington, D.C.: Smithsonian Institution Press, 1996), 118.

85   B. J. Olewiler, *A Woman in A Man's War: Reflections of a Red Cross Donut Girl in WWII* (Bloomington, IL: Xlibris Corporation, 2003), 23.

86   Wikipedia, The Free Encyclopedia, "Richard Halliburton," date of last revision: 7 July 2022 19:41 UTC, date retrieved: 18 June 2024 21:04 UTC, permanent link: https://en.wikipedia.org/w/index .php?title=Richard_Halliburton&oldid=1096959888, page version ID: 1096959888.

87   Ramsey, "'Girls' in Name Only," 54.

88   "Railroads During World War II," Publications International, Ltd., date retrieved: 18 June 2024 21:09 UTC, permanent link: https:// history.howstuffworks.com/american-history/great-depression -railroads.htm.

89   Elliot Carter, "Washington During Wartime," Architect of the Capitol: The Hidden History of Washington, D.C., date of article: 11 August 2016, date retrieved: 18 June 2024 21:13 UTC, permanent link: https://architectofthecapital.org/posts/2016/7/30/washington-at -war.

90   "How the Federal Government Used the National Mall During Wartime," Histories of the National Mall, by the Roy Rosenzweig Center for History and New Media, George Mason University with funding from the National Endowment for the Humanities, date

retrieved: 18 June 2024 21:18 UTC, permanent link: http://mallhistory.org/explorations/show/wartime.

91   Ramsey, "'Girls' in Name Only," 46.

Chapter 5

92   Barnes, Personal story, opinions, observations, and recollections.

93   In 2020 dollars, the policy was worth approximately $28,500. See Paige Gulley, "After all, who takes care of the Red Cross's morale?" (Orange, CA: Master's Thesis, Chapman University, Fall 2021), 54.

94   Rosemary Norwalk, *Dearest Ones: A True World War II Love Story* (New York: John Wiley & Sons, Inc., 1999), Letter of June 12, 1944, 12.

95   Blanche had a still camera and a movie camera with her during her overseas service but, unfortunately, only used them sparingly. The developed film is in the possession of the author.

96   Olewiler, *A Woman in A Man's War,* 30, 33.

97   Norwalk, *Dearest Ones,* Letter of June 15, 1944, 14.

98   David Reynolds, *Rich Relations, The American Occupation of Britain, 1942–1945* (London: Random House, 1995), 200, and footnote 1 for Chapter 13.

99   John A. Prosser, Order No. 347, ARC Headquarters, July 1944. However, once assembled for embarkation, there were 52 women in all. They are named in an article that appeared in the Sinker newsletter, published in London by the ARC. Volume 1, No. 27, August 4, 1944; Collection of the American Red Cross Clubmobile Service, 1940–1998, Identifier: MC 550: CD-1, Schlesinger Library, Radcliffe Institute, Harvard University.

100 James H. Madison, *Slinging Doughnuts for the Boys: An American Woman in World War II* (Bloomington, IN: Indiana University Press, 2007), 18.

101 For example, when clubmobiler Virginia Storts signed her receipt for the military equipment she was issued at the New York Port of Embarkation in September 1944, it included the following items: 1 Belt Pistol; 1 Helmet Steel M-1; 1 Liner Helmet M-1, New Type; 1 Can Meat, M-1932; 1 Canteen M-1910; 1 Cover Canteen Dismounted M-1910; 1 Cup M-1910; 1 Fork; 1 Knife; 1 Spoon; 1 Headband Adj. New Type; 1 Neckband, No. 4 Med.; 1 Pouch, First Aid Packet M-[19]24; 1 First Aid Packet. See Collection of the American Red Cross Clubmobile Service, 1940–1998, Identifier: MC 550: CD-1, Schlesinger Library, Radcliffe Institute, Harvard University. See also Todd Parnell, *Mom at War: A Story of Courage and Love Born of Loss* (Springfield, MO: PELP Publishing, LLC, 2005), 23–24.

102 Norwalk, *Dearest Ones,* Journal entry for 12 July 1944, 28.

103 Norwalk, Journal entry for 13 July 1944, 28.

104 Norwalk, Journal entry for 14 July 1944, 29.

105 Norwalk.

106 Wikipedia, The Free Encyclopedia, "RMS *Queen Elizabeth,*" date of last revision: 7 July 2022 22:21 UTC, date retrieved: 1 July 2024 17:13 UTC, permanent link: https://en.wikipedia.org/w/index.php?title =RMS_Queen_Elizabeth&oldid=1096977736, page version ID: 1096 977736.

107 Wartime records of troop ship crossings indicate that the *Queen Elizabeth* had 5,060 passengers on this trip and 1,102 officers and crew.

108 Norwalk, *Dearest Ones,* Journal entry for 14 July 1944, 29.

109 Barnes, Letter to her parents, 1 August 1944.

110 Madison, *Slinging Doughnuts for the Boys,* 18–19.

111 Adjutant General's Office, *Army Song Book,* in collaboration with the Library of Congress and published by order of the U.S. Secretary of War (1941).

112 Barnes, Letter to her parents, 1 August 1944.

113 Madison, *Slinging Doughnuts for the Boys,* 18–19; and Parnell, *Mom at War,* 25–26.

114 Norwalk, *Dearest Ones,* Letter of 19 July 1944, 32.

115 Norwalk, Journal entry for 19 July 1944, 32.

Chapter 6

116 I.C.B. Dear and M.R.D. Foot, eds., *The Oxford Companion to World War II* (Oxford & New York: Oxford University Press, 1995), 809–10.

117 Olewiler, *A Woman in A Man's War,* 95.

118 Wikipedia, The Free Encyclopedia, "Firth of Clyde," date of last revision: 19 June 2024 11:48 UTC, date retrieved: 19 June 2024 15:35 UTC, permanent link: https://en.wikipedia.org/w/index.php? title=Firth_of_Clyde&oldid=1229914493, page version ID: 122991 4493.

119 The V-1 was a highly explosive, pilotless, radio-controlled aircraft that looked like a miniature jet plane. It was the first of Hitler's so-called "vengeance weapons" deployed for the terror bombing of London. The "V" came from the German word "*Vergeltungswaffen,*" meaning weapons of reprisal. It was a "haphazard terror weapon of little military value, except to put an enormous new strain on the British public." See Stephen E. Ambrose, *Citizen Soldiers: The U.S.*

Army from the Normandy Beaches to the Bulge to the Surrender of Germany, June 7, 1944–March 7, 1945 (New York: Simon & Schuster, 1997), 56. The V-1 was developed at the Peenemünde Army Research Center on the Baltic Sea in 1939 by Wernher von Braun and Walter Dornberger under the auspices of the German Luftwaffe.

120 "A Short Guide to Great Britain for Military Personnel Only," U.S. War and Navy Departments (ca. 1943); and Violet A. Kochendoerfer, *One Woman's World War II* (Louisville: The University Press of Kentucky, 1994), 43–44.

121 Kochendoerfer, *One Woman's World War II*, 43–44.

122 Norwalk, *Dearest Ones*, Letter of 20 July 1944, 34.

123 Blanche kept a small daily diary from July 22 to August 9, 1944. Unfortunately, she did not continue writing in it once she started her first field assignment near Kettering, England. [In the possession of the author.]

124 Norwalk, *Dearest Ones*, Journal entry for 21 July 1944, 37.

125 Norwalk, Journal entry for 21 July 1944, 37–38.

126 Winston G. Ramsey, *The Blitz: Then and Now, Vol. 3* (London: Battle of Britain Prints International, 1990), 408–9.

127 Barnes, Diary entry for 23 July 1944.

128 Barnes.

129 Norwalk, *Dearest Ones*, Journal entry of 23 July 1944, 39.

130 Barnes, Letter to her parents, 1 August 1944.

131 Wikipedia, The Free Encyclopedia, "Grosvenor Square," date of last revision: 13 January 2024 00:04 UTC, date retrieved: 19 June 2024 15:56 UTC, permanent link: https://en.wikipedia.org/w/index.php?title=Grosvenor_Square&oldid=1195244989, page version ID: 119 5244989.

132 Norwalk, *Dearest Ones*, Journal entry of 25 July 1944, 42.

133 Norwalk, Journal entry of 25 July 1944, 43.

134 Gibson, *An Autobiography*, Red Cross Organizational Chart, 360.

135 Barnes, Diary entries for 25 and 26 July 1944.

136 A handout directed to "New Clubmobile Personnel," dated July 1, 1944, from the ARC's Clubmobile Department, Room 31, 12 Grosvenor Square, W.1. Radcliffe Library, Harvard University.

137 Olewiler, *A Woman in A Man's War*, 43.

138 Barnes, Letter to her parents, 1 August 1944.

139 Olewiler, *A Woman in A Man's War*, 43–44.

140 The recipes for making coffee and doughnuts in a Green Liner clubmobile were as follows:

Coffee for 100 to 125 people
2¾ pounds of coffee
5 gallons of cold water
Bring water to a boil; boil for two minutes
Turn off heater
Leave coffee standing 20 minutes
¾ pounds of sugar to every 5 gallons
1½ times of milk
Doughnuts
Weigh 5 pounds of doughnut mix
Weigh 2 pounds, 10 ounces of water
Sift flour
Take temperature of flour
Subtract from temperature of water
Add water to flour
Mix well
Heat of fat before starting should be 375 degrees
     See ARC File of Phyllis Ruth Lawson Birchard (1943–1945), Radcliffe Library, Harvard University.

141   Barnes, Letter to her parents, 1 August 1944.

142   Korson, *At His Side*, 268.

143   Norwalk, *Dearest Ones*, Journal entry for 30 July 1944, 49.

144   Rexford, *Battlestars & Doughnuts*, 13.

145   Barnes, Diary entry for 28 July 1944.

146   Barnes, Letter to her parents, 1 August 1944.

147   Barnes, Diary entry for 7 August 1944.

Chapter 7

148   Barnes, Personal story, opinions, observations, and recollections.

149   Wikipedia, The Free Encyclopedia, "Eleanor of Castile," date of last revision: 19 June 2024 05:11 UTC, date retrieved: 26 June 2024 17:40 UTC, permanent link: https://en.wikipedia.org/w/index.php?title=Eleanor_of_Castile&oldid=1229874444, page version ID:1229874444.

150   *Kettering: Queen Eleanor Country* (Gloucester, England, 1994), 31.

151   Korson, *At His Side*, 267.

152   Rexford, *Battlestars & Doughnuts*, 11.

153   Olewiler, *A Woman in A Man's War*, 42–43.

154   American Red Cross website, www.redcross.org/content/dam/redcross/National/history-wwii; and Korson, *At His Side*, 293.

155   Barnes, Letter to her parents, 4 October 1944.

156 Barnes, Letter to her parents, 27 January 1945.

157 Jay A. Stout, *Hell's Angels: The True Story of the 303rd Bomb Group in World War II* (New York: Berkley Caliber, 2015), 201; *Kettering*, 8, 33; and Roger A. Freeman, *The Mighty Eighth: Units, Men and Machines (A History of the U.S. 8th Army Air Force)* (Garden City, NY: Doubleday & Company, Inc., 1970), 154, 55.

158 Brian D. O'Neill, *Half a Wing, Three Engines, and a Prayer: B-17s Over Germany* (New York: McGraw-Hill, 1999), Introduction, *xxiii, xxiv*.

159 O'Neill, *Half a Wing*, 19–20.

160 When the Hell's Angels Bomb Group was deactivated on July 26, 1945, its war record included several honors and Eighth Air Force "firsts":

   • First B-17 to complete 25 Eighth AF combat missions—*Hell's Angels*

   • First B-17 to complete 50 Eighth AF combat missions—*Knockout Dropper*

   • First B-17 to complete 75 Eighth AF combat missions—*Knockout Dropper*

   • First Eighth AF Bombardment Group to complete 300 missions from bases in England

   • Two combat crewmen awarded the Congressional Medal of Honor

   • Four combat crewmen awarded the Distinguished Service Cross Medal

   • A total of 364 combat missions—the most flown by any B-17 Bomb Group, 10,721 aircraft sorties flown, 26,346 tons of bombs dropped, 378 enemy aircraft destroyed, and 104 probably destroyed

   Harry D. Gobrecht, *Might in Flight: Daily Diary of the Eighth Air Force's Hell's Angels 303rd Bombardment Group*, 2nd ed. (San Clemente, CA: 303rd Bombardment Group (H) Association, 1999).

161 Freeman, *The Mighty Eighth*, 287.

162 Brian D. O'Neill, *Aviation Elite Units: 303rd Bombardment Group* (Oxford: Osprey Publishing Ltd., 2003), 108.

163 O'Neill, *Aviation Elite Units*, 108.

164 O'Neill, *Half A Wing*, 125.

165 Barnes, Letter to her parents, 24 August 1944.

166 Eleanor Stevenson and Pete Martin, *I Knew Your Soldier: An Intimate Picture of Our Boys Overseas by the Red Cross Girls Who Knew the GIs Best* (Washington, D.C.: Penguin Books, Inc., 1945), 29.

167 Wikipedia, The Free Encyclopedia, "Ernie Pyle," date of last revision: 29 May 2024 01:31 UTC, date retrieved: 26 June 2024 18:30 UTC, permanent link: https://en.wikipedia.org/w/index.php?title=Ernie_Pyle&oldid=1226183357, page version ID: 1226183357.

168 Ernie Pyle, *Here Is Your War: Story of G.I. Joe* (Cleveland: Pocket Books, 1945), 89–90.

169 O'Neill, *Half A Wing*, 124; and O'Neill, *Aviation Elite Units*, 22–23.

170 Barnes, Letter to her parents, 29 September 1944.

171 O'Neill, *Half A Wing*, 124.

172 Barnes, Letter to her parents, 24 August 1944.

173 O'Neill, *Half A Wing*, 23.

174 Stout, *Hell's Angels*, 406.

175 Rexford, *Battlestars & Doughnuts*, 3.

176 Madison, *Slinging Doughnuts for the Boys*, 29.

Chapter 8

177 Barnes, Letter to her parents, 21 October 1944.

178 Barnes, Personal story, opinions, observations, and recollections.

179 Rexford, *Battlestars & Doughnuts*, 11.

180 Olewiler, *A Woman in A Man's War*, 56.

181 Olewiler.

182 Rexford, *Battlestars & Doughnuts*, 11.

183 Barnes, Letter to her parents, 21 October 1944.

184 Barnes.

185 Madison, *Slinging Doughnuts for the Boys*, 30.

186 Ramsey, "'Girls' in Name Only," 47.

187 Reynolds, *Rich Relations*, 216.

188 Nick Wynne and Richard Moorhead, *Florida in World War II: Floating Fortress* (Charleston, SC: History Press, 2010), 210.

189 Reynolds, *Rich Relations*, 223.

190 Although in 1944 Princeton University was not admitting African Americans as undergraduates, in 1943 the University did establish an Army Officers' Exchange Program which included a few African Americans. Before the United States entered World War II, there were only five African American officers in the U.S. military. By war's end there were over 7,000. See "Black GIs in Britain," The Mixed Museum (London, 2021), date retrieved: 26 June 2024, permanent link: https://mixedmuseum.org.uk/brown-babies/black-gis-in-britain/; and Wikipedia, The Free Encyclopedia, "Military History of African Americans," date of last revision: 24 July 2023 03:14 UTC, date

retrieved: 2 August 2023 22:04 UTC, permanent link: https://en
.wikipedia.org/w/index.php?title=Military_history_of_African
_Americans&oldid=1166844115, page version ID: 1166844115.

191 Only six months earlier, in April 1944, Camilla Moss, the Director of
the African American Red Cross club in Basingstoke, England,
resigned in protest over what she referred to as the "infiltration of
prejudices" in Red Cross policies and management. "I see us fighting
fascists but not fascist principles, for in our midst we continue to
harbor doctrines of racial supremacy which belie the [cause] for
which we are fighting." Reynolds, *Rich Relations*, 316–17.

192 Barnes, Personal story, opinions, observations, and recollections.

193 Olewiler, *A Woman in A Man's War*, 73–74.

194 O'Neill, *Aviation Elite Units*, mission of 21 November 1944, 111.

195 Dear and Foot, *The Oxford Companion to World War II*, 50–53.

196 O'Neill, *Aviation Elite Units*, 121.

197 O'Neill, *Aviation Elite Units*, 111.

198 Barnes, Letter to her parents, 20 December 1944.

199 O'Neill, *Aviation Elite Units*, 111.

200 O'Neill, *Aviation Elite Units*, 121–22.

201 Barnes, Letter to her parents, 27 January 1945.

202 *Encyclopedia Britannica Online*, "Destruction of the Maine," date
retrieved: 26 June 2024, permanent link: https://www.britannica.com
/event/destruction-of-the-Maine.

203 In the author's possession.

Chapter 9

204 Gulley, "After all, who takes care of the Red Cross's morale?," 29–30.

205 Gulley.

206 Gulley.

207 Korson, *At His Side*, 279.

208 Gulley, "After all, who takes care of the Red Cross's morale?," 29–30;
and Olewiler, *A Woman in A Man's War*, 131.

209 Korson, *At His Side*, 279.

210 Korson, 267.

211 Gulley, "After all, who takes care of the Red Cross's morale?," 29–30.

212 Korson, *At His Side*, 279.

213 Korson, 267, Appendix I; Emily Yellin, *Our Mothers' War: American
Women at Home and at the Front During World War II* (New York: Free
Press, 2004), 175, 178; and Rexford, *Battlestars & Doughnuts*, 20.

214 Madison, *Slinging Doughnuts for the Boys*, 154–55.

215 Olewiler, *A Woman in A Man's War*, 87–88.

216 Rexford, *Battlestars & Doughnuts*, 18–20.

217 Madison, *Slinging Doughnuts for the Boys*, 148, 154.

218 Madison, 155.

219 Madison, 158.

220 Olewiler, *A Woman in A Man's War*, 64.

Chapter 10

221 Barnes, Letter to her parents, 3 March 1945.

222 Wikipedia, The Free Encyclopedia, "History of Rouen," date of last revision: 7 May 2023, date retrieved: 29 August 2023, permanent link: https://en.wikipedia.org/w/index.php?title=History_of_Rouen &oldid= 1153710631, page version ID: 1153710631.

223 Wikipedia, The Free Encyclopedia, "Cigarette Camp," date of last revision: 1 December 2022, date retrieved: 29 August 2023, permanent link: https://en.wikipedia.org/w/index.php?title=Cigarette _Camp&oldid=1124893923, page version ID: 1124893923.

224 "The Cigarette Camps, The U.S. Army's Camps in the Le Havre Area," date of last update: 23 June 2024, date retrieved: 30 June 2024, permanent link: https://web.archive.org/web/20150924102539/http:// www.skylighters.org/special/cigcamps/cigintro.html.

225 Barnes, Letter to her parents, 28 February 1945.

226 Anna M. Rosenberg, "Overseas Woman" (newsletter), Volume I, Number I, page 14 (April 1945).

227 Wikipedia, The Free Encyclopedia, "13th Armored Division (United States)," date of last revision: 23 June 2023, date retrieved: 2 September 2023, permanent link: https://en.wikipedia.org/w/index .php?title=13th_Armored_Division_(United_States)&oldid = 1161481265, page version ID: 1161481265.

228 Barnes, *Red Cross Scrapbook, 1944–1945*. In the possession of the author.

229 Madison, *Slinging Doughnuts for the Boys,* 28–30.

230 Maurice Chevalier's (1888–1972) story is confusing, as there has always been misinformation and debate about his activities and loyalties during the war. When the war began in 1939, Chevalier was living in Paris and performing at nightclubs to packed audiences. After France fell to the Germans in 1940, he moved to the unoccupied zone controlled by the Vichy government and kept a low profile. However, after the liberation of Paris in August 1944, French authorities arrested Chevalier and informed him that he had been sentenced to death in absentia, but he was quickly exonerated. The

only piece of information against him was the appearance of his name on a list of suspected collaborators released on Radio London in February 1944, but it was later determined to have been a mistake. Furthermore, it is hard to believe that Chevalier was ever sympathetic with the Germans, or with the Vichy government, given that during World War I, while serving in the French Army, Chevalier was captured and spent two years in a German POW camp. Plus, he always had leftist political leanings inconsistent with fascism. See Alan Riding, *And the Show Went On: Cultural Life in Nazi-Occupied Paris* (New York: Alfred A. Knopf Publishing, 2010); and Maurice Chevalier, *With Love* (Canada: Little Brown & Company, 1960) (Chevalier's autobiography).

231 Chris Lloyd, "Rationing and the Black Market in Paris During the War," Aspects of History, 2021, date retrieved: 30 June 2024, permanent link: https://aspectsofhistory.com/rationing-and-the -black-market-in-paris-during-the-war/.

232 Ambrose, *Citizen Soldiers*, 111–12.

233 Wikipedia, The Free Encyclopedia, "Black Market in Wartime France," date of last revision: 9 September 2023, date retrieved: 9 September 2023, permanent link: https://en.wikipedia.org/w/index .php?title=Black_market_in_wartime_France&oldid=1174568245, page version ID: 1174568245.

234 David R. Henderson, "Black Markets Were a Lifeline for Postwar France," Foundation for Economic Education (23 July 2017), reprinted from EconLog, date retrieved: 30 June 2024, permanent link: https://fee.org/articles/black-markets-were-a-lifeline-for-postwar -france/.

235 Barnes, Letter to her parents, 10 April 1945.

Chapter 11

236 *Encyclopedia Britannica Online*, "Le Havre," date of last revision: 22 Feb. 2019, date retrieved: 25 October 2023, permanent link: https:// www.britannica.com/place/Le-Havre.

237 Andrew Knapp, "The Destruction and Liberation of Le Havre in Modern Memory," *War in History*, Volume 14, No. 4 (November 2007), 476–98.

238 Barnes, Letter to her parents, 10 April 1945.

239 David P. Colley, "On the Road to Victory: The Red Ball Express," 19 August 1997, HistoryNet, permanent link: https://www.historynet .com/on-the-road-to-victory-the-red-ball-express-march-97-world -war-ii-feature/, date retrieved: 1 July 2024; and *"The Red Ball Express,*

1944," U.S. Army Transportation Museum, archived from the original on 26 January 2018, date retrieved: 31 December 2013.

240   "GIs in Germany: First Impressions of the Former Third Reich," The National World War II Museum, 16 May 2020, permanent link: https://www.nationalww2museum.org/war/articles/wwii-allies -impressions-of-germany, date retrieved: 1 July 2024.

241   Olewiler, *A Woman in a Man's War,* 55.

242   Rexford, *Battlestars & Doughnuts,* 63.

243   "American National Red Cross Activities in European Theater of Operations," 17.

244   Olewiler, *A Woman in a Man's War,* 122–23.

245   Korson, *At His Side,* 285–86.

246   Korson, 283.

247   Ambrose, *Citizen Soldiers,* 432; and Dear and Foot, *The Oxford Companion to World War II,* 944.

248   Ambrose, *Citizen Soldiers,* 432.

249   Rexford, *Battlestars & Doughnuts,* 98.

250   Angela Petesch, *World War II as seen Through the Hole of a Doughnut* (Los Angeles: Privately published, 1999), 122.

251   Barnes, Letter to her parents, 16 June 1945.

252   The B-17G Flying Fortress was a four-engine heavy bomber like the B-24, with a slightly smaller wingspan of 103 feet, a crew of 10, and a maximum speed of 287 miles per hour. However, it had a service ceiling of 35,600 feet and a maximum range of 3,400 miles (both superior to the B-24D). It carried 500- or 1,000-pound bombs and its maximum bomb load was 17,600 pounds (double that of the B-24D). For protection it carried thirteen .50 caliber machine guns. See Enzo Angelucci, *The Rand McNally Encyclopedia of Military Aircraft, 1914–1980* (New York: The Military Press, 1983), 287–88. However, like the B-24, it had no pressurized cabin, no heat, no bathroom, and nothing to warm up food or coffee. Both the B-24 and the B-17 served one purpose and one purpose only—to carry a large bomb load long distances and drop them on enemy targets.

253   Robert Morgan with Ron Powers, *The Man Who Flew the Memphis Belle: Memoir of a WWII Bomber Pilot* (New York: Penguin Publishing Press, 2001), 83.

254   *Encyclopedia Britannica Online,* "Women Airforce Service Pilots" by Michael Ray, date of last revision: 21 July 2023, date retrieved: 1 July 2024, permanent link: https://www.britannica.com/topic/Women-Airforce-Service-Pilots.

255   Barnes, Letter to her parents, 10 April 1945.

Chapter 12

256 Dear and Foot, *The Oxford Companion to World War II*, 308.

257 Author's oral interview with George H. Gangwere Jr. (1917–2003), 1995.

258 *Encyclopedia Britannica Online*, "Koblenz," date of last revision: 11 May 2024, date retrieved: 1 July 2024, permanent link: https://www.britannica.com/place/Koblenz-Germany.

259 Barnes, Letter to her parents, 16 June 1945.

260 Wikipedia, The Free Encyclopedia, "Mannheim," date of last revision: 24 June 2024 05:45 UTC, date retrieved: 1 July 2024 17:02 UTC, permanent link: https://en.wikipedia.org/w/index.php?title =Mannheim&oldid=1230698344, page version ID: 1230698344.

261 "The 85th in Germany: Historical Overview," The 85th Engineer Heavy Ponton Battalion in World War II, date retrieved: 1 July 2024, permanent link: https://www.85th-engineer.com/319115462.html.

262 "Heidelberg Thingstätte," *Atlas Obscura*, date retrieved: 1 July 2024, permanent link: https://www.atlasobscura.com/places/heidelberg-thingstatte.

263 Carlos D'Este, *Patton: A Genius for War* (New York: HarperCollins Publishers, 1995), 740–41.

264 Wikipedia, The Free Encyclopedia, "Bombing of Munich in World War II," date of last revision: 27 October 2023 19:25 UTC, date retrieved: 1 July 2024 18:53 UTC, permanent link: https://en.wikipedia.org/w/index.php?title=Bombing_of_Munich_in_World_War_II&oldid=1182199081, page version ID: 1182199081.

265 Frank Sisson with Robert L. Wise, *I Marched with Patton: A Firsthand Account of World War II Alongside One of the U.S. Army's Greatest Generals* (New York: HarperCollins Publishers, 2020), 179.

266 Holocaust Encyclopedia, "Dachau," United States Holocaust Memorial Museum, date retrieved: 1 July 2024, permanent link: https://encyclopedia.ushmm.org/content/en/article/dachau.

267 Olewiler, *A Woman in A Man's War*, 134–35.

268 Barnes, Letter to her parents, 16 June 1945.

269 Eugen Trapp, *World Heritage Regensburg: A Guide to the History and Art History of the Old Town of Regensburg and Stadtamhof* (Regensburg: Schnell & Steiner, 2008), 76–79.

270 Dietrich had starred in numerous films during the 1930s including *The Blue Angel* (one of Germany's first talking films), *Dishonored*, *Shanghai Express, Blonde Venus, The Devil Is a Woman*, and *Destry Rides Again*. She opposed Hitler's dictatorship, and as a result, her films

were banned in Germany. She became a U.S. citizen in 1937 and made more than 500 personal appearances before Allied troops from 1943 to 1946. See "Marlene Dietrich," *Encyclopedia Britannica Online*, date last updated: 21 June 2024, date retrieved: 1 July 2024, permanent link: https://www.britannica.com/biography/Marlene -Dietrich.

271 Barnes, Letter to her brother and sister-in-law, 22 June 1945.
272 Oral interview with George H. Gangwere Jr.
273 Interview.

Chapter 13

274 Barnes, Personal story, opinions, observations, and recollections.
275 "Veste Museum Oberhaus Passau," date retrieved: 1 July 2024, permanent link: https://www.oberhausmuseum.de/en/castle/history/.
276 The road was much narrower in 1945, and it was impossible to turn a large truck around.
277 Ernie Hayhow, *The Thunderbolt Across Europe: A History of the 83rd Infantry Division, 1942–1945* (Munich: I & E Section, 83rd Infantry Division, 1945), 94.
278 Barnes, Letters to her parents, 13 and 20 July 1945.
279 "Red Cross girls here for month," *83rd Spearhead* (official newspaper of the U.S. 83rd Infantry Division), 23 June 1945 edition, published in Passau, Germany.
280 *83rd Spearhead*, 14 July 1945 edition.
281 George T. Simon, *The Big Bands* (New York: The Macmillan Company, 1969), 369.
282 *Encyclopedia Britannica Online*, "Glenn Miller," date of last revision: 12 December 2023, date retrieved: 28 December 2023, permanent link: https://www.britannica.com/biography/Glenn-Miller.
283 Barnes, Letter to her brother and sister-in-law, 22 June 1945.
284 Wikipedia, The Free Encyclopedia, "Leonard T. Gerow," date of last revision: 8 August 2024 14:33 UTC, date retrieved: 22 August 2024, 14:33 UTC, permanent link: https://en.wikipedia.org/w/index.php ?title=Leonard_T._Gerow&oldid=1239242656, page version ID: 12392 42656.
285 The United States military took possession of the *Ostwind* after the war and it was used as a training craft at the U.S. Naval Academy in Annapolis, Maryland, until it was sold as surplus in the 1950s. Then the yacht was owned by various individuals in Florida until finally sold to a Nazi memorabilia collector from Massachusetts in the

1970s. The boat was repeatedly vandalized and finally burned and sunk in Miami Harbor. See Mike Miller, "Hitler's Yacht in Jacksonville," Florida-Backroads-Travel.com, date of last revision:12 June 2024, permanent link: https://www.florida-backroads-travel.com/hitlers-yacht.html; and Rick Spilman, "Adolf Hitler's Yachts—Part 2: *Ostwind* and the Offshore Reef," The Old Salt Blog, date of last revision: 24 April 2022, date retrieved: 1 July 2024, permanent link: https://www.oldsaltblog.com/2022/04/adolph-hitlers-yachts-part-2-ostwind-and-the-offshore-reef/.

286 Miller, "Hitler's Yacht in Jacksonville."

287 Barnes, Letter to her brother and sister-in-law, 22 June 1945.

288 Barnes, Letters to her parents, 13 and 20 July 1945.

289 Wikipedia, The Free Encyclopedia, "Sorbonne Chapel," date of last revision: 24 August 2023 06:05 UTC, date retrieved: 1 July 2024 18:25 UTC, permanent link: https://en.wikipedia.org/w/index.php?title=Sorbonne_Chapel&oldid=1171970453, page version ID: 1171970453.

290 Barnes, Letter to her parents, 14 August 1945.

291 Barnes, Letter to her parents, 26 September 1945.

292 Gangwere.

293 Barnes, Letter to George H. Gangwere Jr., 2 October 1945.

294 ARC File of Phyllis Ruth Lawson Birchard, 1943–1945, Radcliffe Library, Harvard University.

295 Barnes, Letter to George H. Gangwere Jr., 15 October 1945.

296 George H. Gangwere Jr., Letter to Blanche Barnes, 2 November 1945.

Epilogue

297 Ramsey, "'Girls' in Name Only," 11, footnote 30.

298 Madison, *Slinging Doughnuts for the Boys*, 28.

299 Barnes, Letter to Mr. and Mrs. Hans Feil, 3 October 1945.

300 See the dedication page for the list of clubmobilers who lost their lives while serving in the ETO.

301 Senate Resolution 471, Volume 158, Number 75, Wednesday, 23 May 2012, S3519.

Selected Bibliography

Note on Sources

Unfortunately, the original American Red Cross World War II era clubmobile records were lost in a fire back in the 1970s. Nevertheless, the personal recollections and records of dozens of clubmobile girls contain a wealth of valuable information. In addition, the records retained by Virginia Wilson Cook Osgood (1917–1998), the Assistant Director of Clubmobile Personnel in London, is housed at the Schlesinger Library, Radcliffe Institute, Harvard University, in Cambridge, Massachusetts, and they contain copies of many official clubmobile documents.

The primary source for this book, however, is Blanche Gregory Barnes Gangwere's personal story as gleaned from her letters, diary, Red Cross scrapbook, photographs, and 8mm movies (all in the possession of the author); and extensive oral interviews with her conducted by the author between 1978 and 2018. Her story has been independently verified, to the degree possible, and enhanced by the following books, articles, academic papers, government resources, manuscript collections, and internet resources.

Books

Ambrose, Stephen E., *Citizen Soldiers: The U.S. Army From the Normandy Beaches to the Bulge to the Surrender of Germany, June 7, 1944–March 7, 1945*. New York, NY, 1997.

Ambrose, Stephen E., *The Wild Blue: The Men and Boys Who Flew the B-24s Over Germany*. New York, NY, 2002.

Angelucci, Enzo, *The Rand McNally Encyclopedia of Military Aircraft, 1914–1980*. New York, NY, 1983.

Craven, Wesley Frank, and James Lea Cate, *The Army Air Forces in World War II, Volumes I and VII*. Chicago, IL, 1948.

Dear, I.C.B., and M.R.D. Foot, *The Oxford Companion to World War II*. Oxford, England, 1995.

Douglas, Deborah G., *U.S. Women in Aviation, 1940–1985*. Smithsonian Studies in Air and Space, Number 7, Washington, D.C., 1996.

Dulles, Foster Rhea, *The American Red Cross: A History*. New York, NY, 1950.

Dyer, George, *XII Corps: Spearhead of Patton's Third Army*. Philadelphia, PA, 1947.

Freeman, Roger A., *The Mighty Eighth: Units, Men and Machines (A History of the U.S. 8th Army Air Force)*. Garden City, NY, 1978.

Freitus, Joseph and Anne, *Florida: The War Years, 1938–1945*. Niceville, FL, 1998.

Gardiner, Juliet, *Overpaid, Oversexed, and Over Here: The American GI in World War II Britain*. New York, NY, 1992.

Gezzi, Kathleen Havens, *Journey Between Mountains: A Young School Teacher's Experience as a Red Cross Volunteer During World War II and In Post War Europe*. Bloomington, IN, 2006.

Gibson, Harvey Dow, *Harvey D. Gibson: An Autobiography*. North Conway, NH, 1951.

Gilbo, Patrick F., *The American Red Cross: The First Century*. New York, NY, 1981.

Gobrecht, Harry D., *Might in Flight: Daily Diary of the Eighth Air Force's Hell's Angels 303rd Bombardment Group,* 2nd ed. San Clemente, CA, 1999.

Guhzit-Hoyt, Olga, *They Also Served: American Women in World War II.* Secaucus, NJ, 1995.

Hayhow, Ernie, and the I & E Section, *The Thunderbolt Across Europe: A History of the 83rd Infantry Division, 1942–1945.* Munich, Germany, 1945.

Haynsworth, Leslie, and David Toomey, *Amelia Earhart's Daughters: The Wild and Glorious Story of American Women Aviators from World War II to the Dawn of the Space Age.* New York, NY, 1998.

Holden, Henry W. (with Lori Griffith), *Ladybirds: The Untold Story of Women Pilots in America.* Mt. Freedom, NJ, 1991.

Kochendoerfer, Violet A., *One Woman's World War II.* Louisville, KY, 1994.

Korson, George, *At His Side: The Story of The American Red Cross Overseas in World War II.* New York, NY, 1945.

MacDonald, Charles B., *A Time for Trumpets: The Untold Story of the Battle of the Bulge.* New York, NY, 1985.

MacGregor, Morris J., *Integration of the Armed Forces, 1940–1965,* Defense Studies Series. Washington, D.C., 2001.

Madison, James H., *Slinging Doughnuts for the Boys: An American Woman in World War II.* Bloomington and Indianapolis, IN, 2007.

Morgan, Majorie Lee, ed., *The Clubmobile: The ARC in the Storm, A Personal History of and by the Clubmobilers in the European Theatre of War During World War II.* St. Petersburg, FL, 1982.

Morgan, Robert (with Ron Powers), *The Man Who Flew the Memphis Belle: Memoir of a WWII Bomber Pilot.* New York, NY, 2001.

Norwalk, Rosemary Langheldt, *Dearest Ones: A True World War II Love Story.* New York, NY, 1999.

Olewiler, B.J., *A Woman in A Man's War: Reflections of a Red Cross Donut Girl of WWII.* Bloomington, IL, 2003.

O'Neill, Brian D., *Aviation Elite Units: 303rd Bombardment Group.* Oxford, England, 2003.

O'Neill, Brian D., *Half a Wing, Three Engines and a Prayer: B-17s Over Germany*. New York, NY, 1999.

Parnell, Todd, *Mom at War: A Story of Courage and Love Born of Loss*. Springfield, MO, 2005.

Petesch, Angela L., *World War II as Seen Through the Hole of a Doughnut*. Los Angeles, CA, 1999.

Pyle, Ernie, *Here Is Your War: Story of G.I. Joe*. Cleveland, OH, 1945.

Reynolds, David, *Rich Relations: The American Occupation of Britain, 1942–1945*. London, England, 1995.

Rexford, Oscar Whitelaw, ed., *Battlestars & Doughnuts: World War II Clubmobile Experiences of Mary Metcalfe Rexford*. St. Louis, MO, 1989.

Ross, Stewart Halsey, *Strategic Bombing by the United States in World War II: The Myths and the Facts*. Jefferson, NC, 2003.

Shealy, Gwendolyn C., *A Critical History of The American Red Cross, 1882–1945: The End of Noble Humanitarianism*. Lewistown, NY, 2003.

Shettle, Jr., M.L., *Florida's Army Air Fields of World War II*. Roswell, GA, 2009.

Simmons, Graham M., *Consolidated B-24 Liberator*. Barnsley, England, 2012.

Simpson, Rod, *Airlife's World Aircraft: The Complete Reference to Civil, Military and Light Aircraft*. Shrewsbury, England, 2001.

Stout, Jay A., *Hell's Angels: The True Story of the 303rd Bomb Group in World War II*. New York, NY, 2015.

Wayne, Lewis N., and Richard Moorehead, *Florida in World War II: Floating Fortress*. Charleston, SC, 2010.

Weatherford, Doris, *American Women and World War II* (Part of the *History of Women in America* series). New York, NY, 1990.

Wiggins, Jim, *Florida and World War II: A Personal Recollection*. Westminster, MD, 2008.

Yellin, Emily, *Our Mothers' War: American Women at Home and at the Front During World War II*. New York, NY, 2004.

Articles and Academic Papers

Atwood, Anthony, "A State of War: Florida from 1939 to 1945." Florida International University Electronic Theses and Dissertations, 2012.

Bailey, Karon S., "Harriet Englehardt: A Job Worth Having." Alabama Heritage, Summer 2000.

Gough, Allison J., "Messing Up Another Country's Customs: The Exportation of American Racism During World War II." World History Connected, October 2007. Permanent link: https://worldhistoryconnected.press.uillinois.edu/5.1/gough.html. Retrieved: 26 June 2024.

Guglielmo, Thomas A., "Red Cross, Double Cross: Race and America's World War II-Era Blood Donor Service." The Journal of American History, Vol. 97, No. 1, June 2010.

Gulley, Paige N., "'After all, who takes care of the Red Cross's morale?': The Experiences of American Red Cross Clubmobile Women During World War II." Master's thesis, Chapman University, 2020.

Holtz, Maureen, "Clubmobile Gal: A Young Woman's Service with the Red Cross in Europe." World War II History (magazine), October 2017.

Junior League Magazine, July 1945. Schlesinger Library, Radcliffe Institute, Harvard University, Cambridge, MA.

Lamartina, Jerry, "KC woman saw World War II from a different perspective," (relating to Blanche Gangwere). *The Kansas City Star*, 15 July 2014.

Life Magazine, "Red Cross Fun," 8 February 1943; and "Life Visits Red Cross in England," 28 February 1944.

MacGregor, Jr., Morris J., "Integration of the Armed Forces, 1940–1965." Defense Studies Series, Center for Military History, 2001.

Ramsey, Julia A., "'Girls' in Name Only:' A Study of American Red Cross Volunteers on the Frontlines of World War II." Master's thesis, Auburn University, 2011.

Stewart-Smith, Natalie Jeanne, "The Women Airforce Service Pilots (WASPs) of World War II: Perspectives on The Work of America's First Military Women Aviators." Master's thesis, Washington State University, 1981.

Sunday Punch, "Thanks for the Sinker, Sister." 15 December 1944 edition.

Yank Magazine, The Army Weekly, "Somewhere in England." 7 February 1943 (British edition).

Government Articles, Studies, and Documents

Adjutant General's Office, *Army Song Book*, in collaboration with the Library of Congress and published by order of the U.S. Secretary of War (1941).

Baldwin, J. L., *The Weather of 1942 in the United States.* National Weather Bureau, Washington, D.C., 1943.

Collins, Shannon, *WASPs Were Pioneers for Female Pilots of Today, Tomorrow.* DoD News Features, Defense Media Activity, U.S. Department of Defense, 2 March 2016.

Over There: Instructions for American Servicemen in Britain, 1942. Oxford, England, 1994.

Seventeenth Census of the United States, Volume II, Characteristics of the Population. 1940, Part 10, Florida.

Statistical Abstract of the United States, Number 65, Chapter 5, June 1944.

Records of the American National Red Cross, U.S. National Archives and Records Administration, permanent link: https://www .archives.gov/findingaid/donated-collection-explorer/list/anrc.

The History of the Mediterranean Air War, 1940–1945, Volume II, North African Desert, February 1942–March 1943, 2014.

U.S. Army Air Forces, *Accident Reports*, #43-7-24-505, 29 October 1942.

American Red Cross and Associated Publications

At Your Service. American Red Cross, 1947.

Our History, "World War II and the Red Cross," 2024, retrieved 27 June 2024, permanent link: https://www.redcross.org/content/dam/redcross/National/history-wwii.pdf.

Sinker Jr. (the official newsletter of the Clubmobile Association), Plymouth, MA, 1946–1947.

Study and Report of the Organization and Operations of the American National Red Cross Activities in European Theater of Operations. U.S. Army, 1946.

The Sinker (the official newsletter of the Clubmobile Department, ARC). London, England, 1942 to 1946.

World War II and the American Red Cross. A booklet published by the ARC, ca. 1943.

Manuscript Collections

Bush, Althea M. *American Red Cross Clubmobile Operations in Great Britain and Western Europe, April 1942 to July 1946.* Typescript, September 1947, Monograph Collection, Hazel Braugh Records Center and Archives, American Red Cross, Lorton, VA.

Collection of the American Red Cross Clubmobile Service, 1940–1998 (inclusive), 1943–1946 (bulk), MC 550, Schlesinger Library, Harvard University, Cambridge, MA.

Osgood, Virginia Wilson Cook (Donor), *Red Cross Reports, and Clubmobilers and Their Assignments (approximately 136 pages).* MC 550, items 11.1 and 11.2; Schlesinger Library, Radcliffe Institute, Harvard University, Cambridge, MA.

Internet Resources

Encyclopedia Britannica. Permanent link: https://www.britannica.com.

Fay, Elma Ernst, *A Brief History of Red Cross Clubmobiles in World War II.* Permanent link: www.clubmobile.org/history.html.

Gezzi, Kathleen Havens, *List of World War II ARC Donut Dollies* (incomplete). Permanent link: http://www.donutdollyhomestead.com/ListofARCWWIIDonutDollies.html.

Hell's Angels, 303rd Bomb Group website. Permanent link: http://www.303rdbg.com.

National World War II Museum, New Orleans, LA, Digital Collection, in particular Blanche Gregory Barnes Gangwere's oral interview, 6 October 2014. Permanent link: https://www.ww2online.org/vocabulary/red-cross-5.

Wikipedia, The Free Encyclopedia. Permanent link: https://en.wikipedia.org.

Index

About the Author

Robert Gangwere is a retired administrative law, real estate, and ethics attorney, and an active historian and genealogist. He spent decades interviewing his mother about, and researching her service in, the clubmobile program of the American Red Cross during World War II.

If you have questions or comments for Robert, he can be contacted at www.robertgangwere.com.

www.ingramcontent.com/pod-product-compliance
Lightning Source LLC
Chambersburg PA
CBHW061607120626
46550CB00004B/1635